Governing Education

BEN LEVIN

UNIVERSITY OF TORONTO PRESS
Toronto Buffalo London

© University of Toronto Press Incorporated 2005
Toronto Buffalo London
Printed in Canada

ISBN 0-8020-8852-X (cloth)
ISBN 0-8020-8622-5 (paper)

Printed on acid-free paper

Library and Archives Canada Cataloguing in Publication

Levin, Benjamin Ruvin, 1952–
  Governing education / Ben Levin.

  Includes bibliographical references and index.
  ISBN 0-8020-8852-X (bound).   ISBN 0-8020-8622-5 (pbk.)

  1. Education and state – Manitoba.   2. Education and state –
  Canada.   I. Title

  LC91.L48 2005   379.7127   C2004-905735-9

This book has been published with the help of a grant from the Canadian Federation for the Humanities and Social Sciences, through the Aid to Scholarly Publications Programme, using funds provided by the Social Sciences and Humanities Research Council of Canada.

University of Toronto Press acknowledges the financial assistance to its publishing program of the Canada Council for the Arts and the Ontario Arts Council.

University of Toronto Press acknowledges the financial support for its publishing activities of the Government of Canada through the Book Publishing Industry Development Program (BPIDP).

GOVERNING EDUCATION

High levels of cynicism about politics, fuelled by a lack of understanding of the real dynamics of policy and the political process, are dangerous to democracy. So argues Benjamin Levin in *Governing Education*. With this book, Levin seeks to improve public understanding of the way government works, especially with regard to education policy.

Based on his experience as Manitoba's deputy minister of education from 1999 to 2002, Levin offers an insider's account of the events and conditions that governed Manitoba's education policy as a way of illustrating the larger dynamics of the political process. He demonstrates how the actions of governments are rooted in diverse political demands, and, looking at the current state of education and education policy in Canada, comments on its strengths, weaknesses, and opportunities.

Levin combines enlightened analysis with stories of real events told by participants, providing an in-depth exploration of government in action. Informative and engagingly written, this unique study will appeal to readers interested in education, political science, and public administration.

BENJAMIN LEVIN is the deputy minister of education for the Government of Ontario.

The Institute of Public Administration of Canada Series in Public Management and Governance

Editor: Donald Savoie

This series is sponsored by the Institute of Public Administration of Canada as part of its commitment to encourage research on issues in Canadian public administration, public sector management, and public policy. It also seeks to foster wider knowledge and understanding among practitioners, academics, and the general public.

Networks of Knowledge: Collaborative Innovation in International Learning, Janice Stein, Richard Stren, Joy Fitzgibbon, and Melissa Maclean

The National Research Council in the Innovative Policy Era: Changing Hierarchies, Networks, and Markets, G. Bruce Doern and Richard Levesque

Beyond Service: State Workers, Public Policy, and the Prospects for Democratic Administration, Greg McElligott

A Law Unto Itself: How the Ontario Municipal Board Has Developed and Applied Land Use Planning Policy, John G. Chipman

Health Care, Entitlement, and Citizenship, Candace Redden

Between Colliding Worlds: The Ambiguous Existence of Government Agencies for Aboriginal and Women's Policy, Jonathan Malloy

The Politics of Public Management: The HRDC Audit of Grants and Contributions, David A. Good

Dream No Little Dreams: A Biography of the Douglas Government of Saskatchewan, 1944–1961, Albert W. Johnson

Governing Education, Ben Levin

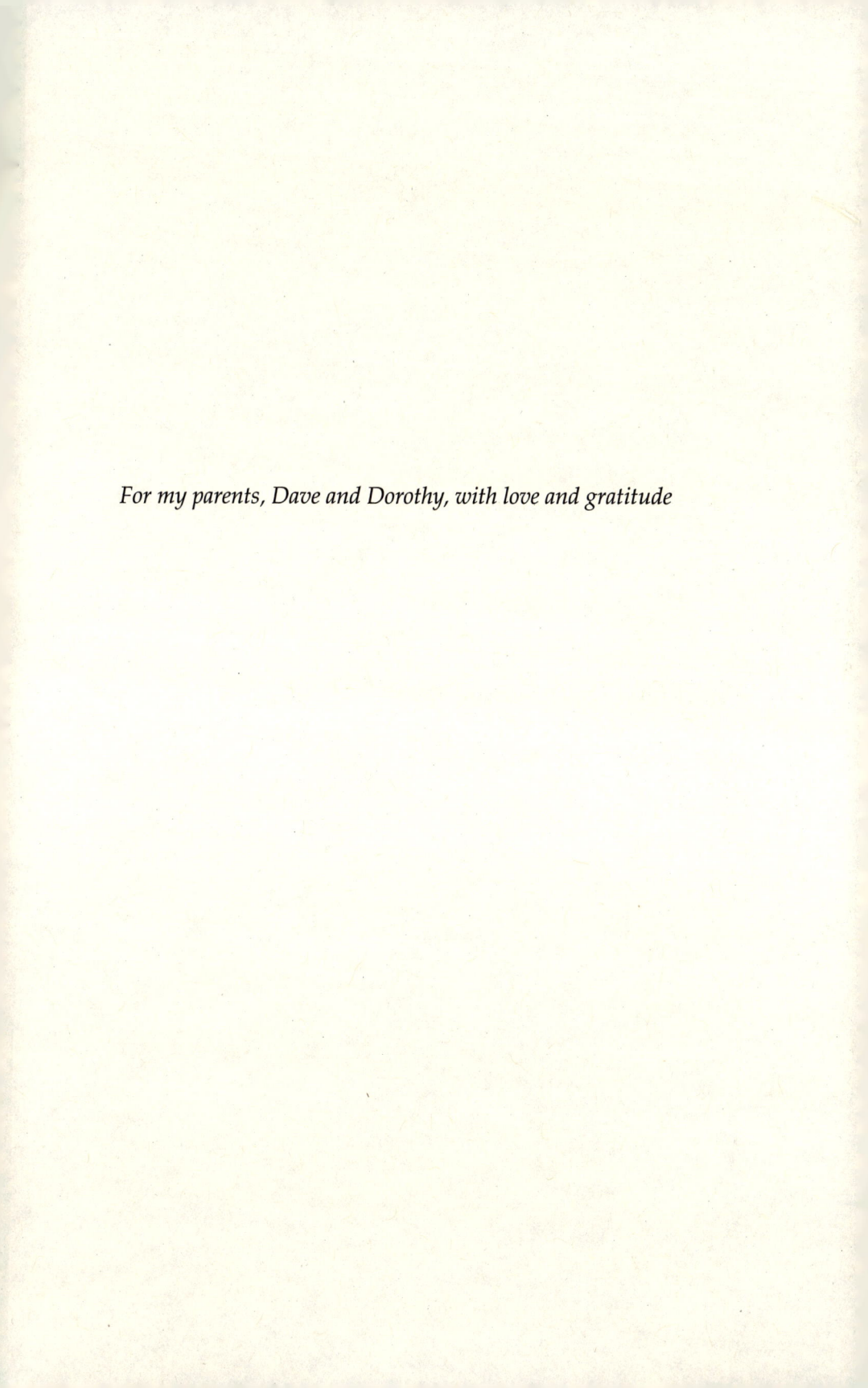

For my parents, Dave and Dorothy, with love and gratitude

Contents

PREFACE ix

ACKNOWLEDGMENTS xiii

Chapter 1 Governing   3

Chapter 2 Education in Canada: Myths and Opportunities   48

Chapter 3 The Grade Three Assessment: Even Doing What People Want Can Be Hard   84

Chapter 4 College Expansion: Unforeseen Problems in Meeting a Commitment   101

Chapter 5 School Funding: Managing the Intractable   119

Chapter 6 School Division Amalgamations: Giving the Public What It Wants   140

Chapter 7 Adult Learning Centres: From Crisis to Opportunity   158

Chapter 8 Focus on What Matters: Managing the Department and Looking After Education   176

Chapter 9 Improving Government and Improving Education   196

viii Contents

Appendix: Chronology of Main Issues and Events in
    Education, 1999–2002   207

REFERENCES   213

INDEX   219

Preface

In the government of Manitoba each year, there is a legislative review of spending estimates. Ministers appear before a committee of MLAs who can ask questions about any aspect of their department's budget, its work, or policies. In 1983 I had just returned to Manitoba and rejoined the civil service as director of research and planning in the Department of Education after completing my PhD and working for the Peel Board of Education in Ontario.

The estimates review for our department began soon after I started, and my unit was the first to be reviewed. The review took place in the main legislative chamber. Our critic was Gary Filmon, soon to become opposition leader and then premier.

The estimates review is the only time civil servants are allowed into the legislative chamber. When the time came, the deputy minister, Ron Duhamel, and I entered the chamber and sat down at a small table placed in front of the minister, Maureen Hemphill. Ron was carrying a huge stack of note paper. As soon as we sat down he began writing notes furiously and passing them to the minister. I was rather puzzled, as the chair of the committee was still going through the preliminaries and no questions had yet been asked.

'Start writing,' Ron whispered to me sharply. But what was I to write in the absence of any questions? 'Just start writing,' he whispered again, meanwhile continuing to do so himself as rapidly as he could. The minister was looking at the notes, crumpling most of them up, and throwing them on the floor.

I realized that I had entered a new world where I did not know the rules at all.

This book is about the challenges of governing in the twenty-first century. Growing public distrust of government poses the danger that people might become disenchanted enough with electoral democracy to render it illegitimate or unworkable. Voter turnouts are declining and young people are especially cynical about or uninterested in politics. These are worrying developments. Unless we understand why and how governments act as they do, we cannot expect improvement. Yet many of the proposals for change are not based on a deep understanding of the realities of government and politics. This book draws on my experience in government, including serving from 1999 to 2002 as deputy minister of education for a new NDP government in Manitoba, to try to show how things really work and what might be done better. As someone who worked in the bureaucracy but with strong political connections, I was well placed to observe both elements of government.

Although this account is set in the province of Manitoba and focuses on issues around education, I hope and believe it will also have a wider application. Each political jurisdiction has its own history, culture, and institutional structure, yet there are also common drivers in all of them. There are even important similarities in many aspects of politics and government between parliamentary systems such as Canada or Australia, and republican systems such as that in the United States. The same is true of policy fields. Education has dynamics that are different from health or agriculture, but the kinds of dilemmas that arise or the ways in which pressures are expressed and acted on are also similar in many ways. On the basis of discussions with many people in a range of provinces, and countries, I expect that readers from other places as well as other policy fields will find they can transfer the accounts and ideas in this book to their own areas of interest.

The view I try to develop in this book is that government is far from perfect but that it is also important; that mistakes and shortcomings are inevitable but that on balance a government can still contribute to important improvements in our society. The same is true of education policy; we cannot make our education system perfect but can make it better. Despite the plethora of proposals, there is no magic bullet or quick fix for the limitations of government or our education system, but with care and attention the balance sheet of achievements against shortcomings can be positive. Public efforts should focus not on dramatic changes that are, finally, unlikely to help very much, but on the kinds of changes in political life, government organization, and public policy that will help push the balance in a positive direction.

The organization of the book is simple. There are two introductory chapters. One describes the start of a new government in Manitoba as a way of illustrating some of the important dynamics that drive government generally. The second chapter is about education policy – what we have in Canada and what we might need. Most of the book is a set of stories about issues that were prominent while I was deputy minister. These stories illustrate the dynamics outlined in the first few chapters and put them in very concrete terms. The book concludes with some ideas for reasonable improvements both in education and in government.

This book is an attempt to describe government as it appears to those who are engaged in it. It is not an exposé or an attempt to attack the bad guys or defend the good guys. I am not seeking to make myself or anyone else look particularly good – or bad. Although I was an insider for these events, the descriptions here are drawn from knowledge that is or could be in the public domain. Very few people are mentioned by name because my purpose is to look at systems and events. The civil servants' oath of office prevents divulging some kinds of information, such as the content of cabinet submissions or the specific differences of views within a government. However I do not believe that these limitations have prevented me from telling these stories in ways that are informative and complete.

I have also tried to avoid taking a partisan stance. I have been a supporter of the NDP for many years, and my connection to the party was part of the reason I was appointed deputy minister of education in 1999. However I believe that civil servants have a duty to be non-partisan, and each time I have been a civil servant I have severed all political party connections including membership, donations, and participation in elections or other partisan events. The reader will certainly hear the stories from my point of view, which means a certain degree of exasperation with the official opposition, as all senior civil servants tend to feel no matter who is in office. This book does not focus on the virtues of the government or the shortcomings of the opposition, but on the larger dynamics that drive and constrain all governments. I see politics not so much as a matter of heroes and villains, but of systems. A book that focuses on flaws and mistakes may have the perverse effect of increasing levels of cynicism rather than promoting sustainable change. The same is true about our education system, where myths also abound.

Although published by a university press, this book is not intended to be a textbook on government or an academic treatise, but rather a picture of government as experienced from the inside. Many books are written about government, but very few of them present a world that feels right to someone who has been there. Some books are focused on explaining the structure and organization of government. Though these are important, it is even more important to have a sense of the complexity, intensity, and unpredictability that characterize government. Government is experienced less as a set of structures and processes than as a kind of endless bombardment of issues and events that have to be coped with. Accounts of this political world, including the one featured in this volume, almost always overstate its coherence and give a greater sense of its control of events than is actually experienced.

To achieve these purposes I have opted to write an account based primarily on my own experience, rather than use a theoretical framework based on a review of the literature on government or politics. In addition to providing sources for factual claims, I do cite selected work that speaks to the themes and issues I am trying to develop. I am drawn to work that highlights the unpredictability and limitations of government by people such as Yehezkel Dror, James March, Deborah Stone, and James Wilson. In the sections on education I have tried as well to provide some introduction to related literature without drowning the reader in references. It is my hope that this book will contribute in a small way to helping people work together to improve both education and government in our country.

Acknowledgments

I want to pay a special tribute to the Honourable Ronald Duhamel, who died while this book was being written. Ron hired me into the Manitoba Department of Education when he was its deputy minister in the 1980s. I learned an enormous amount from him about politics, and government, and about managing people, all of which he understood with great clarity. He was an outstanding leader and a wonderful person, whose untimely death was a great loss to the country as well as to the many people whose lives he touched.

My thanks go to all the people I worked with during my three years as deputy minister. I was honoured when Premier Gary Doer asked me to take on the job; he always treated me with courtesy and respect, and I in turn had enormous respect for his ability to cope so well with the myriad demands of his job. I worked closely with two ministers: Drew Caldwell, who was minister of the Department of Education, Training and Youth throughout my time in government; and Diane McGifford, who became minister of the Department of Advanced Education in January 2001. Drew and Diane, though very different in their styles and approaches, both gave me tremendous support and a great deal of latitude to do the job in my own way. Their special assistants, Annalea Mitchell, Judith Baldwin, and later Susan McMurrich, were also great colleagues. I had quite a bit to do with many other ministers and political staff in the premier's office, as well as in other departments. Politicians and their staff work under pressures that are almost impossible for people who have not been there to understand. The demands on them are enormous and ceaseless. Most of them – in all political parties, I believe – are genuinely motivated by a sense of the public good. They deserve much more credit than they get.

The same is often true of civil servants. There were about 900 people in the Department of Education and Training. I met almost all of them and worked closely with many at one point or another, as well as with many people in other parts of the government and in other governments in Canada and beyond. In any large organization there are some people who are not pulling their weight. But many, many civil servants work very hard for modest rewards because they believe in the importance of what they are doing. It was my privilege to work with many talented and dedicated people in the civil service. To mention names would inevitably mean leaving out some wonderful colleagues. However, I must especially thank the staff who worked in the deputy minister's office during my tenure: Yolande Choiselat, Nicole LaRoche, Diana McClymont, Monique Rowson, and Carla Young. In simply going about their work every day cheerfully and effectively, no matter how difficult the circumstances, they, like so many other colleagues in civil services across Canada, are an example of value for money for the people of their province.

Many people had a role in the development of this book. My University of Manitoba colleague Paul Thomas has long been a source of helpful thinking about government, and he kindly read and commented on several drafts of parts of the book. Many colleagues in the Manitoba government provided useful comments, helped me reconstruct dates and events accurately, and corrected some of my tendencies to generalize unduly. I appreciate the willingness of the University of Toronto Press to produce a book that does not fit the category of an academic work, yet is not quite a 'popular' book either. The editors at University of Toronto Press, including Virgil Duff, Lauren Freeman, and Stephen Kotowych, were helpful at all stages. The reviewers of earlier drafts of the manuscript provided helpful suggestions for improvement.

Despite all this assistance, I emphasize that all interpretations, errors, and omissions are solely my responsibility. Nothing in this book should be held to represent the policy or opinion of the government of Manitoba, the Manitoba Department of Education, or any other official body, either now or at any time in the past.

GOVERNING EDUCATION

CHAPTER 1

Governing

It's 21 September 1999, election night in Manitoba. In a large hall in north St Boniface, near the site where the city of Winnipeg was founded nearly two hundred years earlier, members of the New Democratic Party are gathering for what they hope will be a celebration. The party has been out of power for eleven years. Now they see an opportunity to regain government from the Progressive Conservatives, under Premier Gary Filmon. The polls have been good. The NDP leader, Gary Doer, has seemed the clear victor since the television debate a couple of weeks earlier.

Doer has been leader of the NDP since 1988 and has contested and lost three elections to Gary Filmon. However that record is somewhat misleading. In 1988 Doer was a relatively new cabinet minister when the NDP, far behind the opposition Conservatives in the opinion polls, was thrust into an unexpected election when one of its backbenchers voted against the government on the budget. Then NDP premier Howard Pawley chose to resign in an effort to allow the party to put on a new face. Doer, seen by enough members as the best person to take on this challenge, won the hurried leadership race that spring. The election proved very difficult. The NDP, battered by several unpopular decisions in the previous two years, was badly defeated despite the change in leadership. It became the third party behind the resurgent Liberals under Sharon Carstairs. The Conservatives gained only a minority government. Two years later, in 1990, Gary Filmon won a bare majority, the NDP moved back into second place and into the role of Official Opposition, and the Liberals slipped to third. In 1995 the PCs won another majority, though the NDP again picked up votes and seats while the Liberals largely disappeared. By 1999 people in the NDP were ready for a win.

4 Governing Education

In Manitoba, elections are usually close. As table 1.1 (see p. 11) shows, between 1969 and 1999 the Conservatives won a total of 235 seats and the NDP 233. Elections can be decided by a few hundred votes in each of a small number of swing ridings, so even as the mood in the hall is buoyant, nobody is taking anything for granted.

The polls close at 8 p.m., and about half an hour later the first returns start to come in. The NDP is in the lead almost from the outset, but initial returns are always skimpy and subject to sudden change depending on which parts of a riding are reporting first. The Manitoba legislature has 57 seats, so 29 are needed for a bare majority but 31 are needed for a working majority. The crowd in the hall grows in size steadily as election workers come in from their constituency offices to join the central party. The NDP is shown as leading in 20 ridings, then 25, then 30. Excitement grows. There is a dip at one point as a couple of constituencies move from an NDP lead to a Conservative lead. But by 10 p.m. it is clear that the NDP will win at least 31 seats, and late in the evening a sudden influx of votes in one northern riding brings the final total to 32. When the premier-elect comes into the hall around 10 p.m. to give his acceptance speech, the atmosphere is electric.

That moment – the beginning of a new government – has much to do with why this book has been written. The start of every new administration is marked by great excitement and a sense of possibility. Supporters believe that now that the right people are in office, all good things will be done, all wrongs righted, and glorious days will follow. But the reality of governing is otherwise. Compromises have to be made and mistakes are inevitable. New governments necessarily begin with high hopes, but for a range of reasons, many not of their own making, they do not or cannot fulfil them all. Sometimes the promises are not good ones, but in many cases changes in the situation make it impossible or unwise to do what was planned.

This gap between promises and delivery is one of the reasons there is so much cynicism about politics in Canada, and elsewhere. Opposition parties draw as much attention as they can to a government's shortcomings, while media coverage may also focus on unfulfilled promises or shortcomings in delivery. In such situations people become disenchanted and look for simple explanations, even if these are wrong (Plank & Boyd, 1994). If people believe, for example, that changes in politics are just a matter of electing different people, they will inevitably be disappointed with the results when a new crew is caught up in the same dynamics that shaped all the previous governments. Alternatively, people may believe that it is not important who wins, that all politicians are the same, so voting does not matter. Of course who we elect does matter; governments do differ in important ways. But all governments have to work in a world of political and institutional realities that limit what they can do.

For eighteen months or so prior to that celebration in Winnipeg on 21 September 1999, I had been part of a small group asked by Gary Doer to plan the transition to a new NDP government. Transition planning is necessary for an opposition party because a new government has to hit the ground running. It is too late after the election to start to think about what needs to be done to get a new government in place. Critical decisions about organization, political management, key staff positions, and initial implementation of the new government's program have to be in place on the very first day in office. By election day the transition team had put together such a plan.

The day after the election I took two weeks of holidays from my job at the University of Manitoba to work full time on the transition process. The new government would be sworn in to office two weeks after the election. It is traditional in parliamentary systems that a defeated government avoids making any unnecessary decisions or appointments, leaving those for the new regime after it is sworn in. During the two-week interlude the premier-elect delegated a small group of people – about half a dozen in total – to act on his behalf to begin the transition and also keep an eye on government business.

Towards the end of the transition period the premier-elect asked me to become deputy minister of education for the new government. I felt qualified to do the job, having spent my whole career working in education in a variety of capacities. In the 1970s I had been an elected school trustee before the age of 20 – at that time the youngest school board member in Canada. I had worked in government twice before – running youth programs in the 1970s and holding several senior jobs in the Department of Education through much of the 1980s. For six years I worked closely with the deputy minister of the day, and so was reasonably familiar with that role. I had worked in all areas of the department, including schools, post-secondary education, and adult education. I was also familiar with most of the Manitoba education system and many of the main actors. In 1989 I left government to join the Faculty of Education at the University of Manitoba, where my academic career was also focused on issues of education policy, politics, and economics. Most importantly, I had some strong views – described more fully in the next chapter – on what should (and should not) be done in education by a progressive provincial government.

I did not want to leave the university permanently, so I agreed to take on the deputy's job for two or three years on secondment. I served as deputy minister from October 1999 to September 2002, at which time I returned to my academic position at the university. At first there was a single Department of Education and Training that included post-secondary and adult education. In January 2001 a separate Minister of advanced education was appointed, and I served as deputy to both ministers.

I went into government knowing pretty much what it was like and without wildly optimistic expectations. Even so, the job had many frustrations, as later chapters will show. Sometimes decisions were made too quickly, without adequate consideration, while at other times choices that seemed obvious were endlessly delayed. Attention was constantly diverted, by many other demands, both political and bureaucratic, from what I considered to be the important issues. These frustrations are endemic to every government. They are shared by politicians and administrators in every system. Thus it is not so much a matter of who is in charge, as of the dynamics that affect all governments. This chapter will attempt to illustrate some of those features.

The conflicts, ambiguities, sudden changes, short timelines, and endless pressures that confront any government are extraordinarily intense and very difficult to convey in print. Perhaps this is why there are also so few good novels about politics. These realities are more accurately portrayed in theatre or film, where the enormous emotional component of politics and government can be given greater prominence. But even a TV series like *The West Wing*, though it does capture some of the speed and pressure of government, provides a greater sense of order and thoughtfulness than often exists. In reality, government is shaped largely by contingencies such as the individuals who get elected, the pressures that happen to arise, and the constant effort to bring some degree of order to an unpredictable and often very surprising world.

Government gets a lot of bad press today, not only in Canada but also in many other countries. Although this book is in large measure a defence of government, I acknowledge at the outset that governments are very imperfect organizations. They may fail to do what is important or right, and may actually do things that are bad and dangerous. They are sometimes driven by the pursuit of wrong ends: power above purpose, the short-term over the long-term, the interests of the powerful instead of the interests of the majority. Image becomes more important than substance, and personal agendas may dominate public ones. Truth may become a casualty of political convenience (Savoie, 1999).

Evidence of these faults is all too readily at hand, and has led to many scathing denunciations. A strong recent example is Murray Edelman's most recent book, *The Politics of Misinformation* (2001). Edelman's earlier books (1964, 1988) were strong and very perceptive critiques of the deficiencies of American politics and government, but this book, written when he was 80 years old, is particularly bleak. Linda McQuaig's work (1995, 1998) provides a Canadian analogue, exposing the many weaknesses of our governments. It would be easy to cite many other examples.

These criticisms are widely shared by the public. Confidence in politicians and governments as evidenced in polls has declined substantially over the years (Nevitte 1996). The endless jokes about political venality and ineptitude on the talk shows, the bitter comments one can hear on the street or when working on an election campaign, are evidence that many people have little or no respect for politics or those who practise it. Polls conducted by the Centre for Research and Information on Canada (CRIC, 2002) indicate that Canadians have deep misgivings about their political leaders. Membership in political parties has declined, and, even more worryingly, voter turnout is dropping. There is potential for our system of government to lose its basic legitimacy in the eyes of citizens.

Proposals to remedy the deficiencies of government are also readily available. Those on the political right argue that governments are so untrustworthy that they should be limited only to the most essential functions, leaving other activities to the private sector. Those on the left denounce governments' failure to address seriously the real and pressing needs of society around issues such as the environment, human rights, or social inequality. All agree that governments are just not doing what they should.

Whatever the merits of these critiques of government, they cannot lead to improvement unless they are rooted in a clear understanding of how organizations work and what is possible. The weaknesses of government are not unique. All human organizations display similar problems and all are subject to possible corruption as people seek power. Recent revelations of shoddy or criminal corporate behaviour in Canada and other countries are only the latest examples of how corruption seeps into and sometimes becomes the standard in all kinds of organizations. In the private sector it is clear that the same temptations to abuse authority, line one's own pocket, and pursue private ends at public expense are real and frequent hazards, often kept in check only because of regulation by the state. Even religious organizations, officially dedicated to higher purposes, more than occasionally lapse into practices that fall far short of the ideals they preach, such as hiding or condoning abuses of power. In every setting power tends to corrupt. That is why all organizations and systems – governments, but also private and non-profit organizations – need checks and controls to prevent wrongdoing.

Nor are these deficiencies new. One only has to read Machiavelli to see that the same concerns existed five hundred years ago. Shakespeare's historical plays give graphic evidence of political machinations, though in those days they often led to death rather than electoral defeat. Anthony Trollope's political novels, set in England in the late nineteenth century, show striking similarities, including the concern for media coverage, to the world that I try to describe in this book.

We also need to remind ourselves that governments have been the source of some wonderful human achievements, such as education systems, social security systems, relief of poverty, health care for all, protection of the environment, support for a climate of law, and the provision of physical infrastructure. Compared with much of the world, public affairs and services in Canada operate with impressive quality and efficiency and are one of the reasons our country ranks highly in world comparisons of quality of life. That none of these things is done flawlessly should not blind us to their virtues. In all the talk about malaise and problems it is important to be reminded of what has been done that is important and worthwhile.

Although all organizations have similar failings, several features that are unique to government make both the temptations and dangers of corruption something to be taken very seriously.

Governments are entrusted with enormous power even though they are hedged in by various controls. Governments have the power to coerce, to impose taxes and spend on public purposes, to imprison, to deprive people of rights, to start wars, even under some circumstances to kill and order killing. Decisions of governments on many matters – taxation, health, education, environment, child welfare – can have huge consequences for large numbers of people. One does not have to look far either geographically or historically to see the results of despotic regimes, including some that originally came into office through elections.

Government also occurs in an atmosphere of constant conflict. In part the conflict is driven by the competition for office between political rivals. The opposition is always seeking to discredit the government, and it uses whatever vehicles it can within legal and political limits to do so. The media also contribute to this atmosphere because readers, viewers, and listeners are drawn to stories that involve disagreement or wrongdoing. However, beyond these forces, which will be discussed more fully a little later, conflict is endemic to politics because much of what any government does involves matters where there is considerable disagreement over what to do. A private company is in business to make a profit through provision of goods or services, but governments are about defining and shaping the kind of society we live in, and people disagree, often fundamentally, on these questions. Even where there is agreement on goals or purposes there may be disagreement on how the goals should be achieved. For example, everyone wants better health care but some people want more hospital care while others favour more prevention. Some want health services supplied by the public sector while others prefer a market-based system. These differences mean that in many cases any government action – or inaction – will lead to strong opposition and public debate. Opposition to particular policies or actions can end up serving to discredit the entire political process.

On the other side of the same coin, governments embody our hopes for ourselves as a society and are expected to be about the public good in a way that private organizations are not. Simply put, governments deal with things that matter very deeply to us and we expect better behaviour from them than we do from other organizations. How we organize our education system is more important to more people than whether a particular product is produced by a particular company. Issues such as environmental quality, health, social programs, transportation policy, or policing are fundamentally important. The decisions we make on these matter collectively through the political process often have long-lasting and far-reaching consequences. Thus there is, appropriately, a different standard for governments than for private organizations. It is because they represent our ideals that governments take so much abuse for their failings. The challenges of new political movements or the attacks of Edelman or McQuaig on government are clearly rooted in their sense of idealism. People want government to be better, and are bitterly disappointed when it falls short of their expectations.

Manitoba in 1999

Manitoba is a province of little more than one million people, three-quarters of whom live in or close to the capital, Winnipeg. The population has grown very slowly, and outmigration of young people is a long-standing occurrence. Most of the province is sparsely populated, and, like other areas of Canada, rural depopulation has been proceeding steadily for many years with no sign of stopping. The northern third is virtually uninhabited. There is a substantial immigrant and visible minority population, while the Aboriginal population is about 12 per cent of the total and is growing rapidly, especially in Winnipeg and in the north.

Manitoba is about in the middle of Canadian provinces on most indicators of wealth and prosperity. It has a mixed economy, with no one sector dominant, and so tends to experience neither sudden booms nor sudden busts.

The political culture of Manitoba is largely cautious, with important populist and collective elements deriving from the province's early days of settlement when people depended greatly on their neighbours. By and large voters seem to prefer moderate governments that are close to the political centre. Politically, the province has alternated between Conservative and NDP governments for the last thirty years. The split in political allegiance roughly follows a line from northwest to southeast running right through Winnipeg. To the west and south is Conservative territory; to the north and east is NDP. Winning an election usually depends on slight movements in this line, moving a few seats from one camp to the other. Between 1969 and 1999, as table 1.1 shows, neither party has won more than thirty-four seats, and only once has a party received more than 44 per cent of the votes. If one totals the nine elections shown in the table, the two parties have won almost exactly the same number of seats. The Liberals remain a significant third party, though only once (in 1988) have they been more than a third party. More often they get a substantial vote but win very few seats.

The 1999 election was a substantial win for the NDP by Manitoba standards, giving the party its second-highest share of the popular vote and a comfortable majority (though the party was re-elected even more substantially in 2003). The win was a product of a number of developments that also had lasting implications for the new government.

Most fundamental to the future government were pressures related to the province's fiscal capacity. In Canada in recent years every gov-

Table 1.1
Party standings and the vote in Manitoba elections, 1969–99

	PC		NDP		All Others	
Year of election	No. of seats	% of vote	No. of seats	% of vote	No. of seats	% of vote
1969	22	35.4	28	38.1	7	26.0
1973	21	36.5	31	42.1	5	20.8
1977	33	48.6	23	38.5	1	12.6
1981	23	43.7	34	47.2	0	8.8
1986	26	40.4	30	41.4	1	17.9
1988	25	38.3	12	23.6	20	37.9
1990	30	41.9	20	28.7	7	29.1
1995	31	42.9	23	32.7	3	24.2
1999	24	40.6	32	44.2	1	14.6
Total seats	235		233		45	

Source: Data for the number of seats are from the *Canadian Parliamentary Guide, 2002* (Toronto: Thomson/Gale). Data for percentage of votes are compiled from the historical summaries on the Elections Manitoba web site: www.electionsmanitoba.ca.

ernment has been torn between pressures to spend money on things the public wants and pressures to eliminate deficits and then reduce taxes. The way a political party handles these pressures depends on its internal constituencies and predispositions.

As a party committed to smaller government and lower taxes, the Manitoba Progressive Conservatives had faced the problem of very substantial budget deficits in the early 1990s. To cope with this challenge they cut spending in many areas, including education, and later passed a strict law that required a balanced budget each year except under defined and unusual circumstances. The legislation also required a referendum before any increase in personal income tax rates. Manitoba's own-source revenues tend to grow relatively slowly, and for this relatively poor province revenues depend substantially on federal transfers, which were themselves cut sharply by the Chrétien government after 1994. The province was in a fiscal straitjacket and the balanced budget legislation tightened all the straps.

Although the Filmon PC government was less active in the area of privatization than some other provincial governments, it still made a number of forays in this direction. The most notable was the sale of the Manitoba Telephone System in 1996, the proceeds from which were fundamental to the government's ability to produce balanced budgets thereafter. There were some other privatization moves in health care, as well as a climate in education policy that supported private schools, school choice, and so-called entrepreneurship in school financing (see Chapter 7).

These developments were strongly opposed in some sectors. Public debate included many statements of concern about the declining state of public services. Cuts in funding to public services and programs were the subject of many protests. The sale of the Manitoba Telephone System aroused very strong opposition and led to some of the stormiest scenes in the legislature in many years. As the decade went on, politics in Manitoba, as in many other provinces, became increasingly fractious.

Much of the NDP's political constituency wanted to see program renewal and expansion in health, education, and social services. After years of financial pressure under the Conservatives they looked forward to better times for important social programs. The new government would face huge challenges in all areas of social policy because of years of financial restraint. Many areas of provincial infrastructure had also suffered, including capital for health and education. The province faced huge challenges in providing greater opportunity for a rapidly growing Aboriginal population, an issue identified by every department in the briefing materials prepared for the new government at the time of the election. The pressures on the public purse would be many.

At the same time, prior to the 1999 election and after some fierce internal debate, the NDP had committed to keeping and respecting the balanced budget legislation. Gary Doer's view was that the party had to make this commitment if it was to be seen as a credible government by voters. However in a province that tends to have modest growth, keeping the legislation in place meant less revenue available to meet all the pressures for additional spending.

Tax cuts were another tough issue. The Progressive Conservative governments in Ontario and Alberta were cutting taxes aggressively in the 1990s. The NDP government in Saskatchewan, in a province with a long history of outmigration, felt compelled to make its own tax cuts, though smaller ones, to keep some equilibrium with Alberta. Could Manitoba be the only province west of Quebec that did not make any tax reductions, even if this would further reduce revenues? The decisions on these issues had, of course, important implications for education as one of the main areas of provincial spending.

Also important in the 1999 Manitoba election were revelations concerning the Conservative effort to win a number of ridings in the 1995 election by finding and financing from Conservative party sources supposed third-party candidates who would split the vote in an effort to help the Tory candidate win (Smith, 2003). This scandal was the subject of a public inquiry in 1998, and the subsequent finding, that senior Conservative government officials had taken part and then attempted to cover it up, had hurt the Filmon administration.

The 1999 NDP campaign (in which I played no direct role) focused on five key commitments: on health care, on 'hope for young people,' on crime, on keeping Manitoba Hydro as a crown corporation, and on balancing the budget and reducing property taxes. During the campaign these commitments were given more detail and some smaller additional promises were made, but the party wanted to focus on a small number of main commitments it could later demonstrate it had kept. Knowing that the fiscal pressures would be considerable, the party had kept its promises modest and provided careful costing of each of them during the election campaign. (The commitments related to education, under the 'hope for young people' theme, are discussed more fully in Chapter 2.)

People

The term *politician* seems to suggest a class of people who have something in common. However, about the only thing that all politicians have in common is that they are actively engaged, at a particular moment, in electoral politics. Otherwise they are a highly varied lot. It is doubtful that the people in any other occupational group – doctors, teachers, electricians, insurance agents – are more diverse than are the people in politics. The NDP caucus elected in the fall of 1999 included people whose backgrounds were as ministers of religion, civil servants, labour leaders, teachers, nurses, farmers, social workers, leaders of community organizations, lawyers, and university professors, among others. They ranged in age from under 40 to nearly 60. A few had been in politics for many years, while others had just made their entry into provincial politics. There were eight women – a higher proportion than the Canadian norm, which is itself slowly growing.

The NDP had committed to a smaller cabinet than the eighteen members that the Conservatives had going into the election, and to fewer senior civil service positions. The cabinet formed in the fall of 1999 had fifteen members, including five women and two Aboriginal people. As a government, the group was inexperienced. Only one person – the new premier – had previously held a cabinet position. One or two others had been in the caucus but not in the cabinet prior to 1988, when the party was last in power. A number of others had held office at the municipal or school board level.

Knowing that ministers would all be new to the job, the transition team had recommended a series of orientation and briefing meetings for new MLAs and ministers, but in the press of other demands on a brand-new government most of these plans were not implemented. In some of the key departments the new ministers were initially supported by transition advisers. These were people from outside the system who were supportive of the new government and also knew the way the civil service worked. Their job was to help ministers begin to get a handle on their departments and the issues without being captured by the existing policies and people. The transition advisers were in place for the first few weeks, by which time ministers had their own special assistants and executive assistants in place and the central political management structure was also fully operational. In Manitoba each minister usually has only two political staff, including one person to do constituency work – far fewer than in the federal government or larger provinces.

This group of politicians embodied the reality that people enter politics for the most varied of reasons. Some politicians are truly ambitious for themselves. Some have deep commitments to particular public issues or a rather general wish to do some good. Some are drawn to politics by personal connections – a friend or family member, for example. Some love the excitement that politics can offer. Still others end up in the race almost by accident, because somebody thought they might be a good candidate and talked them into running. Once elected, people may stay because they like it, they get used to it, or because they do not have other options. Since human motives are usually complicated, for many people more than one of these factors may be in play.

One result of this diversity, of course, is that there really isn't a typical politician. All politicians are engaged in politics and so are concerned about voters, public opinion, issues, and elections; still, they do not think alike, neither generally nor with regard to particular issues. People do come into politics with ideas about the world and what should be done or not done. Some politicians begin with ideas that are well developed and strongly held, at least on some issues. Others have much vaguer and more flexible views. Almost everybody has some strong opinions but very few people have strong views on every issue.

Outsiders think of political parties as being of one mind, but in Canada there is often more diversity of opinion within any political party than there is difference between the parties. There were members of the NDP who would have been comfortable in the Conservative party and vice-versa. Moreover, people in the same party, or even in the same cabinet, may dislike each other, perhaps because they disagree on policy questions or simply at a personal level. For example, two people may have similar views on many issues, but may see each other as rivals for certain positions. Stories are certainly told about political leaders who go out of their way to make things difficult for potential successors because they happen not to like them. The intensity of political life tends to exacerbate these tensions because there is so little 'down time' in which to build relationships or defuse problems.

It is important to keep in mind that cabinets have to be made from the people who were elected. In a province like Manitoba the government side will elect thirty to thirty-five members, so a premier always has a limited choice as to who to put into the cabinet. Moreover, in forming a cabinet the talents of potential ministers are only one consideration. The premier also has to take into account the need to satisfy various important constituencies within the party, to include various regions of the province, and to take gender and ethnic equity into account. Every government will include some ministers who are very talented and others who are less so.

The fifteen ministers appointed in 1999 – increased to sixteen early in 2001 – varied in the influence they wielded. As in every government, a few ministers had a powerful impact on the government as a whole because of their political stature or their policy skills or their previous experience. Others had quite a bit of say over their own work but were less concerned with or had less influence on government-wide issues. Still others were less influential in all respects. These status differences become quickly and widely known inside the government, not only to ministers but also to senior officials who soon learn which ministers are able to get their agendas into and through the cabinet and its committees or have the ear of the premier.

Organizationally, the new NDP government in Manitoba operated with few cabinet committees. The Treasury Board and the Community Economic Development Committee (CEDC) had important roles in finance and economic policy, respectively. Other committees were set up on particular priority issues such as the Healthy Child Committee, which was charged with putting into place the government's election commitments on its agenda for children. Most issues were handled by the cabinet as a whole, including review and ratification of decisions made by committees such as the Treasury Board.

Differences among people mean that political issues may never be resolved fully, even within a government.[1] Education can be a particularly difficult portfolio in this respect, because, as in the Manitoba cabinet, many members had been teachers, school board members, and university professors, and so felt that they had some contribution to make on education issues. In any field, though, even when a policy on an issue has been hammered out and agreed to, there may be ministers who agree reluctantly and who would like nothing better than to raise the issue again if circumstances suggest the possibility of a different decision. As a government saying goes, 'That's final ... unless it isn't.'

Another consequence of the diversity in any cabinet is that it may matter a great deal who sits in which particular seat. One education minister may be strongly interested in schools while another might be more oriented to post-secondary or adult education. Drew Caldwell was a minister of education who brought to the job particular interests in, among other things, municipal government, heritage and conservation, and Canadian history, as well as a knowledge of rural Manitoba. His strong interest in school district amalgamations (Chapter 6) turned out to be critical. Diane McGifford as minister of advanced education cared deeply about gender issues and about the situation of people living on the margins of society, so her department paid more attention to accessibility issues than might have been the case with someone else. These are individual predilections; another person in the role might have brought different emphases.

These differences matter because individual ministers in most governments do have considerable scope to define and pursue issues. Decisions on high-profile policy matters are usually made collectively in cabinet or by the premier. However, there are simply too many issues for all or even most of them to get this kind of attention. During my time as deputy minister, the cabinet discussed many educational issues, though some of these were left to the minister with some advice from

---

1 Janice MacKinnon's book (2003) on her experience as Saskatchewan's finance minister shows how deep the differences in views were within the Romanow NDP government, but the same could be said of every government.

colleagues, and quite a few other issues, important in education but not necessarily to the government as a whole, were handled in the Department without much direction from the central government apparatus.

A minister's experience, style, and personality therefore matter a great deal. Some ministers see everything through their constituency interests while others tend to have a much broader view. Some have experience in managing organizations but many do not. Some have spent years in their field while others may have very little background in a new area of responsibility. Some are keen readers and want to know about many details of programs and department activities while others are much more focused on the political implications and see their role as being out in the community. Some are self-confident and highly effective with public groups but others may be quite shy and dislike public events. It seems odd to talk about shy politicians, but there certainly are some, including the occasional person who is afraid of speaking in public. More than a few politicians do not much like public events even though they know these events are a key part of their work. Some ministers are excellent communicators while others have difficulty conveying a message. Some ministers have strong personal agendas of things they want to accomplish while others do not. Some ministers have wonderful people skills while others can be petty tyrants. These differences affect not only how ministers go about their work, but their ability to take on various issues and the way their staff and departments manage.

One of the challenges of being a minister is how to get good feedback on your performance (if, indeed, you want such feedback; not everyone does). Other people usually want things from ministers and so tend to flatter them. Government is so hierarchical that it would be highly unusual for a civil servant to argue with a minister even if the civil servant was absolutely sure the minister was wrong. And very few deputy ministers would be willing to tell their minister that she or he was not approaching the job in a constructive way. As a civil servant, when you have a terrible minister you simply suffer through it as best you can.

Public Opinion

Everything in government occurs in the shadow of elections. Every government is thinking all the time about how to improve its prospects for being re-elected. For politicians the task can be put simply, though it is far from simple to accomplish: it is to be elected and to stay elected as long as possible. To do this politicians must convince voters that their party is better able to manage the challenges facing the province or country. Politics is a competitive process, in which individuals and parties bid for public support. No wonder politicians are highly sensitive to public opinion.

One frequently hears this dynamic spoken of with cynicism, as in 'politicians are only interested in being elected.' Of course they are, in exactly the same way that hockey players are interested in winning the Stanley Cup or authors are interested in having their books widely read and admired. What else can they do? That is how politicians achieve their goals. We vote for certain people because we think they are most likely to do what we believe needs to be done. Voters would not be better pleased by politicians who did not care whether we liked what they did. Indeed, one can also hear exactly that criticism – that once people are elected they stop caring about what people think. In my experience the latter is rarely the case. The British cabinet minister in the TV series *Yes, Minister* always reacted with dismay when his chief civil servant, Sir Humphrey, called for taking a courageous stand, since this meant doing something unpopular. Former prime minister Brian Mulroney talked about having the courage to do things that were unpopular. Of course in this case the eventual result of doing unpopular things was that the federal Progressive Conservative party was reduced to two seats in 1993, and thus lost its chance to do other important things. We vilify our politicians for currying favour and for ignoring our wishes, so we can hardly be surprised if they go to great lengths to try not to offend on one account or the other.

This is a crucial point in understanding the political process. In the short term a government can do things that are unpopular, but in the long term, public opinion determines who holds office and what direction public policy takes. Politicians' actions are more closely watched and more quickly judged than those of most people. Hence the aphorism that opposition parties do not win elections so much as governments lose them. Staying elected depends on enough people believing that you are doing enough of the right things. Considerations of popular opinion are and must be fundamental to the work of politicians. It is impossible to imagine what a democratic process would look like otherwise.

Satisfying public preferences is hard to do. The first difficulty is that it is hard to know what 'the public' wants. Voters are not necessarily well informed (Lapia & McCubbins 1998; Milner 2001). People can and do have strongly held views based on astonishingly little evidence – sometimes a personal experience, other times an account of someone else's personal experience. People are generally not given to the calculation of probabilities but are strongly influenced by stories and events (Kiesler & Sproull 1982). Because unusual events stand out, they tend to be given greater weight. Things that are relatively unimportant in the larger scheme, or soon forgotten, can become all consuming in the public mind, at least for a short time, especially when fanned by political opponents and the media.

That people are ill-informed on most issues is hardly surprising given the multiplicity of issues in the public domain at any one time. Even if we were interested, it is hard to see how most people could possibly be reasonably well informed on even a significant number of issues, many of which are highly complicated. So on a large number of issues, whether it be global warming, private health care, transport policy, or the state of our schools, most of us as citizens often form our views based on skimpy evidence. Polling late in 2002, when the Kyoto Protocol ratification was under discussion, showed that most Canadians supported this accord but actually knew very little about what it was (Ipsos-Reid 2002). The same would be true of many other issues.

People's opinions on political issues do not need to be reasonable or consistent. It is quite possible – indeed, it is common – for people to want things that are mutually inconsistent. For example, voters may, and often do, want lower taxes, less borrowing, and more spending all at the same time. They may want greater freedom of choice in schooling while also wanting all students to study the same things in the same way. Canadian polling has shown that people want schools to give more emphasis to every subject (COMPAS 2001) – clearly impossible unless the school day or year is to be made longer, which people do not favour.

Another problem is that preferences are not easily aggregated (Arrow, 1970; Mackenzie, 2000). It is possible for people to prefer option A to option B, and option B to option C, but also option C to option A. This seems illogical, but voters do not have to be logical. Much depends on how a question is posed, which explains in part why different polls on similar issues can come up with quite different results. The inability to rank order preferences poses enormous problems for governments as they attempt to ascertain what people want them to do.

The Role of Evidence

For politicians, what people believe to be true is much more important than what may be true in fact. A number of politicians have told me on various occasions that while the evidence I was presenting for a particular policy might be correct, the poli s not what people would accept. As former Ontario deputy mi McGill University president Bernard Shapiro put it, 'Al¹ ⌐sions are made by leaping over the data' (Shapiro, 1991). ⌐ Proust put it, 'the facts of life do not penetrate to the sphere in ⌐h our beliefs are cherished ... they can aim at them continual blows of contradiction and disproof without weakening them; and an avalanche of miseries and maladies coming, one after another, without interruption into the bosom of a family, will not make it lose faith in either the clemency of its God or the capacity of its physician' (Proust, 1928/1956).

Beliefs drive political action and voting intentions much more than do facts. Witness the strength and depth of public support for various measures that clearly fly in the face of strong evidence. Many people continue to believe in capital punishment as a deterrent for crime, or that welfare cheating is a bigger problem than income tax evasion. A good example in education would be the amalgamation of school districts (discussed more extensively in Chapter 6). Many voters instinctively feel that fewer school districts will save money by reducing duplication of effort. The research evidence says otherwise, but the fact that nine Canadian provinces have reduced the number of school boards in recent years shows the power of public beliefs even if they are not well-founded. Other examples are the belief that eliminating tuition fees would substantially increase participation in post-secondary education, or that 'retaining students in grade' (failing them) will improve achievement. Both are widely believed even though a strong body of evidence indicates otherwise. Where beliefs are very strongly held political leaders challenge them at their peril.

While discussion and argument are one important way in which political disagreements are handled, there is growing interest all over the world in the use of research and evidence to inform public policy. Even while most governments in Canada have reduced their staffing in areas of research and policy support, they are increasingly trying to learn about 'what works' so as to be able to point to good grounds for their decisions. Insofar as research is linked to science, and science is highly credible to the public, the use of research is one way to show one's commitment to the public good.

The role of research and evidence in politics is increasingly complex (Levin, 2002). As with consultation, sometimes research is taken seriously, and a government genuinely wants to find out whether policy A will be more effective than policy B. Sometimes research plays a vital role in raising new issues leading to government action. The rise of interest in early childhood development in Canada, leading to the national Early Childhood Accord of 2000, was largely brought about by the effective promotion of a growing body of evidence about the vital role that early childhood plays in lifelong outcomes. Many other instances, from fields as diverse as health, environment, agriculture, or industrial development, could easily be cited.

Although governments are interested in research, they are also cautious about it. Sometimes people's opinions do not square with the best available evidence. It is very dangerous for any government to ignore what people believe to be true, no matter how much evidence one has on one's side. Also, evidence can be used against you very easily as it gets filtered through the interpretive lenses of news media or lobby groups. Because research is so seldom unambiguous, it can be drawn upon to support a political point, which is one reason governments are not always anxious to do or publish empirical work that evaluates their policies and programs. You get little credit in politics for being honest about your shortcomings. As a former minister said to me, 'A dog learns not to fetch the stick you use to beat it.'

While research is of growing importance, it is rarely the final arbiter of political decisions. For one thing, research is seldom definitive on an issue of importance. The half-full cup is, of course, also half empty. There is always another angle on the issue in which one person's positive becomes someone else's negative. This is one reason many people believe, wrongly in my view, that 'you can prove anything with research.' Also, human affairs change, sometimes rapidly, making knowledge out of date or of limited value. It is more accurate to say that research is one contributor, and sometimes a very important one, to the building of public opinion, which can lead in turn to government action. We can and should do more policy research in Canada, and make better use of it, but this does not mean that research will ever tell us definitively what we should do.

The Opposition, the Media, and Mistakes

Government is the only arena in which there is an official opposition whose job it is to make things look bad. This is a fundamental aspect of government whose impact is not adequately appreciated by most people. It is the job of the opposition to oppose and to present alternatives. Its members will work hard to show how government actions are wrong. In doing so they will not always be particularly concerned with balance or fairness. Any and every mistake can be used against a government. Wrongdoing that in the private sector might never become public at all, or, if public, might elicit only some brief negative comment, can force the resignation of ministers or the fall of governments.

Relations between governments and oppositions are strange to watch. The same people who yell accusations at each other in the legislature can occasionally be seen chatting amicably in the hallway or working out an agreement during a debate. This odd situation grows out of the nature of the government process.

On one hand, some factors draw the sides together. Everyone in government is engaged in the same activity, an activity that is poorly understood by others. No one understands the demands and frustrations of political life like other politicians, so there is some tendency to affinity just as people travelling abroad tend to be drawn to others from their home country. Moreover, elected members even on different sides spend a great deal of time together and go through some powerful shared experiences, such as late night sessions, heated debates on issues, and election campaigns. Getting the business of the legislature done requires a certain element of cooperation. There is constant negotiation and frequent agreement between the parties as to how work will proceed. Because beliefs vary so much within each party, it is quite possible that people may like some members on the other side. There may even be something that looks like a friendship across the House.

On the other hand, these people are opponents struggling for the same prize: holding office. Each side genuinely feels, generally speaking, that the other has the wrong approach and if elected will do damage. Thus neither side is particularly scrupulous about the means it uses to discredit the other. Accusations of incompetence or bad faith are a staple of political debate, and are often directed at individuals. Each side may feel that the other is going beyond the bounds of reasonable action in making accusations. Even when agreements are made, they may be broken suddenly if one side sees a potential political advantage. All of this can lead to considerable anger and bad feeling. Some political opponents have a visceral dislike for each other. This shifting back and forth between a no-holds-barred brawl and a polite exchange of views creates very unusual interpersonal dynamics.

The Official Opposition is aided in its work by the media. The media are certainly subject to enormous criticism for their role in public affairs (e.g., Edelman, 2001; Nadeau & Giasson, 2003). In later chapters I make some very critical comments on the role of the media, whose coverage tends to focus simplistically on heroes and villains, or winners and losers. Neither the journalists who write the stories nor the editors who make decisions about what to run and how to spin stories are always well informed on the substantive issues. There is little follow-up on issues in the longer term. The media distrust government and tend to look for problems and negatives. A reporter once told me that it was not important for the government to release its research reports, since '[he] wouldn't believe any report you issued anyway.' The result is an endless game between politicians and the media in which each side needs but also dislikes and distrusts the other. Government is a major source of stories for the media, while the latter are a vital source of publicity for politicians. A huge amount of energy in government goes into trying to manage media coverage of issues, though often with little success (Levin, 2004).

At the same time, the media also have their own pressures and constraints. Like any business, the electronic and print media are seeking more readers and viewers. The reality is that people are largely attracted by stories that feature conflict, problems, and fairly simple approaches to right and wrong. Many more people are likely to pay attention to a story about a lost child, say, than to one about the decline of an industry (Neuman, Just, & Crigler, 1992). However the relationship between the media and its readers and viewers is complex, and influence runs in both directions (Cappella & Jamieson 1997). While I believe the relationship on both sides could be improved, it is important to be realistic about the dynamics that drive the media, just as it is for politics and politicians.

Although many people decry negativity in politics, politicians use this strategy not necessarily because they like it, but because they think it works. Negative advertising during elections is less common in Canada than in the United States because Canadians do not respond well to it. If conflict is what attracts public attention, then conflict is what politicians will create, since public attention is what they must have. A politician friend once told me that he got far more publicity and recognition from a certain public relations gesture – though he well knew it had little real impact – than from any number of thoughtfully articulated policy papers, so he planned to continue the public relations gesture.

While an opposition is an important part of the democratic process, there is a potential 'tragedy of the commons' in the dynamic.[2] To the extent that political processes focus on the negative and the critical, even when the issues are not really substantive, they prevent us from learning what we might do to make improvements. A focus on the negative can also increase voter cynicism about politics, which in turn leads to even more focus on the negative since this is what too often resonates for people. Low levels of voter turnout in a number of countries indicate that there is substantial disenchantment with politics generally, which must surely be a worrisome trend. Yet as long as the incentives push political action in this direction, we are unlikely to see a change in pattern.

The adversarial nature of politics leads to a focus by governments on avoiding mistakes. Because so much attention is given to what is wrong, errors can result in very large political costs. A good example is the decision by many provinces in the 1990s to save money by reducing the number of nurses. Nursing shortages a few years later turned out to be a potent political issue that in places like Manitoba contributed significantly to the defeat of a government.

A culture in government of mistake avoidance means that politicians inevitably have to pay attention to details that no senior private-sector manager would consider because they always have to be worried that something small can turn into a large political problem. For example, opposition parties are fond of picking on so-called 'perks,' such as government travel or pensions. The travel and expense claims of ministers are regularly scrutinized by the opposition and the media in the hope that something can be turned into a cause célèbre and used to paint the government as arrogant or spendthrift. Opposition parties even argue that it should be possible to fund their promises through saving money currently being 'wasted.' Yet ministerial travel even at its most outlandish will never account for any meaningful percentage of the budget. Spending a few thousand dollars less here or there may be desirable, but it will not balance the budget or pay for programs. Yet it is often easier for an opposition to make a public case for wrongdoing on these small issues than on the big matters of public policy.

---

2 A tragedy of the commons (Hardin, 1968) occurs when the result of everyone acting in their own interest turns out to be bad for everyone. One example has to do with grazing animals on common land. Each person benefits by getting the most grazing for her or his animals, but the result of this approach may be that the entire area becomes unusable for any animals.

The pressure to avoid mistakes has been increased by developments such as the growth in auditing and the development of freedom of information. Both vehicles have important uses in increasing the transparency of government, but both can also be used in a politics of blame that moves attention away from important public issues to relatively trivial mistakes. Chapter 7 provides an instance of this.

The main responsibility for managing a government's response to all these issues resides in the central management structure. In all Canadian provincial governments, the Premier's Office is critically important. Almost every important issue, and certainly every issue with significant political implications, will get attention from the premier's staff. Premiers may also have to resolve issues where ministers disagree.

Premiers need to manage both a political agenda and a government system. Some premiers work with a single key adviser who looks after both the political and the bureaucratic. Others operate with two people, one on each 'side.' Under any model, though, key people in central government include the chief political adviser, the chief civil servant, and the chief communications manager.

The new NDP chief of staff to the premier was Bob Dewar, who had also been the chief organizer of the NDP election campaign and had worked extensively in the labour movement. The chief policy adviser, the secretary to cabinet for policy, was Paul Vogt, who had been the head caucus staff person while the NDP was in opposition. Donne Flanagan was appointed as communications director. Paul and Donne each had a small group of staff to manage, respectively, all the policy and communications issues, not only for government as a whole but for all the departments and agencies. As in other Canadian governments, these staff were appointed directly by the premier and cabinet into roles that are acknowledged to be political.

Premier Doer was very sensitive to the accusation that the NDP is a 'tax and spend' party. He wanted a small Premier's Office and a small political staff, to demonstrate his commitment to the prudent use of resources. While the transition group on which I served felt that the government's heavy agenda would require a few more people to manage, the premier refused to have any increase in the number of staff positions in his office from the previous administration, whether it was political staff, communications staff, or senior civil service managers. The result was a very small central staff. In the 1960s and 1970s provincial governments in Manitoba had put central planning groups in place to try to provide overall direction. Saskatchewan under Alan Blakeney in the 1970s had 75 people in its executive group (Blakeney & Borins, 1998). In 1999, even though government was bigger and quite a bit more complex, the total central political staff, including those concerned with policy and communications, numbered only about a dozen people. This is a small cadre with which to manage an ambitious policy agenda as laid out in the election campaign, a 15,000-person civil service, a wide array of relationships with outside institutions and organizations, and all the attendant political pressures. During my time in government, the central staff were very capable and worked extremely hard but despite this were often in the position of struggling to keep on top of all the issues, let alone provide strong longer-term direction.

Influence

Politics is about influence, so it is crucial to understand the processes through which political decisions are made. Whatever their own views may be, politicians want and need to understand what people think about the issues they are facing. This understanding is necessary, whether a government is deciding what to do or endeavouring to sell its position publicly. As people are better educated and better organized, the number and intensity of the pressures on politicians has risen.

The term *people* has several layers to it. There is in government intense interest in 'public opinion' writ large. This is why governments like polling and focus groups. They want to know what 'the person in the street' thinks or feels on issues of the day. However it isn't just general opinion that matters, but how strongly held and how important that opinion is. People have opinions on many issues, but for most of us there are only a few issues that will influence our behaviour, including how we vote. For instance, people are widely in favour of conservation when polled, but this belief may not even be deep enough to get them to recycle their newspaper. So governments are interested not only in how many people have a certain view but also in how strongly held that view is. For this purpose polling is a less satisfactory instrument (although pollsters have methods of identifying strength of feeling), and there is a tendency to rely on other indicators.

As one example, people who phone or write to a politician about an issue are generally much more concerned about it than the average person. That is why letters and phone calls, or, increasingly, e-mails are viewed as important. On the other hand, mass-produced, fill-in-the-blanks letters or postcards are less important precisely because they require less effort by the citizen.

While public opinion in a general sense is important, even more important are the views of key people and organizations. Over the last ten or fifteen years there has been an explosion of consultation on the part of governments. At one time a government would more likely handle its own policy and political work and then announce its position. That is seldom possible any longer. People expect and want to have a say on many public issues, often at more than one stage of the policy process. As a result governments are constantly conducting consultation activities of one kind or another: white papers, reports, public forums, task forces, commissions, surveys, and so on. In 2001 the Manitoba government tried to get a sense of how much consultation was going on across departments, and came up with well over 100 simultaneous processes. It would appear that citizens might need to quit their jobs in order to devote their full time to participating in consultations!

In Education while I was deputy we undertook several important consultation processes. One of the most extensive was related to the development of the K–S4[3] Agenda for student success, which involved hundreds of people in a series of regional meetings across the province (see Chapter 8). The government created a Commission on Class Size and Composition in the fall of 2000, which held public hearings all across the province in 2001. We also organized several major public events around two new priorities: the Manitoba Training Strategy and the College Expansion Initiative. Almost every policy proposal we made was discussed in some way, at least with the main organizations involved before it was finalized. In his early days as minister of education, Drew Caldwell held a series of meetings with about fifty people representing the main interest groups in the school system. Even the decision to amalgamate school districts occurred only after eighteen months of discussion, including analyses and reports by school districts on their preferred options. So important were these processes that in

---

3 In the 1990s Manitoba changed its high school designations from Grades 9 to 12 to Senior 1 to Senior 4, a change that took quite a bit of effort but had, as far as I could see, no substantive benefit. What is called K–12 (kindergarten to Grade 12) in other provinces is known as K–S4 in Manitoba. I had wanted to reverse this change because it was so useless, but was convinced by staff that a reversal would be just as much work, and just as unproductive, as the original change had been.

2001 our department appointed a full-time staff person to improve the management of our varied consultation processes with the public and with the main groups and organizations. At the same time, formal consultation processes are not always useful. Our department had in 1999 several advisory bodies that we eliminated because they were not accomplishing anything beyond holding meetings.

Not all consultation is serious. Sometimes there is a genuine wish to find out what people think; on other occasions consultation may be intended to provide cover for a decision that has already been made. The civil service may develop consultative processes, but may at the same time have its own strongly preferred options. On other occasions consultation turns out very differently than intended. For example governments sometimes like to deal with a thorny issue by turning it over to a commission of some kind, but such processes often yield recommendations that governments do not much like, such as proposals to be much more active or spend more money. Despite these limitations, growing consultation is a fact of political life.

Not everyone gets an equal opportunity to make her or his views known to government. Groups that are better organized and better financed simply have more opportunity to get their point across. Those who benefit least from our current policies are often also the least likely to have a strong voice in the political process. Many consultation processes are dominated, sometimes overwhelmingly so, by groups that are directly concerned. The 'average person' – whoever that may be – is not a major participant. For example, in consultations on educational issues the vast majority of briefs and appearances come from groups of educators: school boards, teachers, administrators. As awareness of the importance of consultation is growing, governments are looking at alternative ways of gathering input from a broader range of people, such as on-line surveys, focus groups, or polling.

Formal consultations are also only one small part of the process of influence. Governments are continually subject to pressure on almost every issue, usually from multiple quarters, to do contradictory things. The pressures can be unrelenting. A huge range of people and organizations devote time and attention to influencing government decisions. These processes work in multiple ways, from formal submission of position papers and meetings with ministers to much more informal chat when people meet. Responding to these positions, whether in person or in writing, is a main part of political work and often requires great delicacy in what is communicated to avoid giving offence.

In all their interactions and consultations politicians are generally interested in trying to respond positively to people's ideas and wishes. Sometimes a government will be prepared for a knock-down public battle in which it takes on opponents very directly. Aside from the specifics of the issue, there can be political benefit from this kind of battle if it convinces supporters that a government is serious about its agenda. Indeed, even people who are neutral on the issue may respect a government that appears to be acting strongly on its beliefs. The NDP government's decision shortly after its election to ban from Manitoba schools the Youth News Network, a commercial venture that proposed to pump advertising into schools in exchange for donations of computers, was in part intended to demonstrate a firm commitment to a principled action even in the face of substantial conflict.

Confrontation is, however, generally not the preferred mode. It is costly in terms of energy and political capital. In most cases the goal is to try to convince as many people as possible that their concerns are being addressed in some way, even if they do not entirely like the approach being taken. Most people would probably be surprised at how much time in government is spent trying to mollify people who are committed political enemies and who are unlikely ever to vote for the party in power. Yet their views still matter. Often opponents of the government get more attention than supporters, much to the annoyance of the latter.

Politicians are also influenced by their personal networks, the people they know and care about. These networks can include personal friends as well as constituents or important political allies. Here, too, political access is not equally distributed. Senior business and community leaders can always get a meeting with senior political people. A few words from the 'right' person can sometimes, but not always, have a powerful impact. The right person is not necessarily someone in a position of official power, either. Many stories are told in the political world about important decisions being shaped by the opinions of a spouse, an old friend, or, as told about one national leader, a hairdresser.

After a very short time in office, politicians come to realize that almost every contact they have is about influence. For people who left a particular occupation to enter politics it can be wrenching to realize that your former colleagues are now more interested in influencing what you are going to do than in you as a person. It often becomes impossible for ministers to have the kind of passing chat on issues that most of us enjoy with our peers.

Political Issues and Government Agendas

The five central commitments of the 1999 NDP election campaign have already been mentioned. Although every government comes to office with a set of policy ideals or commitments, the reality is that much of what governments attend to is not of their own design or preference. Government agendas are certainly shaped in part by political commitments, party platforms, and the views of key political leaders. Indeed, keeping election promises has become an important focus of political concern in recent years as part of an effort to counteract public cynicism about government.

In addition to party policy, political agendas are also influenced often to a much greater extent by external political pressures, changing circumstances, unexpected events, and crises. If the economy turns sour and revenues drop, if natural disasters occur, if new domestic developments take place, governments must respond in some way, even if that means taking attention and resources away from other activities that were high on the priority list. As Dror puts it, there is 'at any given moment a high probability of low probability events occurring. In other words, surprise dominates' (1986, 186). As an issue comes to be highly salient, other important issues inevitably drop out of sight.

The events of 11 September 2001 provide a perfect example of how something coming literally out of the sky can change everyone's sense of what is important. Security issues, which had been quite low-key in Canada, suddenly became of central concern. Related matters, such as Canada–U.S. border flow, foreign aid, and the health of the airline industry also rose suddenly on the agenda. Many other issues that had been in the news and on people's minds were suddenly shunted aside. Billions of dollars and immense amounts of time and energy were suddenly redirected to new purposes. In Manitoba, too, the government felt it important to respond to these events through new legislation and policy on a number of security-related issues. A special cabinet committee was set up, and for at least a few months a considerable amount of time and energy was diverted from other issues to security.

Of course 11 September is a dramatic example, but the point is a broader one. Issues do go in and out of the public mind and therefore in and out of political favour. The environment, which was a strong public concern a decade or so ago, faded for years until it was recently revived by the Kyoto accord and related issues. Unemployment is a big concern when levels are high, but naturally much less so when levels drop.

Similarly, government deficits were a huge issue a decade ago but are no longer high on the Canadian public's list.

While some political pressures relate to very important, long-term issues, others may concern small, short-term details. One cannot assume that the former will always be more important than the latter. Sometimes very small items can turn into huge political events (Bovens & t'Hart, 1994). For example, a single untoward event can undermine an entire system that may actually be working reasonably well, as those involved in health care or child welfare know only too well. Ninety-nine per cent of children may be receiving wonderful care, but if one child dies or is abused the entire system will be under scrutiny. Just imagine the public and media response to a minister who reacted to the death of a child in custody by pointing out that nothing is perfect and the vast majority of children were well looked after.

Governments are particularly susceptible to issues that take on public salience through the mass media. Because most people get their information about public events from such media, an issue that is played up in the media often becomes something a government must respond to, even if the issue is not part of the government's policy or plan. Media coverage is itself motivated by a number of considerations, but long-term importance to public welfare is not necessarily one of them. Stories often focus on the situations of individuals, even where these are not at all representative of the typical situation (Neuman, Just, & Crigler, 1992). Novelty is also an important requisite for the media in order to sustain reader or viewer interest, so that governments are likely to be faced with an ever-changing array of issues supposedly requiring immediate attention.

And then there is the press of ongoing business. Whatever politicians or the media may be concerned about, the business of government has to go on, and this in itself generates a huge array of issues. Funding decisions have to be made, policies reviewed and revised, and problems attended to. Any government will have thousands of decisions of this kind to make each year. The many issues involved in any large-scale operation – hiring people, paying them, establishing offices, determining what services will be provided where – need political attention at least occasionally.

At any given moment any government in this country is active in a wide range of policy arenas, from health care to highways, from pollution to child care, from education to industrial policy. Within each of these arenas there is usually a host of more specific issues. Should provincial park camping policies be changed? Should water-monitoring practices be reviewed? Should standards for X-ray technicians be changed? Should teacher certification rules be altered? Many of these issues are highly complex. People may spend their whole careers in a particular field without feeling they understand the issues fully. Yet on each issue government is supposed to decide what needs to be done based on the most complete information, while also taking into account the myriad of views that may exist among different sectors of the population. Of course the civil service is there to advise, and various external groups press their point of view, but in the end the key decisions are made by elected people. The scale of the task is overwhelming, and even more so for the head of government, who is supposed to know about all of them. Is it reasonable to expect that fifteen or twenty ministers, who may have no background in most of the areas with which they are dealing, can make intelligent decisions all the time on so many different issues? Yet there is no alternative, since decisions have to be made.

The problem of attending to issues is made worse because it is hard for any government to focus on more than a few things at a time. Tom Axworthy, who was former prime minister Pierre Trudeau's chief of staff, noted that a government could reasonably expect to take on in a serious way only four or five issues during a term in office (Axworthy, 1988), because any serious effort requires a substantial commitment of effort at all levels of the system for an extended period of time. It is not possible to give serious attention to and work hard on twenty-five or thirty different things at the same time, let alone the hundreds and thousands of issues that any government must deal with. In terms of their attention and ability to act, governments face a huge mismatch between what is desirable and what is possible.

Governments are often exhorted to focus on the big things and leave the details of management to the civil service. However the dynamics of government make this a doubtful strategy. It is hard if not impossible to predict what issue may suddenly become important. A decision that seemed a routine procedural matter can suddenly leap to public prominence. Think of decisions about what immigrants will be admitted or deported, or which criminals will be paroled, or where a new office will be located. Very few such decisions make it into the public eye, but when one does, politicians will get no benefit from arguing that these are the kinds of routine decisions that civil servants make.

There is, consequently, never enough time to think about issues in sufficient depth. Important decisions are often made very quickly, with quite limited information and discussion. This is not because politicians necessarily like making hurried or uninformed decisions – though, sometimes, when the political stakes are clear, a quick decision is appealing – but because this is what the office requires. Senior government leaders, both politicians and civil servants, work under tremendous time pressures as well as pressures of public opinion, in which they are expected to make knowledgeable decisions about all the issues facing them within very short timelines and without major errors. This is, of course, impossible. It is nonetheless what we expect from our leaders.

The pressure of multiple issues is also one of the reasons that policy implementation tends to get short shrift. As soon as one decision has been made there is enormous pressure to get on to the next issue. Even with the best intentions, it is difficult to get back to something from months ago to see how it is progressing, since meanwhile so many other issues have arrived on the doorstep demanding immediate attention. Given all of this, it is impressive how knowledgeable and well-informed political leaders often are.

The impact of these requirements on individual politicians is enormous. A cabinet member not only has responsibility for her or his own area of jurisdiction – which can itself be enormously complicated and fraught with difficulties – but is also supposed to participate in all the collective decision-making in cabinet and caucus, to look after a constituency, and to attend all kinds of public events. There is no respite from these demands. A politician may leave her or his office, but almost every social encounter will also lead to new pressures or requests. Being a politician is a 24/7 job, as the new e-language would put it. No wonder the pressures on friendships and families are so enormous in political life.

Political work is not only intensely demanding in terms of time and ideas, it is emotionally draining as well. Politicians spent a lot of time listening to people, whether colleagues, opponents, constituents, or lobbyists, all of whom feel very strongly about things. They hear horror stories, sad tales, angry complaints. Sometimes they are saddened by what has happened to someone, something they cannot do anything about. Sometimes they are infuriated by someone's stupidity. Often their feelings are stirred. Political discussion and debate, whether in the legislature or in any other setting, runs hot and gets people worked up.

When you add to all that an unending work schedule and the sense that there is much more to do than can possibly be done, it is not hard to understand why feelings run high.

Consider a small jurisdiction such as Manitoba. Drew Caldwell, the minister of education with whom I worked throughout my time as deputy, was newly elected to the legislature in 1999 and had previously been a town councillor and part-time teacher. When named minister he acquired responsibility for everything to do with elementary, secondary, and post-secondary education as well as with adult education and training – programs, credentials, funding, facilities, and staffing, as well as for resolving the various disputes that inevitably arise concerning these matters. In most of these areas he had some, but often limited, background knowledge, and so needed to work intensely to learn about them all. Within a few weeks he had 200 requests for meetings from school districts, parent groups, teacher organizations, post-secondary institutions, local community groups, support-staff unions, and so on. He had to give political and substantive direction to staff on every aspect of these systems, many of which involve great subtleties and complexities. At the same time, every week he went to a cabinet meeting at which a whole range of issues from all of his colleagues were also on the table for discussion. He went home at least once a week to his own riding in Brandon where he would spend almost all his 'free' time on constituency matters. He was also trying to attend various political functions, including those in other constituencies, to help his colleagues. It was, and remains, a very tough life.

Political Life

The summer of 2000 was a demanding one for the government. It was their first sustained session of the legislature, which lasted through most of the summer. Everyone was learning new procedures and roles. People had not had any holiday in the summer of 1999 because they were preparing for the election. They then had to organize and begin the work of a new government. They had no holidays in the summer of 2000, either, because the legislature was sitting. The weather was hot, and offices in the legislative buildings are not air-conditioned.

Finally, on 23 August, very late at night, the session adjourned. Many elected people and political staff took a week or

> two of holidays. For Drew Caldwell, however, there were no holidays, since school started the following week and he could not be on holidays when children were just going back to school. He was not alone in the legislative building, however. Early the following week, he ran across Premier Gary Doer, who was disappointed that so many people were away when there was so much to do!

Processes

The government of Manitoba has consisted in recent years of approximately 15,000 civil servants organized into between fifteen and twenty departments. The total provincial budget in 1999 was just over $6 billion, of which more than 35 per cent was spent on health, just under 20 per cent on all levels of education, 12 per cent on social services, and the other third on everything else: economic development, transportation, infrastructure, culture, environment, parks, agriculture, and so on.[4] On the revenue side, 27 per cent came from income tax, 15 per cent from sales tax, and 28 per cent from federal transfers, the rest coming from a range of other sources. As a have-not province, Manitoba needs strong financial support from the federal government.

Managing this large and complex operation involves a number of formal processes, especially elections, budgets, and the sitting of Parliament or the legislature. These elements shape much of what governments do and how they do it.

The importance of elections has already been mentioned but cannot be stressed too much. The fact that federal and provincial elections in Canada are typically about four years apart has a great deal of influence on governments' planning. It is widely accepted that difficult measures are best taken early in a mandate, partly because there is more time for people to get used to them or for necessary adjustments in policy to be made. On the other hand, there is more time to find out that a key policy has not worked well. As the next election approaches, governments focus increasingly on what they think they need to do to get re-elected. Often but not always this means more caution. Making sure that the

---

[4] Data are from the Manitoba budget, available on the government's website: www.gov.mb.ca.

promises of the last election have been fulfilled becomes increasingly important. A government that sees itself as vulnerable or falling behind may feel that bold measures are needed at the end of its term to restore its credibility.

The influence of the electoral cycle extends beyond the planning of major policies. It also affects many operational questions. A new government is likely, if only for practical reasons, to retain many of the procedures it inherits, such as budget formation or policy development. As a government gains experience it is more likely to try to change some of these to suit its own needs and character. On the other hand, the rigours of political life often lead to key people, both politicians and their main advisors, becoming tired. New ideas are less plentiful. Less energy may generally mean that things slow down. A new government, or a re-elected one, will also make key personnel changes early on. As the next election approaches political staff often tire of the intense pressures of work, but it gets harder to recruit new people for what may be a very short-term assignment.

Budgets and legislation are the central vehicles through which governments put their policies and priorities into practice. Few organizational processes have been as much criticized and yet as little changed as government budgeting. Despite all the talk about zero-based budgeting, management by objectives, business re-engineering, and many others, the incremental budget remains firmly entrenched everywhere. As Wildavsky (1986) pointed out, the persistence of incremental budgeting is due to its efficiency and effectiveness; for all its weaknesses, it does accomplish the task of establishing a budget in a reasonable time frame while keeping the focus on the changes that are likely to engender either support or opposition.

While a budget is tabled once a year, budgeting is an endless process in government. At any given moment there is likely to be concern with at least two budget years, the current and the next one. Sometimes the year just ended is also in the picture due to an audit or year-end report.

A budget is as much a political document as an economic one. From a political communications point of view it reinforces a government's central themes and messages – reduced taxes, or balanced budgets, or spending in key areas. It is an opportunity to boast of successes and deflect potential criticisms. Budgets are produced for public consumption in various forms, including flyers to households, web sites, and 1–800 telephone information lines.

The budget matters greatly to the bureaucracy, since it lays out the resources departments will have available as well as some of the tasks they must accomplish. However, in the face of changing circumstances adjustments to budgets are inevitably required as a year goes by. Revenue may decline requiring cuts in expenditures, or unforeseen spending needs may arise, or political considerations may lead to a readjustment of priorities during the year. The cabinet committee that reviews spending during the year – in Manitoba the Treasury Board – is often the most powerful committee in the government because it controls to a large extent the response to changing circumstances, and, as already noted, changing circumstances are often critical to governments. The minister of finance is almost always one of the strongest and most important people in the cabinet.

The difficulties in budgeting have been exacerbated by some of the dominant political trends of the last decade. Governments across Canada committed themselves to reducing or eliminating deficits and then to reducing taxes. At the same time, a number of factors have put pressures on spending, notably in areas such as health and education. Most Canadian provincial governments have made very significant cuts in spending and staffing in the last decade. Each cut makes it harder to find the money for the next one without creating serious program difficulties. Moreover, most of the cutting has taken place in good economic times when revenues were growing. If Canada experiences a significant economic downturn with falling tax revenues, many provincial governments will be in dire straits, caught between balanced budget legislation and tax cut promises on the one hand, and the clear public wish to preserve high quality public services on the other.

In Manitoba the Conservatives made significant reductions in public spending and increases in various fees in the 1990s in their effort to balance the budget without increasing income or sales taxes. Manitoba spends two-thirds of its budget on health, education, and social services. Own-source revenue growth in Manitoba tends to be smaller than the regular demand for increases in social spending, even without taking account of unexpected crises in areas such as flooding or drought or forest fires. The result is a constant pressure to try to respond to political demands without money.

The consensus of many commentators on parliamentary government is that the parliament or legislature does not matter all that much any more, especially for a majority government. Power has become more centralized in the executive arm of government, especially in the offices of prime ministers and premiers. Even cabinet ministers, some feel, are not all that important any more (Savoie, 1999).

Even so, much of the work of government is still organized around sittings of the legislature. The main events of the year in government include the Throne Speech and the budget, both of which are related to the legislature (unless the recent Ontario attempt to produce a budget without a sitting legislature becomes a norm). These events require a great deal of preparation. From the standpoint of much of the public, a Throne Speech may be at most a one-day wonder, but within government, preparation of the speech takes months, including much attention from the most senior political people. The bureaucracy will forward hundreds of ideas for consideration for inclusion in the speech. Decisions on what will or will not be mentioned, and how each issue will be presented get worked over repeatedly. The speech itself may be revised twenty or more times before a final version is ready – quite often at the last possible moment. The budget, as just discussed, is a much larger enterprise, but also often comes down to a whole series of important but last minute decisions – not only about what money will be provided for what purposes, but about how the various decisions as well as the whole package will be portrayed. The budget speech, too, often goes through dozens of versions.

In Manitoba from 1999 to 2002 the legislature sat twice each year, for about a month in the fall and for three to six months in the spring and summer. When the House is sitting, a large amount of ministerial time is taken up with it. Ministers have to be present in the House several hours each day. They have to manage their own issues and legislation. This means that they have much less time for departmental issues, meetings with stakeholders and the public, their political work, and for other business. Everything else, including cabinet meetings, tends to get compressed or put off. Senior staff, too, have a considerable amount of their time diverted from other work to managing or responding to issues in the House.

Sittings of the House are also important because they provide a political platform for the opposition through debate, and, especially, question period (QP). For the public, question period may be of little importance. Few people outside the political system pay much attention to it. However politicians and political staff give it a great deal of attention because it can attract substantial media attention. Huge amounts of staff time in government are spent preparing ministers for QP – anticipating possible questions, putting together possible responses, responding to questions that do get asked, gathering data, and thinking about the best lines of attack and defence. Even without any crises, over the course of a year the bureaucracy and political staff will put together hundreds of pages of material for each minister related to possible question period issues and preferred responses. Because of the volume of briefing material, most governments have a standard format for these papers in order to make them more usable for ministers, and they get organized into huge binders that ministers can take into the legislature in case they need the information. The requirement to anticipate trouble creates a large amount of work that is of doubtful value on any other count.

When an issue becomes controversial and the House is sitting, that issue can literally absorb the entire attention of a minister, senior staff, and many others. When the opposition senses that a minister is weak on a particular issue they will redouble their attacks. Some of the response work takes place in an atmosphere that can come close to being panic-stricken. If an issue appears to be heating up, the demand for background and options from staff to be provided immediately becomes intense. In the fall of 2001, almost the whole of question period for more than a month was devoted to issues related to adult learning centres (see Chapter 7). This meant that the Minister's time, my time as deputy, and the time of six or eight other department staff connected with this issue were largely given over to preparing for or responding to questions on this one issue, both in the legislature and from the media. Other issues were largely driven off the agenda for a couple of months.

My experience, however, was mild compared to that of my colleague, the federal deputy minister of Human Resources Development Canada (HRDC), who had to cope with a string of allegations of inappropriate grant-giving that lasted for months and took huge amounts of staff time at all levels of the organization, but especially at senior levels, in explaining what had happened and identifying possibilities for improvement. One result of the HRDC scandal was that reporting requirements on contracts throughout the federal government were tightened significantly. The cost of these changes in terms of additional staff, reporting, and computer systems was enormous. Provincial governments and community organizations receiving HRDC funds were affected because HRDC imposed substantial new accountability requirements on its many, many undertakings with us. Yet there was never any public consideration of whether the new requirements were cost-effective or overkill. The government would have looked defensive if it had raised the issue, while the media and the opposition were happy with a series of events that made the government look bad.

Of course it is important to identify and correct problems. Governments do make mistakes, and procedures and systems do require improvement. The Opposition and the media can contribute to this improvement by drawing attention to flaws or problems. My point is that the nature of the political process focuses on assigning blame rather than giving sober consideration to how improvement can best be brought about. Sometimes a solution is worse or more expensive than the problem it purports to address.

Most legislation gets very little public attention. Even well-informed voters are likely to know only a few of the bills that a government has presented in the most recent session. A government's legislative agenda is typically a combination of work that has to be done and legislation that is seen as politically important. An example of the former would be changes to the Public Schools Act to make it possible for school-board members to participate in meetings via technology, so that rural trustees can avoid travelling in very bad weather. An example of the latter would be the provision in the legislation on school-district amalgamations (see Chapter 6) to allow the minister to review school-district budgets if the spending increases were seen as excessive. Sometimes these two categories intersect, so that a bill is both substantively and politically important. At other times bills of considerable importance get almost no public attention. If the media report on legislation at all, it is generally only on legislation that is controversial. One reason that governments give more rhetorical names to their legislation – such as the Better Schools Act in Ontario – is to gain more public attention.

Whether or not legislation is controversial, it needs an enormous amount of time and attention. As a law is developed a great deal of discussion usually occurs with staff and the lawyers who do the drafting of the precise wording of each clause. A draft bill may go through dozens of revisions, especially if it is politically sensitive. Legal requirements, program needs, and political considerations all have to be thought about and reconciled where they differ. Attempts are made to anticipate problems and prevent misinterpretations. Despite all this work, amendments are often necessary at the last minute as the bill is debated, either to deal with substantive concerns that have been raised or to try to resolve some of the political conflict.

Legislation: The Real Process

In June 2000 the Manitoba government introduced legislation to reverse the changes in collective bargaining for teachers made by the Progressive Conservatives in 1996. The premier had committed to these changes while in opposition. The legislation was very controversial in the education sector. The Manitoba Association of School Trustees (MAST) took out a full-page ad in the *Winnipeg Free Press* attacking the changes. Two evenings of public hearings were scheduled on the bill, and some seventy groups, mostly school boards and teachers associations, signed up to make presentations to the committee of the legislature that conducted the hearings. Media coverage was extensive.

The hearings took place on two very hot nights in late July. The committee room is not air-conditioned. The windows were open but there were no screens, so mosquitoes were everywhere. People waited patiently for hours for their ten minutes to speak, interrupted occasionally by disputes between government and opposition committee members over procedures. Most delegations said about the same thing, often in the same words. The school boards attacked the legislation for its potential cost and the teachers groups defended it as giving teachers reasonable collective bargaining rights that would help them educate students.

The first night the hearings lasted until 3 a.m., and the second night until about 1 a.m. Although some presenters waited for hours for their ten minutes before the committee, a number of others gave up and left. In the end the government did make some minor amendments to the bill, voted down all amendments offered by the opposition, and the bill passed.

The Bureaucracy

The world of the government bureaucracy is in many ways completely different from the world that ministers and politicians inhabit, yet governing requires that the two worlds work together effectively. The political level of government needs the civil service in order to achieve its goals and fulfill its promises. It also needs the civil service to keep it aware of other issues and needs that require attention or could turn into political problems. The civil service cannot function without the direction and legitimacy that elected people supply. Both functions require close cooperation and strong working relationships, yet a number of factors militate against good working relationships between the political and bureaucratic sides of government.

Consider the first purpose: to fulfil political commitments once in office. Election promises are usually rather general, partly because political communication does not allow too many specifics and partly because in the heat of a campaign there is often no time to do the work on the details. Considerable work is almost always required to move from a political commitment to an actual policy or program, and that work is done primarily by the civil service. A good example of this process is discussed in Chapter 3, which looks at the NDP commitment to replace the Grade 3 standards test with a start of year report to parents on key reading and math skills. Compared to many election commitments this one was fairly specific, yet there were still a large number of issues to be worked out, and in the course of working those out the commitment came to assume a particular shape and form. The same process happens with every political commitment.

At the same time, most of what government does is relatively routine and largely happens outside the sphere of political interest. Because governments are involved in so many different issues and tasks, it would be impossible in any case for a small number of politicians and their advisors to monitor and control them all. In every department there are routine, ongoing programs to be managed. Services are delivered, cheques are issued, credentials are examined, people are hired and paid, contracts are let, buildings are built or leased, rules and procedures are established or changed. Hundred or thousands of such activities are going on all the time. They constitute the nine-tenths of the iceberg that is under water and invisible.

Getting these activities done well is important for several reasons. Of course we have a public interest in providing good services to people. It is better for everyone if government services are efficient, effective, and user-friendly. As James March (1991) has noted, all the emphasis on leaders as heroes and on glamourous but unusual events distracts us from the realization that the success of most organizations is much more dependent on doing all the little things right than it is on a few big successes. In the longer run all the operational details have a powerful effect on overall success.

Aside from the intrinsic value of good service, deficiencies can quickly generate large political problems. People who do not get their pension cheques on time or for the right amount tend to be quite miffed, and say so. As the Ontario government discovered, if water quality is not adequately controlled, the ensuing problems can rapidly create high political costs. The same is true in many, many areas of government: something seemingly insignificant can turn into a huge political issue.

Every government is searching for resources that it can use for its highest priority activities, so every gain in program efficiency has the potential to create some additional capacity to address those priorities. For all these reasons there should be a strong interest in delivering high-quality, efficient services, which in turn requires strong working relationships between civil servants and politicians.

Unfortunately, there are powerful factors that militate against those strong relationships. These have to do with the very different orientations, values, and cultures of the bureaucratic world and the political world.

Political parties always come into office from opposition. For several reasons, being in opposition is terrible preparation for being in government. Governments almost inevitably take office with a low level of regard for the civil service because they have just spent years in opposition criticizing almost everything it does. After years of seeing the civil service as delivering wrongheaded policies badly, it is hard for politicians to shift suddenly to see them as effective mangers of one's own priorities. Moreover, oppositions have very little access to the civil service and so often see civil servants, especially the senior ones, as being closely aligned with their opponents. A new minister comes from years of watching the deputy minister working closely with the former minister. This does not build immediate trust. In 1988, when the Conservatives replaced the NDP (I was then a senior official in Education), our new minister seemed convinced that most of the senior officials in the Department had close personal and political links with the NDP. Political staff who arrive with a new government naturally share this distrust. Because they are often the people with the strongest influence on ministers, they tend to deepen the divide. At best, it can take months for ministers and their senior officials to develop the kind of close working relationship that is necessary for effective government. Sometimes the desired level of trust never develops. Yet it is hard to see how it could be otherwise.

Another problem of moving from opposition to government is that while the opposition focuses largely on finding mistakes, criticizing, and looking for the weak link, government leaders need to be able to see the big picture, focus on what is really important, and take a longer-term view. The shift is hard. New ministers are often very focused on the same things that interested them while in opposition – the details of programs, or particular spending decisions. They are understandably anxious to avoid being open to the same kinds of criticisms they were previously levelling at others. Yet their job is now quite different. They have to provide overall policy direction to large and complex programs. The more time that is spent on looking at the details, the less time there will be for doing the things that could really make a difference in the longer term. Yet many new ministers, unless they get and take good advice to the contrary, will spend vast amounts of time on the details of relatively unimportant programs, or involve themselves in individual staffing decisions, or try to monitor each cheque or letter that goes out the door.

The distrust created by moving from opposition to government is exacerbated by differences between the culture of politics and the culture of the civil service. Political life, as I have already suggested, is fast-moving, unpredictable, focused on large-scale issues and attempts to shape and gauge public opinion. Bureaucratic life is almost the opposite. Bureaucracies run on rules, standard procedures, and careful attention to detail. Things tend to move slowly. The emphasis in the political world on avoiding mistakes strongly reinforces these inherent tendencies of large bureaucracies. The nature of and forces that drive the bureaucracy are well described by James Wilson (1989) in his book, *Bureaucracy*.

These elements of bureaucratic culture are highly frustrating to politicians and political staff, who tend to interpret them as obstruction or incompetence. Political staffers are often scornful of the bureaucracy. They expect everyone to have the same commitment to the goals of the government as they do, to work the same endless hours that they do, and to be willing to do anything to increase the government's success. Many civil servants, on the other hand, see the political level as shallow and self-serving. Civil servants who have deep, lifelong commitments to their field of work are incensed by politicians who are interested only in what can be put in a press release, or who are unwilling to take any time to learn about the area for which they are now responsible. Having seen many governments come and go, they may be inclined to resist passively decisions they dislike and to wait for change. Of course this attitude simply reinforces the suspicion and disdain at the political level. I have written about these tensions in more details elsewhere (Levin, 1985, 1986).

The problem of trust is especially acute for deputy ministers in Canadian governments, who occupy a key role between the politicians and the civil service. They have to be able to face in two directions. On the one hand, it is their job to carry out the decisions of the elected government, even if they do not particularly like those decisions. That is why deputies are appointed by the premier and the cabinet 'at pleasure,' and not by individual ministers. On the other hand, it is the job of deputy ministers to make recommendations on what to do and to advise ministers on the potential consequences of their decisions. A good deputy must have a clear sense of what the government is about, what its priorities are, and the kinds of measures it is or is not likely to want to pursue. However a good deputy also has to understand the field of service she or he represents, and to make the case to the political level about what effective public policy in that field requires, as well as raising the potential downsides of government's intentions. It can be a fine balancing act.

Manitoba has had a history of making changes in some key senior civil service positions when the government changes. In 1977 the new premier, Sterling Lyon, very publicly fired a number of senior officials who were seen as closely connected with the outgoing Schreyer NDP administration. In 1981 the NDP also made some key changes on taking office, most notably replacing the province's chief civil servant, known as the clerk of executive council, who had served under several previous governments. However, dismissal of senior officials remains relatively uncommon in Manitoba; it is more common to put trusted people into key positions as and when they become vacant. The great majority of senior civil service jobs in Manitoba at that time continued to be occupied by career civil servants who served both Conservative and NDP administrations. Indeed, one of the changes made by the Filmon PC government was to remove some levels of civil service positions from cabinet purview as a way of enhancing civil service neutrality.

When the Conservatives were elected in 1988 they replaced the clerk of executive council with their own appointee, Don Leitch, who was not at that time a civil servant and who had ties to the Conservative Party.

The NDP in 1999 replaced Leitch, but rather than appointing a person affiliated with the NDP they chose a career civil servant, Jim Eldridge, who had been responsible most recently for federal-provincial relations. Eldridge's appointment to this key role was seen by Premier Doer as a way to demonstrate his commitment to a neutral and professional civil service.

The Conservatives had also put a trusted political person, Julian Benson, in place as secretary to the Treasury Board, the group of ministers responsible for spending decisions and hence the most powerful cabinet committee. Benson was thought to have exercised considerable influence in the Filmon government. Towards the end of the Conservative mandate, Benson was caught up in the scandal around vote-rigging in the 1995 election and resigned his position. He was replaced by a career civil servant, Don Potter, who remained in that position after the NDP took office.

In fact, the new NDP administration made very few changes in the senior administration. Eugene Kostyra, a minister in the Pawley NDP government in the 1980s, was appointed as secretary to the newly created Community Economic Development Committee (CEDC) of the cabinet, with deputy minister rank. Kostyra was given responsibility for issues that were economically important, especially if they were also politically sensitive. The number of departments and deputies was reduced as part of the new government's promise to have a smaller cabinet and fewer senior civil service positions. Three other former deputies were removed from their positions because the new government saw them as being closely tied politically to the Conservatives. Two of these positions were eliminated as part of the reduction. The new premier met with the deputies' group in the first few weeks of the government's tenure, to reassure them that the government intended to respect a neutral civil service and would not be making many changes. In fact, I was the only new deputy minister appointed in the government's first year in office.

In light of this careful approach to the civil service, it is not surprising that the kinds of frustrations just described existed in the Manitoba government. While many civil servants worked well with the new government and good levels of trust developed, in other cases ministers and senior political staff did not feel they were well served by the civil service in terms of understanding and implementing the government's policy commitments.

The Challenge of Governing

Government is a very tough world, full of pressures, tensions, and contradictions. A new government begins with strong policy commitments, but the pressures of political influence and events are highly distracting. The work is complex and unrelenting, while expectations are so high they can rarely be met and scrutiny is extensive and unforgiving. In some ways it is an impossible task, made more difficult because often the people taking it on do not really know what they are getting into. The challenge facing the Manitoba government in 1999, both in education and more generally, was the management of all these demands and pressures while keeping faith with their core beliefs and central election commitments, in spirit as well as in the letter. How would it be possible to balance the demands for an active agenda on many different fronts with the need to maintain a balanced budget?

CHAPTER 2

Education in Canada: Myths and Opportunities

I agreed to take on the role of deputy minister of education in Manitoba because I believed there were important things to be done and that these things required government action. For most of my career I have been critical of Canada's education system, feeling that it could and should be better than it is. I have been concerned especially with the lack of respect that students are often given, especially students who do not want to conform to the systems' expectations. I have also worried about the significant number of students who do not do well in school or in post-secondary education and the degree to which social issues, especially poverty, shape educational outcomes. Looking back on my three years in the job, though we did not solve any of these problems, I am pleased by many of the things we accomplished, and also heartened that Manitoba did not adopt some of the counterproductive and negative education policies used in some other provinces.

This chapter begins with a very brief overview of the structure and politics of education across Canada and in Manitoba. This is followed by a discussion of the reasons for education's prominence as a public issue, the kinds of criticisms that are made, and how these compare with the best evidence we have on the actual performance of the system. The kinds of reforms made by governments in the last few years are described and critiqued, and the chapter concludes with suggestions on the kinds of policies that might be most likely to improve educational outcomes.

Education in Canada is a large and complex enterprise involving a myriad of difficult policy and political questions. In recent years in Canada we have seen considerable debate and conflict on a variety of educational issues, such as the quality of schools, the rights of teachers, financing of schools, appropriate tuition levels in universities, student debt levels, official languages, and others. Teacher strikes have occurred in several provinces, as have strikes of college and university faculty. Polling shows consistently that education is an important issue to many Canadians (Leithwood, Fullan, & Watson, 2003). Education in Canada is, in my view, in reasonably good shape. Improvement is certainly possible, but the most common policy approaches in recent years are unlikely to get us where we want to be.

The education sector in Canada includes the kindergarten through high school system, the post-secondary system, and adult education. It is a big sector. In most provincial budgets, education is the second largest item after health care. Canadian schools in 2001 enrolled about 5.4 million students, had about 320,000 graduates, employed about 300,000 teachers, and spent about $40 billion. Canadian post-secondary institutions in 1999 had 1.2 million full-time students, some 70,000 teaching staff, and spent about $20 billion (Education at a Glance, 2002, 48–9).

The Manitoba education system in 1999 included schools, colleges, universities, and a relatively small number of other training and adult education organizations. A variety of pieces of provincial legislation provided the governance structure for the major institutional structures.

The provincial public school system consisted of 200,000 students attending about 700 schools organized into 54 school districts. (A fuller picture of this structure is given in Chapter 6.) Manitoba does not have a separate school system for religious minorities as exists in Ontario or Alberta. About 5 per cent of the student population attended private schools (officially called 'independent' schools), most of which received significant funding from and were regulated by the province. The province also contained sixty-two First Nations, almost all of which operate their own schools under federal legislation. All public school teachers were members of the Manitoba Teachers' Society (MTS), the single provincial teachers' organization. Collective bargaining for teachers was regulated under the Public Schools Act. Since the 1950s Manitoba has resolved teachers' contract disputes through binding arbitration, while prohibiting strikes or lockouts.

At the post-secondary level the province had four universities and four community colleges. In addition to provincial legislation that created the colleges and each of the universities, the post-secondary system was also regulated through the Council on Post-Secondary Education (COPSE), a board appointed by the government with statutory authority in areas of funding, program approvals, institutional evaluation, and so on. The council was in some senses arms-length from the government, as officially its chair reported directly to the minister. However because the department had no other staff working on post-secondary education, the council also played the de facto role of advising and supporting the minister and the government on issues concerning post-secondary education. This was sometimes awkward. The former executive director, Leo LeTourneau, joked about having to write to the minister on behalf of the council, and then having to draft the replies for the minister to his own letters. However, on the whole the structure worked reasonably well, and did have the advantage of providing a bit of distance between the government and the institutions.

The four universities were the University of Manitoba, the largest, offering almost all the professional and graduate programs; the University of Winnipeg, a smaller, primarily undergraduate arts, science, and education institution; Brandon University, a small institution with a diverse set of programs; and Collège universitaire de Saint-Boniface, a small francophone institution with its own legislation and board of governors, but affiliated with the University of Manitoba. The universities collectively operated a northern delivery system and a system under separate provincial funding to provide distance education courses across the province. In all, the universities enrolled about 22,000 full-time and 17,000 part-time students in regular programs in 1999, as well as another large number of students in their various continuing education programs.

The community college system, roughly parallel to the universities, is described more fully in Chapter 4. Total college enrolment, not including continuing education, was 8,000 full-time and 5,000 part-time students in 1999, which gave Manitoba one of the lowest rates of college participation in the country.

Post-secondary education in most places is becoming more diverse and harder to define. Manitoba in 1999 had a variety of institutions in this area beyond the public colleges and universities. These included a technical college that operated both college and high school programs, several institutions run by Aboriginal organizations, and more than 50 private companies offering vocational courses or training to more than 500 students. The latter were regulated by the province under legislation and partly subsidized through Manitoba's Student Aid program, which in 1999 was among the least generous in the country, with almost all aid being through loans. The province also had one of the lowest rates of take-up on student aid across the country, with only about 20 per cent of students receiving support from the program (personal communication, M.L. Spangelo, June 2003).

To give a sense of the size of the effort, in Manitoba in 1999–2000, public expenditure was $1.3 billion for schools, about $400 million for post-secondary education, and about $70 million for all other forms of adult education and training. The proportions in other provinces are very similar. As outlined more fully later in this chapter, these proportions are not appropriate to our changing needs and understanding of education; the shares devoted to early childhood and adult education are too small in relation to the whole.

Education in Canada is the constitutional purview of provinces and territories, though the federal government is involved in a variety of ways, especially in post-secondary education where it has increased its programming significantly in recent years. All the current signs are that the federal government wants to play a more important role in education, a strategy that will be strongly resisted by many provinces. Another former provincial deputy minister of education, BC's Charles Ungerleider, has recently called for a federal office or minister of education (2003). Whatever the merits of such a proposal, it seems exceedingly unlikely to occur given the nature of Canadian politics and constitutional arrangements.

Provinces tend to go back and forth between having one minister and department responsible for all of education, and having a separate department and minister for some combination of post-secondary education, adult education, and training. At any given time some provinces are combining two education ministries into one, while others are separating one into two. Early childhood development, while increasingly linked in policy thinking to education, is usually in a different ministry.

There is no right way to set up the structure. The argument for a single department is greater policy coherence, or, sometimes, the desire to have a smaller cabinet, as was the case in Manitoba in 1999. At that point there was a single minister of education and training who had responsibility for schools, post-secondary education, and adult education, as well as training and labour market issues. However there were two deputy ministers – one for K-12 education and one for post-secondary education and training – both reporting to the same minister. Shared corporate services personnel reported to both deputies, including Human Resources, Finance, Technology, and Native Education. One minister with two deputies was a very unusual arrangement, but as it is with so much in government, the people involved managed to make it work reasonably well.

The new government initially reverted to a single Department of Education, Training and Youth, with one minister and one deputy responsible for all areas of education from kindergarten to post-secondary education, training, and adult education. In January of 2001, about fifteen months after the election, Diane McGifford was appointed minister of advanced education, with responsibility for post-secondary education. The argument for a separate minister in post-secondary education is to give greater political attention to these other areas of education. The political demands of the school system are enormous, so if there is only one minister, post-secondary education and training tend to get much less attention.

Although a second department was officially created, in practice there remained a single department with a single deputy, though I reported to two ministers. (When asked about the task of reporting to two ministers I used to joke that far from being a problem it was an advantage, in that now for the first time when the minister wanted me to do something I could excuse myself on grounds of the demands of the other minister.) In a cabinet shuffle in September 2002, just after I left the government, Ron Lemieux was appointed minister of education and youth while responsibility for training moved to Diane McGifford, who now became minister of advanced education and training. However there continued to be one deputy minister and a largely unified departmental operation through the 2003 election.

The combined department in 2000 had about 900 staff and a budget of about $1.3 billion, a large organization by any standard. More than 90 per cent of the money flowed out in grants to schools, colleges, and universities, and in student loans and bursaries. Staffing had been reduced significantly during the 1990s, and we eliminated another 50 positions, primarily in the schools area, in the 2000 budget. Thanks to some tremendous work by our human resources staff and line managers, nobody was laid off despite this large reduction in staff. Prior to the election, the department had had two deputy ministers, a third position at deputy rank (the full-time chair of the Council on Post-secondary Education), and five assistant deputy ministers. One of the first steps the new government took, again as part of the election commitment to reduce the number of senior managers, was to eliminate the full-time position for the chair of the council and to reduce the number of assis-

Table 2.1
Organizational Units of the Department of Education and Youth and the Department of Advanced Education and Training

Activity	Functions	No. of Staff	Budget (millions of $)
Administration	Ministers' offices, deputy's office, corporate services of all kinds	70	5.5
School programs	Support for curriculum, special education, and other aspects of school programs	250	21
Bureau de l'éducation française	Responsibility for all aspects of French education	70	8
School for the Deaf	School and residence for severely hearing-impaired students	55	3.6
Schools finance	Operating and capital grants to public schools (plus $200 million from PSFB*)	17	790
Training	Youth programs, adult education, provincial training, apprenticeship	280	42
Labour Market Development Agreement	Federally funded support for training	120	55
Student aid	Financial assistance for students	70	50
Post-secondary education	Operating and capital support to colleges and universities	15	360

Note: These numbers cannot be reconciled to the Manitoba Public Accounts because they involve restatements of amounts from several different accounts to their actual functions.
*Public Schools Finance Board (see page 126)

tant deputy ministers from five to three. The civil servants involved were moved to other significant positions.

Table 2.1 gives an approximate description of the main organizational units of the two departments, including their budgets and staffing for the 2002/3 fiscal year.

The department had some but not all of the usual characteristics of a government bureaucracy. One important feature in education is that a large proportion of the staff is made up of people who see themselves as career educators rather than career civil servants. However, Manitoba's Department of Education, like other departments, operated in the usual hierarchical government way. Information was not well shared across the organization. Links across units were weak; people often knew little about what was going on in other parts of the organization. There was a general habit or belief that change happened in education by issuing orders to the education system. The research and analytic capacity was weak; many of these positions had been eliminated during the budget cuts of the 1990s. A huge amount of work and effort went to feeding the machine – churning out documents, reports, cheques, accountability measures, briefing notes.

These problems were by no means unique to the Department of Education; they are typical of most government departments and of many large organizations in other sectors as well. A minister of education in England once referred to his department as a 'knowledge-free zone.' Common they may be, but these characteristics do make it more difficult to develop and implement a powerful and positive agenda, an issue to which I return in Chapter 8.

Within the rest of the education system the governance arrangements that have developed over more than a century are quite complex.[1] Although taken for granted by Canadians, by world standards our education system is highly decentralized. Almost every sector has a substantial degree of autonomy. More than 90 per cent of education spending in Canada is by school boards, colleges, and universities rather than directly by governments. The result is that a great number of groups have an active interest in education policy, including the institutions that operate programs, as well as their students, staff, suppliers, and employers – in short, almost everybody in the country.

All provinces have local elected school boards that operate public schools under provincial legislation. The long-term trend for many years in Canada, though, has been for provincial governments to become more powerful and school boards less so. Many provinces have also delegated some official role to local school councils through legislation, though this role is primarily advisory; only in the occasional school have school councils played a very strong role. In post-secondary education government control comes more through funding than through governance; arrangements for Canadian universities generally give the institutions substantial autonomy with their own boards of governors, often under provincial legislation. Community colleges are

---

[1] See Young & Levin (2002) for a more complete discussion of the organization of schools and school systems.

less autonomous than universities, but still have a significant degree of authority over their own affairs. In adult education and workplace learning the Canadian system is not yet well enough developed to have a stable legal or institutional structure but has many participants, mostly small, and including an active private sector. Extension or continuing education work carried on by schools, colleges, and universities is another significant part of this sector.

The politics of education in Canada have been changing in the last twenty years. For many years as the education system grew, policymaking was largely based on discussions among the key established groups. Of course when money was reasonably plentiful it was relatively easy to obtain consensus on actions. However as part of broader shifts in the role of the state, beginning in the 1980s the old institutional politics of education began to disintegrate. As education became a high priority political issue, the range of interested parties grew. In tandem with decreasing deference to professional groups everywhere, efforts were made in many places to bring new parties into the political equation, most notably parents, businesses, and, in some cases, private schools.

Education politics in Manitoba, as in the rest of the country, had long been dominated by the main interest groups. For schools these included the provincial organizations of teachers, school trustees, and superintendents. School administrators were part of the Manitoba Teachers' Society. In post-secondary education the university and college presidents and boards, faculty groups, staff unions, and student groups had played the main roles. Not surprisingly, these groups varied considerably in their size, cohesion and organizational capacity to lobby government or influence public opinion.

The influence of these groups also depended on which party was in power. The school trustees, dominated by rural members, tended to be more influential with the Conservatives. While Manitoba school boards have more authority and autonomy than boards in most other provinces, school boards everywhere lack a substantial base of public support, which is a main reason that provinces have been taking more control over many aspects of schooling. Trustees in Manitoba, as in other parts of Canada, have tended to get much more exercised over issues of funding, taxation, and teacher salaries than over matters of education despite some good effort from their leadership to shift that orientation. For example, when in 2000 the NDP government reversed some of the Conservatives' changes to collective bargaining for teachers, MAST took out full-page ads in the newspapers attacking the move. However, when education funding was frozen or reduced for five consecutive years in the 1990s by the Conservatives, the trustees, while certainly not happy, did not undertake any public advertising against the government.

The NDP has always had closer ties with teachers than with school boards. The 1999 NDP government included half a dozen elected members of the legislative assembly (MLAs) who were teachers as well as at least two former school board members. The Manitoba Teachers' Society did not take the same kind of partisan political positions as did teacher organizations in some other provinces, such as BC. Nor did the MTS affiliate with the broader labour movement in Manitoba. However teachers were clearly very unhappy with many of the education policies of the Conservatives, including their approach to funding of schools and the limits they imposed on collective bargaining for teachers. Many teachers were active in the NDP, and the views of teachers on the need to support public schools and the public sector generally were much closer to typical NDP beliefs. After the election, relations were far from smooth, though; the MTS was often quite critical of the government and never seemed to feel that it had the degree of influence on education policy that it wanted.

Parent organizations in Manitoba were generally weak, although parents in particular communities could and did mobilize quite effectively on particular issues, such as the threatened closure of a school. Although many other organizations had views on particular education issues, the only organization outside the education sector that had a consistent influence on education policy during my time as deputy minister was the Association of Manitoba Municipalities (AMM), partly because Drew Caldwell, as a former councillor in Brandon, had been active in the AMM and knew many of its leaders.

The lines were not as clear in the post-secondary arena, but generally the NDP were closer to student and faculty groups and the Conservatives a little more inclined to side with the boards and administrations of the institutions.

During the 1990s Canada saw considerable conflict in education, manifested in strikes, demonstrations, and very sharp public disagreements among the parties on the best approach to education policy. There has been increasing pressure, described later in the chapter, to move away from a single public education system through a variety of measures, such as a greater focus on testing and comparing of schools and students, parental choice of schools, increased funding of private schools, and reduced tax support. These ideas are supported by some powerful segments of the community, notably business leaders (Livingstone & Hart, 1998). On the other side, many parents and educators continue to advocate actively for a strong universal public education system. The disputes on these issues are sharper and more disruptive than used to be the case for education policy issues.

While strong opposition is never comfortable for a government, the decision to move away from consensus policy-making was made quite deliberately by most governments as part of their political strategy. As education became an important area for public policy change, and given the unwillingness of governments across the country to increase spending substantially, conflict with the system became inevitable. Some governments felt that attacking the status quo would be politically popular, and that it would be easy to discredit those who sought to oppose change or to argue that nothing could be done without more money. In Canada governments have often attacked teachers and governing boards as being defenders of the status quo and as 'special interests.' As large-scale change was accompanied by frozen or reduced funding, the politics of education became more intense and more conflict-ridden. Governments that had at one time rarely made an important move without advance discussion with the main stakeholders began to announce far-reaching changes without any discussion.

The calculus that attacking the system could be popular with voters has been proved to be substantially correct, at least in the short run. In several provinces, teachers, as the best organized of the established groups, have tried to organize political opposition to their governments without success. In Ontario, Alberta, Manitoba, and elsewhere governments were re-elected in the 1990s despite – or perhaps partly because of – reforms that were strongly opposed by teachers. The established organizations have not recognized the degree to which the politics of education are changing. While the number of pressure groups is increasing, it is harder for any specific group to make its case. It is increasingly important to have broad public support and to do the work necessary to mobilize allies and public opinion. Although schools continue to enjoy relatively high levels of public support and confidence, there is less and less public patience with the claims to autonomy of any expert or professional group. Neither schools nor post-secondary institutions have built the kinds of close ties with their learners and their families and communities that would allow them to mount effective political opposition to a provincial government. (For a discussion of these issues in relation to Canadian teacher unions see Naylor, 2003.)

School boards typically lack public credibility and have not done the work needed to make themselves significant political actors.

This weakness is not surprising. Organizations that see themselves as under attack are not inclined to adopt bold new political strategies. Yet the fact that voter turnout for school board elections is low has made it almost impossible for school boards to defend their authority from provincial incursions. The lack of political support for universities by their former students, and the ways in which schools often marginalize parents, have had the same effect.

Growing polarization and conflict also characterized education politics in Manitoba in the 1990s, though to a lesser degree than in some other provinces. As the Conservatives began to pay increasing attention to education (as described a little later), they were less and less inclined to be guided by the established organizations. The main Conservative program for schools, announced in 1994, was not supported by any of these groups. Many of the government's legislative changes in education in the mid or later 1990s, in post-secondary education as well as for schools, faced vocal opposition from groups within the system.

At the same time, the level of hostility around education in Manitoba, though considerable by 1999, never reached the pitch that occurred in a number of other provinces. The changes made by the Conservatives were less drastic than those in several other provinces. In a small province people tend to know each other not just in their current roles but from various previous encounters. For example, by 1999 I had been actively involved in education for nearly thirty years. During that time I had worked with many of the key leaders in education in my time as a researcher, a school board member, a civil servant, and a university professor. Furthermore, one tends to see those colleagues in other settings, such as social events. Other people in leadership roles would also have multiple contacts with their peers. John Carlyle, my predecessor as deputy minister, also had a substantial career in education and knew many people when he moved into the deputy's role – and when he left government and became superintendent of one of the larger school districts. There were always at least some lines of communication among the main parties, and even when there was strong conflict on some issues, people could be, and were, working together effectively on other issues. Manitoba has been able, to its advantage, to preserve a considerable degree of goodwill and cooperation among the main partners in the educational enterprise.

Where is 'the public' in its thinking on education? Consistent with the propositions made in the previous chapter, polling indicates that Canadians have very mixed views on schools. Polls (Livingstone, Hart, & Davie, 2003; Leithwood, Fullan, & Watson, 2003) indicate a split between the large number of people who are reasonably satisfied and think that schools are getting better, and another large group who think they are getting worse. Polls also show that Canadians have as much or more confidence in their schools as they do in most other institutions or sectors (Guppy & Davies, 1999).

Education is a high-profile social policy issue for several reasons. It is a large sector involving many people. Almost everyone has some direct connection to schools or post-secondary education, whether it is through one's children, one's work, or one's neighbours. Everyone went to school, and everyone has an opinion about how education ought to be conducted. Education is also linked with higher incomes and other positive life outcomes for individuals, so families naturally want their children to have a competitive advantage. In uncertain economic times people are even more likely to be concerned about securing their children's future.

Some of the public concern about education also arises from the oft-cited link between educational outcomes and economic success, a connection strongly promoted by governments around the world in recent years. Many government position papers espouse the view that good educational outcomes are essential to a nation's ability to generate good jobs, good incomes, and economic growth. In recent years this focus on the economic aspects of schooling has also come to include an emphasis on increasing skills in science, mathematics, and information technology.

In addition to its economic importance, education is seen as a primary means to address a variety of social problems such as improving fitness, combating crime, reducing drug abuse, increasing tolerance, and generally improving social cohesion. Whenever a new social concern arises, one of the first proposals is that the schools should address it.

Expectations for schools have been increasing in recent years, in Canada and worldwide. Given the increasing level of education in the population, this should be no surprise. More educated people are, we hope, more able to identify needs and press authorities to address them. As a former Minister once said to me during a difficult time, only half in jest, 'You know, if we hadn't educated them so well, they wouldn't be bothering me now.' Polling shows that people with more education have higher expectations for schools, as they do for all other institutions, and lower satisfaction levels with what is provided (Guppy & Davies, 1999).

Changing demands on our educational system, however, are not just a matter of people's preferences. The objective situation around education has also changed significantly over the last couple of decades. Higher credentials are increasingly important in the labour market. High school completion, which used to be a ticket to reasonable employment, is now of little value as a labour market credential in its own right (HRDC and Statistics Canada, 1998). Participation in postsecondary education has multiplied with enormous implications in many directions.

The scope of education has expanded both vertically and horizontally. Vertically, we are witnessing increasing concern for very young children and for adult learning throughout the life span. Schooling has traditionally been concerned with children aged from about 6 to about 16, expanding a few decades ago to about age 24 as higher education has become more important. This is where we have created substantial public institutions, put laws in place to govern them, and where we spend the great bulk of the public money for education. It is also where most of the political attention goes, partly because as institutions and systems become better developed they generate a variety of pressure groups and interests.

At the same time, increasing recognition has been given to the importance of education beyond schools, colleges, and universities. A very important change in public policy has been the acceptance of the importance of the first years of life as setting a foundation for learning. Countries around the world are realizing that more attention has to be paid to early childhood development (McCain & Mustard, 1998; OECD, 2001a). There is also increasing awareness around the world that people need to continue their formal learning later in life. At the same time, as jobs change it becomes essential for workers to be able to develop new knowledge and skills. Thus the growing interest around the world in adult learning, workplace learning, and ongoing skill development (OECD, 2003).

No institution could accomplish as much as we want from our education system. We want and expect our educational institutions to create perfection – model citizens and model workers with high levels of motivation and skill as well as all the right social attributes. This is an impossible task. Not only is it impossible to achieve all these purposes at the same time, but some of the purposes are mutually exclusive. To take one example, it is hard to see how an institution can develop both obedience and critical thinking at the same time. Schools are unlikely to be able to resolve social problems that the rest of society cannot.

The fact that the expectations are unreasonable, however, does not mean that they are going to change. We want all these things for our children and ourselves, schools are essential in achieving these purposes, and we are not going to give up on any of them.

These disparate expectations generate one of the central policy problems of schooling. The wish for mass success and elitism at the same time leads inevitably to contradictions. We say we want all children to succeed, but when they do, schools are criticized for reducing standards. We want everyone to have the opportunity for post-secondary education, but are at least half convinced that institutions that admit too many students are really not all that good. It is hard to reconcile the requirement to distribute rewards differentially based on merit, with the requirement to promote equity and success for all.

Diverse expectations are also a main reason schools are subject to so much criticism. Institutions that are expected to do everything will inevitably fall short. A public that expects everything will inevitably be disappointed. Education always has been and always will be subject to criticism for its failures. History is replete with arguments that students of the day were not doing as well as those of previous generations (Bracey, 1995). University professors, in particular, have always lamented that the skills of new students have declined since the good old days, though each new round of criticism is dutifully reported as if it were entirely new. In Canada in the last twenty years, as in many other countries, criticism of schools and of post-secondary education has not been lacking. Canadians have been subjected to a steady diet of media coverage, books, and government reports all commenting, if not on how much better our schools used to be, at least on how much better they need to be.

As an instance of our fondness for an imagined golden age in the past, consider this U.S. list of ten criticisms of public education:

1. The public schools are controlled by 'professional educationists,' schools of education, school superintendents, experts in departments of education, and the national organizations of educators.
2. Progressive education has taken over the public schools leading to a crisis in standards.
3. Intellectual training has been replaced with soft social programs in many schools.

4. The spirit of competition, an important incentive for learning, has been eliminated by the 100 per cent annual promotion policy and the multiple-standard report card.
5. Lax discipline in the public school is contributing to the increase of juvenile crime.
6. The teaching of classical and modern foreign languages is infrequent in the secondary schools.
7. High school students, even the bright ones, are avoiding science and mathematics.
8. The public schools are neglecting gifted children because they are geared to teaching the average child.
9. The public schools are neglecting the training of children in moral and spiritual values.
10. Academic standards of schools of education are low: their programs of study are of questionable value, and the intellectual qualities of future teachers are poor.

Do these sound familiar? Yet these criticisms are from a U.S. National Education Association publication written in the fifties (NEA, 1957), an era which many of today's critics see as a golden age of education. And this is just one example of how today's complaints about schools are not really new, but have been made in practically every generation. To take another instance, in the October 1947 edition of *Reader's Digest* – shortly after the Second World War – given a map of Europe, Americans could on average identify only five of twelve countries correctly. The average person with 'college training' (much less common in 1947 than today) could only identify seven out of twelve correctly. The same issue (back cover) contained an item reporting that a survey of high school teachers has 'revealed this startling and disturbing fact: Many high school students today simply do not know how to read.' Complaints about the quality of education have always existed, and are inevitable because of our high expectations.

The reality is not nearly as dismal as the critics claim. Canadian education certainly has shortcomings, but it also has great achievements and shows considerable continuing strength. There is much to be proud of as well as much more to accomplish. In the welter of conflicting claims about education, a few key trends can be identified that are critical for understanding both the present situation and potential policy options for education in Canada.

First, levels of participation and attainment in education have been rising steadily in Canada, as in most other countries. More students are completing secondary school than ever before – nearly 90 per cent according to the most recent studies from Statistics Canada. Participation rates in post-secondary education are among the highest in the world, and new forms of adult education and training have been developing. The 2001 census shows that between 1991 and 2001 the proportion of adults in Canada aged 25 to 34 with college or university training increased from 35 per cent to nearly 50 per cent – a huge increase in a single decade. The proportion of the same age group with less than complete high school fell from 23 per cent to 15 per cent. More than 60 per cent of Canadians without high school are 55 years of age or older.

As far as can be determined from the available evidence, levels of student achievement in Canada are quite good by international standards. Canada did very well in the 2000 Program for International Student Assessment (PISA) conducted by the Organization for Economic Cooperation and Development (OECD). Canadian students (15-year-olds were tested) were among the top achievers of the thirty-two countries in all three domains of reading, science, and mathematics (www.pisa.gc.ca). Given the Canadian preoccupation with our status vis-à-vis the United States, it is worth noting that Canadian students outperformed U.S. students substantially in every area.

The PISA assessment is particularly interesting because it focuses on skills for lifelong learning rather than on specific curriculum objectives. Not only were our overall results in PISA good, but Canada was also among the countries with the smallest gap between the highest and lowest levels of achievement. I was particularly surprised to hear, at an international conference on PISA in 2002, the German federal minister of education talk about how Germany had much to learn from Canadian education. For many years Germany has been held up as a model of education for Canada, yet Germany's PISA performance was dismal. A single test should never be given too great a weight, but the Canadian PISA results are reasonably consistent with data from other international assessments such as the International Adult Literacy Survey (IALS) or the Third International Assessment of Mathematics and Science (TIMSS), and with evidence from the School Achievement Indicators Program (SAIP), a Canadian achievement testing program funded by the federal government and run by the Council of Ministers of Education Canada (CMEC).

Although the general picture of educational attainment and accomplishment in Canada is quite positive, there are also some negatives on our scorecard. In early childhood education Canada has made some significant progress in recent years through a federal-provincial accord on child development, but our programs and services are still less developed than those in many other OECD countries (OECD, 2001c). Some subpopulations are not benefiting sufficiently from education. One can identify in particular Aboriginal Canadians, people with disabilities, and immigrants as groups whose educational attainment lags behind the rest of the population (Canadian Education Statistics Council, 2000). Although high school dropout rates have fallen, there are still students leaving high school without graduating or with weak skills. Attrition rates in post-secondary education remain higher than desirable. Canada has a large number of adults who when young were not able to attain very much formal education, and, according to the International Adult Literacy Survey, a substantial number of Canadian adults in the workforce have relatively low levels of literacy (OECD Human Resources Development Canada, 1997). Improvement in this situation seems important to our social welfare as well as our prosperity. Although Canada's performance in adult education and workplace learning has been improving, it is still not strong by international standards. The private sector in Canada in particular does not support training nearly to the same extent as in the United States (Conference Board of Canada, 2001). Despite the rhetoric of the need for high skills, many Canadians also report that they have more skills than they are allowed to use in their work (Livingstone, 1999).

Despite these reservations, the overall record is one that should make us proud. Given the high expectations we have for our educational institutions, levels of achievement will never be high enough, and improvement is always possible, but the evidence certainly does not support the view that there is a crisis in students' skills or in the performance of our schools, colleges, and universities.

Education Reform

Whatever the realities of the performance of the education system, because of its high-profile, education has been subject to innumerable reform projects by governments around the world. The good side of these reforms is that they have had as their goal, at least officially, the desire to improve student outcomes and often to reduce disparities in outcomes across society. The problem is that in education, as in other policy fields, political dynamics often favour simplistic approaches even when the evidence suggests that these are unlikely to be effective.

Education policy has to be understood in the context of broader events and pressures. In Canada in the 1990s actions in education were shaped by governments' wish to limit overall public spending to reduce deficits and later to cut taxes. Under these conditions, more money could not be a solution to any of the problems of education. Indeed, many education reforms seem to have been motivated as much by the desire to spent less money as by any deep-seated convictions about how to improve schools or post-secondary education. While the expectations are high and growing, education's share of provincial attention and budget has declined in most provinces. Per-pupil spending on schools in Canada rose steadily for forty years after the Second World War, but in the 1990s it actually dropped somewhat in some provinces (Interprovincial Education Statistics Project, 2002). In the most extreme case, per pupil spending in schools adjusted for inflation dropped in Ontario by nearly 12 per cent from 1994 to 2000. Colleges and universities have also had to contend with decreases in their budgets in real terms. For a system accustomed to steady growth in real terms, declines in budgets were a huge shock. More than 80 per cent of the operating budget in education goes to salaries of teachers and other staff, so budget cuts inevitably mean staffing reductions and loss of the associated services.

Five areas of policy have dominated recent reforms in schooling across Canada. These changes have focused on governance structures, financing mechanisms, testing of students, curriculum requirements, and the status of teachers.

In the area of governance all provinces have created some kind of school-based councils with a majority of parents either to advise the school, or, in some cases, to make decisions on some matters. All provinces except Saskatchewan have reduced the number of school districts. Another common governance reform has been devolution of greater authority away from school boards to individual schools. At the same time, many provinces have increased the powers of the provincial minister and department of education, mostly at the expense of school boards, in an attempt to create greater uniformity in practice. A final common governance change involves giving parents more choice as to the school their child will attend.

In the area of finance, provinces have attempted to control the growth of expenditures on education. Several provinces have increased the provincial share of school funding to 100 per cent, or close to it, as a way of trying to control overall expenditure levels and also reduce disparities in spending among communities within the province. Because so much of education spending is in the form of salaries, several provinces took steps to limit the pay of teachers and others using measures such as legislated limits on bargaining, or legislated rollbacks of negotiated wages and working conditions. The problems of education funding are discussed more fully in Chapter 5.

During the 1990s all provinces reviewed and generally increased the amount of provincial testing of students, an issue taken up in Chapter 3. In some provinces the growth was more substantial, in others more modest. Provinces vary in the grades and subjects they test, but the typical pattern is to try to test major subjects (English or French and mathematics at least) at several grade levels. Reporting of results also varies, from the very high-profile release of school and grade results in some provinces to a much lower-key process in others. Much depends on whether results are released in a form that encourages school-by-school comparisons.

Another common element across provinces was to increase and tighten curriculum requirements. More emphasis was put on the 'basic' subjects of language and mathematics, typically at the expense of less time for art, music, or social studies. Some provinces limited students' options in high school by requiring more compulsory courses. New curricula were developed in many provinces, or in several cases by consortia of provinces, in an attempt to increase the demands on students. For example, western provinces collaborated on a new high school mathematics curriculum that saw material in Grade 9 that was more demanding than Grade 12 courses used to be.

A final important common policy area had to do with teachers. In most provinces the effort to restrict spending on education and to increase testing and standardization put governments in direct conflict with teachers' organizations. Over the last decade Canadian teachers have been subject to quite a few policy changes that have made their working conditions less satisfying. These range from wage rollbacks and limitations on bargaining to policies that most teachers have strongly opposed, such as overall budget reductions or more authority for parents or public comparison of school-by-school test scores. Some provinces took direct action to change the status of teaching by introducing teaching tests (as in Ontario) or compulsory recertification (also in Ontario), or by removing school principals from the teachers' organization (Ontario and BC). Canadian teachers found the 1990s a discouraging decade in which they felt undermined by governments.

Almost all these trends can be seen in play during the eleven years the Progressive Conservatives were in office in Manitoba. In the schools sector there was little of import in the first few years. In 1991 a commission (Panel on Education Legislation Reform, 1993, was set up to review the Public Schools Act, but only a few of its recommendations were enacted. In 1993, a commission was established to look at reducing the number of school districts, but its recommendations were not implemented (see Chapter 6). The main Conservative policy effort in schools, called New Directions, came in 1994. New Directions called for substantial changes in school curricula, including more demanding programs of study and fewer options for students. It also proposed increasing use of technology, changes in teacher education, a substantial increase in provincial testing of students, a greater role for parents in setting school policy through the creation of school councils, and the introduction of parental choice of schools. The announcement of the plan in July 1994 was followed by an intensive period of implementation, including a large number of new curriculum and other policy documents. (A fuller account of these events can be found in Levin, 2001.)

Although some aspects of New Directions were controversial, much of the plan would have been reasonably well accepted if its implementation had been smoother and if there had not been, at the same time, other significant controversies. As it was, neither the Department nor the school system were able to meet all of the very demanding timelines in New Directions, such as those for producing new curricula. Some of the specific proposals in New Directions, such as giving individual teachers the right to suspend students from school, or prohibiting teachers from serving on parent councils in their children's schools, were changed in the face of opposition. Minister of Education Clayton Manness speculated at one point about eliminating recess to provide more instructional time, a possibility that was quickly abandoned. The resources required to implement the commitments on student testing were not provided, so the goals and timelines were changed several times. At the same time, the government was freezing or cutting its funding for schools and taking action to limit teachers' collective bargaining rights. The implied stance of the government – that Manitoba schools were not nearly good enough and were too expensive – provoked a great deal of unhappiness from teachers. The combination of increased testing, budget reductions, public criticism, and policy reversals made New Directions highly unpopular in the system despite some of its positive aspects. By 1999 a number of the major planks in the program, such as new curricula, had largely been implemented, while others, such as increased testing, had not. However, the profession was very unhappy, as were many parents who saw the effects of the budget pressures on schools.

Compared to events across the rest of Canada, the Manitoba reforms were rather moderate. Most other provinces brought in more draconian measures in almost every sector, including deeper budget cuts, more restrictions on teachers, more centralization of authority to the province, and more testing.

Post-secondary education policy gets less political attention than do schools and has been less subject to government intervention, for a variety of reasons. Fewer people are involved, whether as students or workers, than in schools. Issues around adults, even young adults, are less compelling in terms of public and media interest than are issues around children. Post-secondary institutions are harder to understand and less directly under state control than are schools. And everyone went to school, whereas only a minority of Canadians, though a rapidly growing one, has had direct experience in post-secondary education. The sector has not, however, been immune, especially in the last few years as the federal government has involved itself very directly in post-secondary education issues.

Provincial governments in Canada have tried to do several things through policy changes in post-secondary education. As in all other areas, a preoccupation has been controlling costs. Not only are post-secondary institutions expensive, costing quite a bit more per student to operate than do schools, but substantial growth in enrolments has magnified the problem. Governments all across the country have limited their funding to a greater or lesser degree depending on their circumstances. Some provinces made substantial cuts, such as Ontario in the Harris years. Others, such as British Columbia or Quebec, increased funding but at a rate slower than required to compensate for cost and enrolment increases. In most provinces university tuition fees rose rapidly as more of the burden of paying for post-secondary education was shifted to students, while non-loan forms of student aid were reduced or eliminated.

In most provinces governments also tried to pay more attention to the technical training part of post-secondary education as part of their focus on economic growth. Several provinces invested in expansion of their community colleges. Ontario changed the name of its ministry to Training, Colleges and Universities to reflect its priorities.

The oft-held view is that investing in shorter-term training in technology produces better economic payoffs than does a general higher education such as a Bachelor of Arts. This argument was especially strong in the late 1990s because of shortages of workers in fields such as computer science or the highly skilled trades. The best available evidence does not, in fact, support the superiority of shorter-term technical training (Human Resources Development Canada, 2001), but here, as in so many places, the facts are less significant than are public beliefs.

The focus on the non-university sector is also fueled by the love-hate relationship that governments have with universities. In 1990 Stuart Smith, former Ontario Liberal leader, conducted a review of the status of university education and public policy (1991). Smith found that people in government, both politicians and senior civil servants, were highly critical of universities, finding them elitist, smug, unwilling to change, unproductive, and expensive. The depth of the bad feeling surprised even Smith, a political veteran. There is no evidence that this disdain has lessened. At the same time, governments need universities. The latter educate the elite – the children of the privileged – but they also produce many of the most highly skilled people in society, control access to many high-status occupations, and are important generators of the ideas and products that fuel our economy.

Governments have therefore tried to develop policy towards universities to make the latter more responsive to changing public policy needs. The emphasis has been on funding programs in high priority areas (such as science and technology, or more recently health care), on requiring institutions to take in more students with the same resources, on strengthening connections between research and industry, and on setting public accountability requirements through vehicles such as performance indicators. The strategy, if that is not too grand a term for what has typically been a series of one-off measures, has been one of constant pressure on the institutions.

The federal government, on the other hand, has made in the last few years a series of commitments to post-secondary education. In the early years of the Chrétien government, the federal government cut its transfers to provinces substantially, which was one of the reasons that provinces reduced funding to post-secondary education (though the desire to finance tax cuts was another, at least in many provinces). The federal government came to the conclusion that giving provinces a substantial amount of money that they might or might not spend on post-secondary education was a far less desirable strategy than putting a much smaller amount of money directly into targeted areas of post-secondary education. Examples include student financial assistance (through the Canada Millennium Scholarship Foundation, and, more recently, increased graduate fellowships) and support for research (through the Canada Research Chairs, the Canada Foundation for Innovation, and paying for indirect costs of research). In this way the federal government can spend less money and get much more political credit – a choice that might well be called a no-brainer! The provinces are, of course, quite unhappy because they are left to pay the ongoing costs of post-secondary education with less federal support. However their earlier (and continuing) unwillingness to give the federal government credit for its funding made the federal change in approach entirely predictable, even if not necessarily good for the overall health of post-secondary education in Canada.

In post-secondary education the Conservatives made several important policy changes. In 1993 they passed legislation that gave Manitoba's community colleges a substantial degree of independence; prior to this the colleges had been part of the government bureaucracy, reporting through an assistant deputy minister, which significantly limited their ability to be innovative. Under the new legislation, colleges were given boards of governors and much more autonomy, although the government retained substantial control in many areas.

In 1992 the government established a commission, under former premier Duff Roblin, to examine the role of universities in the province (University Education Review Commission, 1994). The Roblin Commission reported in December 1993. One of its main recommendations, surprising given its mandate, was that community colleges should be strengthened substantially. In fact, the commission recommended that participation rates in colleges in Manitoba should be doubled. In 1996 the government passed legislation creating the Council on Post-Secondary Education. The council would be a new arms-length agency with policy and funding responsibility for universities and colleges. Previously, universities had been funded and regulated through another arm's-length agency that was now to be replaced by COPSE, while colleges were directly controlled through the Department of Education. Although the creation of COPSE was not generally controversial it was strongly opposed by some groups of faculty and students who felt it would infringe on what they saw as university autonomy.

The larger concern for the post-secondary institutions, as for schools, was the decline in provincial funding coupled with reduced support for students. Funding to Manitoba's colleges was frozen or cut in 1991-92 and 1992–93. For the universities, funding was cut every year from 1993 to 1998, except one year when it was held at zero. Overall this meant that university funding decreased in real terms by some 20 per cent. In their attempt to maintain their budgets the institutions raised tuition substantially, so that standard university tuition for the Faculties of Arts and Science rose by more than 130 per cent over a decade, from less than $1,400 in 1989 to nearly $3,200 in 1999. Also, as the government struggled in the 1990s with its commitment to reduce its deficit without increasing income taxes, it eliminated its Manitoba bursary program and replaced it with student loans. Funding to a set of special opportunity programs serving largely Aboriginal students was cut. (It must be said here that the federal government, which had cost-shared these programs, eliminated its contribution in 1990; the Conservative government continued to provide at least some funding, though at a much reduced level, to the programs throughout its time in office.) Overall, students faced higher costs, with more of their support in the form of loans to attend institutions that were under serious financial pressure.

All these reforms have so far had rather modest impacts. They have certainly put the post-secondary system under stress as enrolments grow but funding is capped. An immense amount of energy in most universities now goes into generating revenue, whether from research, private-sector partnerships, fund-raising, or increased tuition fees. Institutional focus has also been redirected in many places towards areas designated as priorities by governments. Yet the basic shape of post-secondary education has not changed very much. In some areas that are government priorities, such as prior learning assessments or outreach to underserved populations, progress has been modest, at best. There are still massive problems in recognizing credentials from other institutions. Universities especially remain quite autonomous and highly decentralized institutions that have a hard time moving quickly on new initiatives.

In the other areas of education policy the story is easier to tell. Early childhood development has been an area of growing attention in Canada, fuelled partly by the federal-provincial Early Child Development Accord of 2000. Though some important progress has been made in improving the situation of very young children, policy and infrastructure in Canada still lag far behind many European countries (OECD, 2001c).

In adult education and workplace education Canada has almost no policy or institutional structure to speak of. All the rhetoric about lifelong learning has yet to be matched with any real strategy on the ground. Apprenticeship has been improving, but slowly and in small measures. The Labour Market Development Agreements between the federal government and the provinces, the prime vehicles for financing training, are completely inadequate, both in size and in structure, as a way to support effective ongoing learning in the workforce. To take just one example, a company that could improve its results and either protect or increase jobs by doing so cannot get support for training, but if it lays off its workers, these workers are then eligible to be trained. This is a completely indefensible, catch-22 approach that is so mired in federal-provincial disputes over jurisdiction and funding as to appear unresolvable. Some good efforts to improve workforce training have been made through vehicles such as sector councils, but these are so small as to be almost inconsequential.

What Would Meaningful Education Reform Look Like?

The recent reforms in education in Canada are characterized in large part by their distance from actual teaching and learning. They seem to assume that if we change the structural arrangements around schools, improvements in learning will somehow follow. Both logic and evidence make this a doubtful proposition. However, as shown in the last chapter, education policy is the result of a myriad of factors and influences.

The counterproductive nature of much recent education policy in Canada is becoming increasingly evident. Attacking the quality of schooling may play on public concerns in the short term, especially for a new government, but in the long term it saps morale and reduces commitment in the system. Provinces that have attacked the quality of their schools and teachers have found it harder to recruit and keep teachers, leading to a new problem of teacher shortages. Cuts in funding have led to school closures, program reductions, and parental opposition. Most importantly, a strategy based on more tests and so-called tougher standards is unlikely to demonstrate the improved outcomes it promises because these policies do not create more effort and thus better results. These reforms produce acrimony, but not improvement.

In contrast, an increasing amount is known about the kinds of policies that are most likely to produce improvements in educational outcomes. Although research in education seems to have a poor reputation, we actually have learned quite a bit over the last thirty years about 'what works' to improve student learning. An extensive treatment of this question deserves a book of its own, but in the box 'The Elements of a Strong Education Policy,' and in the following pages, I outline very briefly what I consider to be a sound education strategy based on the best available evidence. These directions provided much of the focus for my work as deputy minister.

The Elements of a Strong Education Policy

1. Looking beyond the school
    Early childhood
    Adult education
    Parent and community involvement
    Building bridges across education sectors
    Links to broader economic and social policy
2. Schools
    Reducing gaps in achievement
    Increasing student motivation
    Strengthening teachers' skills
    School planning and reporting
3. Post-secondary education
    Increasing accessibility
    Increasing supports for success
    Supporting innovation

Looking beyond the School

Educational success is about much more than formal education. The most important single predictor of educational outcomes continues to be family socioeconomic status. To put it bluntly, children who grow up poor are much less likely to be successful as adults. Yet income inequality has grown substantially in Canada in the last ten years. More than 15 per cent of Canadian children, and well over 20 per cent in Manitoba still live in families with inadequate incomes (Campaign, 2000). Other kinds of status – Aboriginal, visible minority, disabled – are strongly associated both with higher poverty and with poorer educational and other life outcomes. Moreover, the nature of the local community appears to have an independent impact on students' achievement, so that students with similar backgrounds may be more or less successful depending on the kind of community they live in.[2] Accordingly, if we want significant improvements in educational outcomes we will have to have policy approaches that go beyond the actions of schools, colleges, universities, and other formal institutions.

In this regard, the growing focus on early childhood education and development is particularly important. We have good evidence that people of any age can make important changes in their lives with appropriate motivation and support (Alcorn & Levin, 2000), but it remains vitally important to provide children with the best possible prenatal and early post-natal care. While world attention has been largely on the preschool years, it seems likely that an even better investment would be to focus on the development of children from conception through to about age 3. The benefits of preventing low birth weight or fetal alcohol syndrome or early nutrition deficits are huge – clearly greater than any other later intervention that we have available.

The corollary of early childhood development is effective adult education. Children who grow up in difficult circumstances are, of course, connected to adults who are in difficult circumstances. Canada is still weak in the area of adult education in comparison with many other countries (OECD, 2003). Although we do not have the kind of crisis of literacy that is sometimes portrayed in the media, Canada does have a substantial number of adults who have not completed high school and who have low skill levels. As the recent Manitoba experience (Chapter 7) shows, many adults are motivated to return to school in order to assist or provide a better example to their children. So not only does effective adult education help adults to improve their own situation, it often has benefits for their children as well.

Much of the already limited provision of adult education in Canada, however, is not of very high quality in that it has high attrition rates, is poorly linked to credentials with labour market value, and does not provide enough or the right supports to students whose history of failure has limited their self-confidence and their learning skills. There is still much to do to improve the provision of adult education and to give opportunities for learning to all those who are interested in and capable of benefiting from them.

---

[2] A variety of studies in several different countries have demonstrated this point, including data from the National Longitudinal Study of Children and Youth in Canada, reported recently by Willms (2003).

The significance of adult education draws attention to the general importance of families and communities in shaping educational success. The problems that students may show in school are often blamed on parents. In fact, almost all parents genuinely want their children to succeed in school though they may lack the abilities to help effectively. But efforts to draw parents and the larger community into strong partnerships with schools remain too few and too small. To be sure, many Canadian schools have tried hard to reach out to parents, and some very exciting efforts have been made. (For an interesting example see Hunter, 2000.) But in general these practices depend on exceptional efforts by individuals or on soft money from grants, and when the individuals leave or the money vanishes, so does the work. Very few schools or school systems have permanent positions or budgets for the work of family and community liaison.

This involvement can take many different useful forms. It is important to give parents more information about what their children are learning in school and help them understand how they can most effectively support their children's learning. We also need better ways of helping parents advocate for their children without setting up irreconcilable conflicts with the school. Community organizations such as service clubs, churches, ethnic organizations, and non-profit agencies can all be sources of support in the form of mentoring, giving consistent messages to students, providing appropriate complementary out-of-school activities, and helping the school understand the community's strengths and challenges more fully.

Despite the rhetoric of lifelong learning, the various levels of education remain largely separate from each other. The connections between schools, early childhood care, post-secondary education, and adult learning are weak. Students often have difficulty moving from one college or university to another, let alone transferring their skills and knowledge readily from one level of education to another. Developments such as prior learning assessment have the potential to help us move towards a much more integrated approach to learning, but they are in their infancy and still receive very little support.

Educational success is strongly linked to broader social indicators, and it is clear that some improvements in education will only come from broader changes in society. Some examples from early childhood development have already been mentioned, but other examples are also easy to identify. Children who change schools frequently because they cannot find adequate housing are less likely to be well cared for educationally. Every teacher in a high-poverty school can talk about the impact on children of having adequate nutrition. Richard Rothstein (2002) has pointed out that substandard housing may contain flaking lead-based paint that may be eaten by very young children, causing lead poisoning with dire consequences for their learning. A coat of new paint is a relatively easy and cheap intervention.

These examples all reinforce the importance of having good connections between education policy and other social policies. The availability of employment, the level of wages, and the adequacy of social programs are important determinants of school outcomes. There is not much point to investing in schools while simultaneously driving down wages or social benefits so that families cannot house or feed themselves adequately. Parents who have to work two jobs including evenings in order to make ends meet are not going to be as able to supervise and support their children. The British government talks often about 'joined-up thinking'; while hard to do, this kind of policy coherence has never been more important.

Changes in Schools

The evidence on the outcomes of schooling, described earlier, suggests that on the whole Canadian students are performing well. However the large gap between the best- and worst-performing students remains a concern. We cannot afford to have even 10 per cent of our young people fail to develop the skills they need to participate in society. The cost to those young people and to the rest of us is too high. So a first priority for education policy at all levels must be to try to reduce gaps in achievement between the top and the bottom. The English experience with its National Literacy and Numeracy Strategies, which I helped to evaluate (Earl et al., 2003), shows that a determined effort can improve the situation. However it requires ongoing effort – what U.S. researcher Robert Slavin calls 'the relentless pursuit of success for all learners.'

A policy focus on reducing gaps would require more careful reporting of achievement levels, not necessarily in the form of provincial testing but in terms of the numbers of students failing a grade, not completing enough high school credits, being expelled from school, being referred to special education, and so on. We do not have a magic answer as to how to help these children improve their performance, but we do know that with care and attention we can do better. In my view, reducing gaps in achievement is the single most important policy emphasis that we need in our schools.

One key to improving performance is improving motivation. Students' level of motivation predicts their performance very well. We know quite a bit about what students find motivating, and it is pretty similar to what works for adults: meaningful work, some autonomy in how the work is done, a sense that one is respected, a good working environment, support from colleagues and superiors, and useful feedback on performance. We should be seeking to increase the presence of these characteristics in schools, because increased motivation by students will lead to improved performance.

The kinds of changes in the demands on schools and the reduced level of deference to professionals everywhere has made the work of teachers harder than it used to be. We are asking teachers to do more and be better. At the same time, in most of Canada, teachers' working conditions have deteriorated markedly in the last decade as budgets have been reduced and they have been subjected to public attacks on their skills. Good people will not enter or stay in teaching if their work is not reasonably paid and reasonably respected.

A respectful approach to teachers does not mean that they should be left alone to do whatever they want. It does mean that teachers need to be adequately paid, that their working conditions matter, and that they need support in their work. Most importantly, we need to give serious support to teachers' ongoing learning. A profession is characterized by continual learning of new approaches and techniques. Teachers, like other professionals, need meaningful opportunities to improve their current skills and to develop new skills. The education system makes a considerable investment of time and money in professional development, but it is widely agreed to be of little value or impact. Better approaches to encouraging and supporting learning by teachers are a vital part of any strategy to improve schooling.

The key to making all the elements of improvement work together is a strong system of school planning and reporting. Schools are subject to so many competing pressures that unless they are able to set some clear goals they run the risk of trying to move in so many directions at once that they make no progress in any of them. Schools, like other organizations, need to define some achievable goals, work towards them, and then report – to the staff, the students, the parents and the broader community – on how much progress has been made and what challenges remain. The reporting should not be limited to one or two measures of academic achievement, but can and should include a range of indicators of student outcomes, including graduation rates, attendance, extra-curricular participation, retention in grade, volunteerism, post-secondary participation, and other measures relevant to the long-term benefits of schooling that people really care about.

Post-secondary Education

As participation in post-secondary education grows, not only in Canada but around the world, it is increasingly important that participation is possible for everyone with the ability and motivation. Canada has one of the highest participation rates in post-secondary education in the world, but we still have large gaps in participation between poorer and wealthier segments of society and for some minority groups (Canadian Education Statistics Council, 2000). There is abundant evidence that many people who do not meet normal admission requirements can succeed in very challenging programs of advanced study, including medicine, engineering, and law, if they have the right supports. We know how to extend accessibility to more people; we just need to do more of it.

Although post-secondary participation rates are high in Canada, attrition rates are also quite high, so that large numbers of students do not complete their programs of study. Some of this instability is inevitable as people's interests and life circumstances change, but many post-secondary institutions, especially universities, still think they are doing learners a favour by admitting them and that those who cannot immediately swim should sink. This is wasteful, not only of the scarce resources of our colleges and universities but even more so for the people involved, who, with a little more help, might have found a way to succeed. Education must be one of the few sectors of our society where high rates of failure are somehow taken as an indicator of success. It is as if manufacturers boasted about their products because so many of these products were tossed off the assembly line for failing to meet quality standards. The point is to do the things that create quality, not to try to weed out its absence. Moving to a system that is truly focused on helping learners meet high standards would be a real and welcome change in our post-secondary system.

In many ways colleges and universities are among the most innovative places in our society. People in these organizations are constantly coming up with new ideas, new theories, new discoveries and inventions. Yet this ferment of innovation at the level of the individual is not always matched by an equal commitment to innovation at the level of the organization. Many post-secondary institutions remain highly conservative, subjecting any potential change to rigorous scrutiny while existing practices continue without much examination. Given the changing needs for advanced education in Canadian society, such as the delivery of learning in workplaces, advanced credentials for professionals, outreach to the large number of adults who are interested in further education but cannot attend full time, or the need to teach in newly developed areas of knowledge, post-secondary institutions need help in increasing their level of innovation. As with schools, our colleges and universities have much to be proud of, but that alone will not help anticipate, define, and meet the emerging challenges of today and tomorrow

NDP Election Commitments on Education

The NDP typically has a political advantage over the Conservatives in Manitoba with regard to voter perceptions of its commitment to social programs such as health and education. Capitalizing on this advantage was an important part of the NDP's 1999 strategy, especially given the cuts made by the Conservative government. A party committee had spent quite a bit of time looking at education policy options between 1995 and 1999, but, in the end – as happens now in all election campaigns – the central campaign management committee had to decide which particular issues would be central to the campaign. During an election only a limited number of issues can be highlighted, and these have to be chosen to support the party's strengths and minimize its potential weaknesses. For example, the NDP has a long-standing policy commitment to eliminating post-secondary tuition fees, but a promise to do so in 1999 would have been clearly beyond the fiscal capacity of the government even had there been popular support for it.

Although health care was the party's most important issue, the NDP made a number of commitments on education issues during the campaign. The general theme – 'Hope for Young People – starting with excellent public schools and making community college and university tuition fees more affordable' was one of the five central commitments released at the beginning of the campaign. Two days later the party committed to a 10 per cent reduction in college and university tuition fees. Several other main pledges are discussed more fully in later chapters: the Grade Three Guarantee (Chapter 3), the 'plan to double college enrolment' (Chapter 4), and the promise to 'invest in our public schools at a rate no less than the growth in the economy' while also increasing property tax rebates and attempting to eliminate the provincial education property tax (Chapter 5). Other education commitments included eliminating the Youth News Network from Manitoba schools, increasing time for arts and physical education, making a commitment that all Grade 8 students would demonstrate a high level of computer literacy, providing every student with an e-mail address, and enabling all high school students to complete a community service credit before they graduate. While making these commitments the party wanted to minimize charges that it could not manage finances effectively, so each promise was carefully costed and the party kept a running total of costs and revenue sources for all its promises.

While the specific election commitments were necessarily more limited than the comprehensive policy agenda sketched in this chapter, the general orientation in the NDP program and among elected members was quite consistent with this larger agenda. The sense of congruence was what allowed me to move forward with a broader agenda (described more fully in Chapter 8).

Managing Multiple Issues in a New Government

In addition to reviewing developments on three major election commitments, later chapters also look at amalgamation of school districts, adult learning centres, and the development of overall education strategy and policy. Amalgamation was a government initiative that was not an election commitment, while the adult learning centres were an issue thrust upon the government by unanticipated events.

Reading about the issues one at a time gives a misleading impression of the experience of government. In fact, all five concerns were on the table from the very beginning of the government's term, and four of the five (the exception being the Grade Three Assessment) were still very active issues three years later when I stepped down as deputy. The work of developing and implementing an overall education strategy was also going on throughout this period.

These were far from being the only important issues that had to be managed during those three years. At times all of them receded from the horizon as other issues dominated. Among the NDP government's very first actions was the ending of all provincial involvement with the

Youth News Network, a private company that gave schools computers and TVs in exchange for the right to broadcast a daily news show with advertisements. This issue was not solved for close to a year. The government's commitments on improving the use of technology in the system were ongoing throughout my time there. Another major preoccupation for much of the year 2000 was the commitment to reverse changes made by the Conservatives in collective bargaining provisions for teachers. The legislation on that issue, in the summer of 2000, brought some of the most heated moments in my time in government. The concerns were revived in 2002 with the report of the Commission on Class Size and Composition that had been created as an outcome of the debate over the scope of collective bargaining.

Several other important areas were also of concern in the schools sector between 1999 and 2002. The Conservative government had created a review of special education that reported in 1998; managing the report's recommendations and their implementation was a challenging exercise. The government was involved in constant negotiations with the Division scolaire franco-manitobaine, the province's francophone school district. A group of francophone parents had a constitutional lawsuit pending against the province for alleged failure to live up to its obligations in minority language education through this period. We also commissioned a review of the governance structure of the division, at their request, and passed legislation in 2002 changing some aspects of that structure.

Among other areas that required frequent attention were teacher pensions, the schools capital program, proposed changes to the school year, the funding of and relationship with private schools, a variety of safety issues related to school buses, and the status and future of the Winnipeg Technical College. In addition to provincial issues, a range of local issues in education inevitably find their way to the political agenda and to the minister's desk. The threatened closing of a small school, a dispute over curriculum, the controversial handling of the case of an individual student, a proposed change in the school day or year – any of these can turn into an issue that, at least in the short term, takes a great deal of attention. In the summer of 2000 a seemingly innocuous change in the legislation governing home schooling provoked protests and demonstrations just as the government was grappling with the controversial changes in collective bargaining for teachers.

In post-secondary and adult education the agenda was at least as busy. The government inherited work on a new northern post-secondary institution and the creation of what was called the University College of the North, which was an ongoing effort. The creation of the institution was formally announced in 2002. The government's commitment to reduce tuition fees in colleges and universities took substantial energy in the first half of 2000, as did the negotiations with the Canada Millennium Scholarship Foundation that were instrumental in re-establishing a provincial bursary program in 2000. The Manitoba Student Aid Program was given its own legislation in 2002, making it harder for a future government to cut the provincial bursary program. The withdrawal of the banks from providing student loans led to a long period of work to review options, decide on a Manitoba approach, and, eventually, develop our own service bureau to provide and manage Manitoba student loans. Capital and operating funding issues with colleges and universities were active at all times. The government made important commitments to expand funding for university capital early on, and these took ongoing attention. A first effort in 2000 to provide capital funding through the Manitoba Public Insurance Corporation generated so much opposition it was soon withdrawn, but the government did find other sources to fund university capital. A serious operating funding problem at the University of Winnipeg was a public issue for some time and came to a head in 2002, though it was only resolved after I left government. A review of the work of the Council on Post-Secondary Education, required under its legislation, was done by an external consultant in 2002.

Very early in its mandate the government began to develop plans to build new hydro dams in northern Manitoba. These projects were to have important training components, so the Department of Education and Training was involved very actively from the outset, not only in the program planning but in very complex and difficult negotiations with the First Nations that were to be equity partners in the new projects. A substantial rebuilding of the apprenticeship system had been initiated by the Conservatives but required ongoing attention. Training issues were also raised frequently as part of larger efforts in areas such as economic development, where negotiations with companies about locating in Manitoba often involved a provincial commitment on training. Much of the training effort is funded by the federal government under the Labour Market Development Agreement, which has been a constant source of discussion between the two governments. For two years (2001–03) Manitoba co-chaired the federal-provincial Forum of Labour Market Ministers, adding an additional set of responsibilities in federal-provincial relations, an area marked by a history of poor relationships and lack of progress on a common agenda.

On a system-wide level, efforts to improve all aspects of Aboriginal education were a priority for the NDP, and often involved complex negotiations with a variety of Aboriginal and other groups. The challenges in Aboriginal education are huge, so there was constant pressure to improve or expand programs, and to support the development of Aboriginal-controlled education programs and institutions. Manitoba depends heavily on federal revenue transfers and federal policy, so federal-provincial relations on a whole range of education issues were active. These included various issues related to minority languages, Aboriginal education, northern training, adult literacy, and others. The Department of Education also participated actively in a number of other central government directions, including a Healthy Child policy with its focus on young children, inner-city revitalization, and local community economic development.

On top of all of these were the ongoing operational issues of running a large organization. The budget process, discussed earlier, takes a huge amount of time, including that of the minister. In an organization of 1,000 people there are constant issues of staffing: retirements, hirings, leaves of various kinds, grievances. Many routine items of government – issuing contracts, producing documents, holding public events, administering tests –also require attention. Managing the budget process is an endless and intense task. Another constant issue was getting people appointed to various government boards and commissions related to education, including the boards of governors of the colleges and universities as well as many others. The process for making these appointments tends to be slow because nominees have to be vetted through the political apparatus prior to being approached, and if they decline the whole process has to start again. Our communications policies, including our internal and external internet sites, required attention and constant upgrading.

In other words, there were always many more issues than time to manage them. Setting priorities was a constant concern, involving delicate balances among competing needs. Political agendas have to be looked after, the basic operating needs of the organization and its people also have to be met, and somehow, on top of all this, important long-term issues have to be addressed. It was a tough challenge!

CHAPTER 3

The Grade Three Assessment: Even Doing What People Want Can Be Hard

'How do you feel about writing the math exam today?'
'I'm so glad we're finally writing it.'
'Why?'
'Because all we've been doing every day for weeks is math, math, math, and I'm sick of it.'
'Are you nervous about the test?'
'No. Our teacher keeps telling us, "Don't be nervous," and she's the only one who is nervous.'

This was a conversation with my 8-year-old daughter in 1996, on the way to school the day of the provincial Grade 3 math pilot test.

Across Canada, as in many other countries, the amount of large-scale testing of students was increased substantially during the 1990s. Not only did most provinces add more tests in more subjects and at more grade levels, but the Council of Ministers of Education, with funding provided by the federal government, developed a pan-Canadian assessment program, the School Achievement Indicators Program, which has conducted testing in core subjects several times. Canada – sometimes a few provinces and sometimes across the country – has also participated in several international testing programs, such as the Third International Assessment of Mathematics and Science and the Program for International Student Assessment, organized by the OECD.

The politics around large-scale testing are intense, and few issues in education are more controversial.[1] There is generally strong public

---

[1] Readers interested in a deeper understanding of the issues around large-scale testing might consult Earl, 2003.

support for such testing, largely because people want some easy-to-understand indicators of how much students are learning (COMPAS, 2001; Livingstone, Hart, & Davie, 2003). Governments may see increased testing as a relatively easy policy strategy, although in practice it has often turned out to be more expensive and more complicated than anticipated. The media like test results that provide stories about the overall level of achievement using a simple set of numbers. The people are interested in data that allow rankings of countries, provinces, or schools, often provided by various kinds of tests.

Educators often have strong misgivings about large-scale testing. Their concerns are of two sorts. One set of criticisms has to do with the deadening effect of such testing on school practices. Teachers feel constrained to alter their teaching and focus on the test skills even where this may mean a narrower and less stimulating curriculum for students, or may lead, as in the conversation at the start of this chapter, to a great deal of repetition of material. Many parents are uneasy about testing, especially of younger students, for the same reasons. Some research suggests that teachers do tend to focus their teaching on tests when these tests are seen as having high stakes for students and schools (Mehrens, 1998). On the other hand, there is not much evidence to suggest that teaching was dramatically different in the years before the recent resurgence of large-scale testing. While teachers feel constrained, the impact on students may be much smaller.

The second concern is that large-scale tests will be used to make unfair comparisons among schools and teachers and lead to 'winners' and 'losers' among schools as parents choose those they think are better. The comparisons are seen as unfair, because, as was noted earlier, student achievement is substantially shaped by influences that are largely beyond the capacity of schools to affect. Many educators worry that when schools are ranked based on their tests, those schools with poor results will be unfairly blamed.

This concern also has some merit. The simple reporting of test results may feed the belief that if only teachers worked harder, or parents were better, or sanctions were stiffer, then student performance would improve. Yet everything we know tells us that improving student outcomes, especially in communities with high levels of poverty, is very difficult and that simple solutions, while publicly attractive, will not work.

Despite these cautions, the worry about unfair comparisons based on tests is, in my view, overstated. Schools are quite ready to give students marks and to compare their performance without evidencing these same concerns about all the non-school factors that may shape students' outcomes. The marks given by schools are more important than provincial tests in determining entry to desired courses and to post-secondary education. We also know that many of the tests teachers use to award marks are of doubtful validity (Black & William, 1998). The concerns about the impact of testing on students apply to school practices as well as to large-scale assessments, yet there is much less criticism of the former, especially from educators.

As well, large-scale testing can reveal important patterns in levels of achievement that warrant greater attention. It can show just how big the gap is between the best- and worst-achieving students so that the need to improve equity in outcomes is made more evident. There is no guarantee that test results will be used for this purpose, and they certainly can be and have been misused, but they can provide one means of looking at system-wide achievement that could be valuable. Polling shows that most parents see large-scale tests as one measure of the success of students and the system, but favour using a range of measures (COMPAS, 2001; Leithwood, Fullan, & Watson, 2003). Support for diverse measures of success fits with the multiple goals people have for schools.

Although large-scale testing has, in my opinion, some value, it has received far too much emphasis in many jurisdictions in the last few years. The idea that testing alone can drive improvements in achievement does not hold up to any reasonable degree of scrutiny. After all, ever since schools began they have been testing students frequently with very public results, yet that does not seem to have had the desired effect. Why would large-scale testing be more successful? Indeed, when one looks internationally, the countries that have the highest student outcomes generally have quite moderate testing programs. They rely on other vehicles – high-quality teaching, strong parent and community support, high expectations – to motivate students to do their best. Some large-scale testing can be part of a balanced approach to educational improvement, but always in a subordinate role.

The key to effective use of student assessment is its connection to subsequent policy and practice around teaching and learning. To be effective, assessment has to support and be supported by good teaching. Testing needs to be linked carefully to the curriculum, it should address the full range of skills we want students to develop, and it should reinforce the kinds of teaching and learning practices we want to see in our schools. It should also help people outside the school system better understand how students are doing. As the Manitoba story shows, doing these things is not easy but it is possible.

In Manitoba in the 1990s, as part of the New Directions agenda, the Conservative government had committed to testing of all students in Grades 3, 6, 9, and 12 in the core subjects (mathematics, language, and, except in Grade 12, social studies, and science). This commitment was never fully implemented because it proved to be too expensive. At the time of the 1999 election the provincial testing regime included a compulsory examination, worth 30 per cent of the final mark, in Grade 12 mathematics and English as well as in French for immersion students and francophones. A provincial test was also available in Grade 6 language (English or French) and in Grade 9 mathematics on an optional basis if school districts chose to use it. Having an optional test was a rather uneasy compromise measure, but worked reasonably well from a political perspective as it left the responsibility for testing decisions at the local level. About 40 per cent of schools participated in these tests in 2000, a number that was too high to justify cancelling the test altogether and too low to warrant making it compulsory.

Finally, there was a provincial examination for all Grade 3 students in language (English or French) and mathematics. Of all the provincial tests, the Grade 3 tests were the most controversial because they involved young children. From the outset the Grade 3 tests had more opposition from both parents and teachers than did any of the others.

In developing a stance on testing, the NDP had some political skating to do. On the one hand, many party activists, including teachers but also parents and others, were strongly opposed to all provincial tests for reasons already outlined. On the other hand, tests are popular with much of the electorate, and the NDP did not want to be seen as being captured by so-called special interests, such as teachers.

The solution to this dilemma was an interesting one. During the 1999 election campaign the NDP said it would continue the existing testing policy in Grades 6, 9, and 12. However, it committed to eliminating the provincial tests for Grade 3 and replacing them with a start-of-year, teacher-based report to parents of Grade 3 children on students' skills in some key areas of reading and mathematics. The promise – made by NDP leader Gary Doer during the election campaign – was framed as a 'guarantee' that all students would be reading and writing in Grade 3 or would have a plan to address any deficiencies. Doer promised he would get rid of the most disliked of the provincial tests and recognize the vital role of teachers in assessment, while preserving most of the existing testing program and emphasizing the importance of reporting to parents on core skills.

More specifically, in an NDP press release (30 August), NDP leader Gary Doer promised that

> Every child will be reading and writing fluently in their grade three year. If not, the teacher and parent must work out an effective plan that addresses the child's problems. That's our Grade Three Guarantee ...
>
> This assessment will take place near the beginning of the school year, to allow for time to address any problems before the child finishes grade three.

Implementing this promise was an immediate priority when the government took office. As with every political commitment, it was first necessary to decide what, precisely, the promise would look like in practice. One clear requirement was to replace the existing Grade 3 standards test with a teacher-led assessment focused on key skills. However, assessing writing at the start of Grade 3 is a particularly difficult task in that the writing skills students are expected to have at this age are still very rudimentary. An early decision was to include reading and arithmetic in the assessment, and not writing. We also had to ensure that the plan did fulfil the commitment that students would either be reading fluently or have an effective plan to address shortcomings.

Short timelines made implementation more difficult. The government was committed to putting the new policy in place for the fall of 2000. From October 1999 this gave us only a few months to design the policy and advise people in the school system of what it would be. This may seem to be plenty of time, but because what we were doing was quite new, we had no models to draw on. Because there were also many other pressures at the same time the process ended up being rushed.

Development of the policy was led by the two assistant deputy ministers with responsibility for school affairs: Dr Gerald Farthing in School Programs, and Guy Roy in the Bureau de l'éducation française. They established a team across their two units to develop some options for the minister's review. The team involved people from student assessment as well as from the curriculum units in both the English and French parts of the department. In Manitoba, as in many other provinces, the assessment and curriculum staff are not necessarily used to working together and tend to see the issues very differently. Assessment and measurement people tend to focus on technical and administrative issues related to assessment. For the previous five or more years they had been totally occupied with designing and implementing new, large-scale testing programs. They were now being asked to do something quite different – define and support a teacher-led assessment process. This required a considerable shift in their thinking and in the necessary skills required. What kind of test could be designed that would have an acceptable degree of validity and reliability without making huge administrative demands on the teachers and the schools? What sort of results would be produced, how would they be analysed, and what could be reported? What skills would be needed in the schools to conduct such an assessment, and how could these skills be developed?

The curriculum consultants, on the other hand, focused on assessment that would support and encourage what they believed to be good teaching practice. They were strongly influenced by professional norms and less interested in either technical issues of good assessment or questions of reporting and accountability. Although both groups worked hard, and steadily improved in their ability to work together effectively, there were certainly some bumps along the way.

Some basic elements of the policy were quickly settled. Each Grade 3 student would be assessed on a limited set of the most important competencies in language and arithmetic early in the fall of their Grade 3 year. Teachers would conduct the assessments but there would not be a standard test or method for doing so. Instead we would expect teachers to use their professional skill and judgment. Parents would get a report that would be easy for them to understand and could form the basis for further discussion between parents and the school where there might be concerns on either side. The reporting and subsequent discussion would be the basis for the 'effective plan' mentioned in Gary Doer's election promise.

Many details, however, had to be resolved. How many and exactly which competencies would be assessed? How much guidance would teachers be given on how to do the assessment? What resources might they need to help them? How would the reporting to parents be done, and how would this reporting relate to the regular report cards that schools produced? How and when would the policy be announced and how could we ensure that it was well understood and effectively implemented?

Many of these issues were subject to intense discussion in the department. We did not have models from other provinces to rely on. Ideally we would have issued a discussion paper with proposals, and invited feedback from the system before making final decisions. However, we simply did not have time to do so in this case, though we did bring together several groups of elementary teachers informally to advise us on some of the key issues.

A number of unanticipated complications arose. The staff working with French Immersion schools felt strongly that it would be unfair to assess French Immersion Grade 3 students on the same criteria as students working in their first language, so we moved the French Immersion reading assessment to Grade 4. While this was a reasonable measure from an educational point of view, it complicated the delivery considerably in that it added a whole new set of students, parents, and teachers to the process.

Which competencies to include turned out to be a difficult issue. The curriculum staff pressed for including more competencies to represent the full set of outcomes in the curriculum. Policy staff, myself included, pushed to have fewer competencies to make the assessment easier for teachers to do and for parents to understand. There was also debate on which competencies to include, since each curriculum had many. In arithmetic, adding and subtracting are done primarily in earlier grades, so this did not appear on the initial set of skills proposed for grade three by the department. However, I believed strongly that parents would be vitally concerned with these basic number skills, and insisted that they be among the competencies included in the assessment. The department wanted to include a competency on graphing, while I thought most parents would not be particularly concerned and that this one could be eliminated. The debate was really between a conception of the assessment that focused, from a professional point of view, on its faithfulness to the curriculum, and a view that focused on providing limited but meaningful information to parents even if important parts of the curriculum were ignored. After much discussion we largely adopted the professional view, and the initial policy provided for assessment of students in seven competencies in reading and fourteen in arithmetic. I was reluctant to overrule the combined judgment of the department's professional staff. The list of competencies for 2000, and the changed list for 2001, are shown in table 3.1.

Another example of the gap between a curriculum view and a public reporting view of the policy concerned the wording of the competencies. Staff in the department tended to use educational terminology that would not necessarily be understandable to parents. Others, myself included, pressed for the use of wording that would be readily meaningful to parents. As table 3.1 shows, over time we simplified the wording, especially in relation to reading.

We also had to decide how to report students' skills. The ratings had to be simple to use and easy for parents to understand. Again we had internal debates between staff who wanted a rather vague wording and others who felt that we had to use language that parents would readily understand. After much discussion we settled on three levels of performance.

Our proposals for the Grade Three Assessment were released in May 2000, much later than we had hoped. We distributed thousands of copies to parents of Grade 2 students and to parent councils, as well as to schools, districts, and provincial organizations. The proposals received quite good support from parents, who were overwhelmingly interested in knowing early in the year how their children were doing. Educators were supportive but worried about the workload implications. A majority of educators did not think the assessment would be useful to parents. This is consistent with other research showing that educators underestimate consistently how interested parents are in school matters (Vincent, 1996).

We spent a considerable amount of time working on effective implementation of the policy. One of the clearest findings in education research is that the development of new practices takes ongoing support. If we want people to do different things in new ways, we have to help them learn to do so. Yet in many cases governments announce complex changes in practice and provide almost no assistance to the system to make the changes. For example, new curricula are often put into place with only a day or two of professional development for teachers, who are then expected to change not only what they teach, but often how they teach. No wonder so many new curricula are left on the shelf while teachers continue with their previous practice.

Although the new policy was an election commitment, the government did not provide any additional money or staff to the department for it, so our efforts to support implementation had to be resourced from existing budgets. This was a challenge because the policy announcement came well into the year, when both staff and money had already been committed to other purposes. However, the assessment and curriculum staff responded well to this challenge. They designed a series of workshops for school district personnel to help them under-

Table 3.1
Changes to Grade Three Assessment Competencies, Numeracy and Reading

Numeracy

14 original competencies, 2000	8 revised competencies, 2001
Sorts 3-D objects and 2-D shapes using 2 attributes; identifies attribute	Sorts objects using one mathematical attribute; identifies attributes such as shape and size
Recalls facts to ten (addition, subtraction)	Recalls addition and subtraction facts to 10 (2 separate items)
Reads and writes number symbols to 100 Counts and skip counts to 100 Describes and compares numbers to 100	Represents and compares numbers, using terms such as *even, odd, more, less, same as*, to 100
Understands place value	Understands place value to 100
Describes number patterns	Identifies, extends, and describes mathematical (repeating and growing) patterns
Creates equivalent sets of coins up to $1.00	
Selects the appropriate standard unit (cm, m) and estimates and measures lengths	Selects the appropriate standard unit (cm, m); estimates and measures length
Measures and compares area using non-standard units Measures and compares capacity using non-standard units Measures and compares mass using non-standard units	
Estimates and computes to solve problems (addition, subtraction) using manipulative materials, symbols, or mental mathematics	Solves and creates addition and subtraction story problems
Manages data and communicates conclusions	Reads and interprets graphs

Table 3.1
(continued)

Reading

7 original competencies, 2000	3 revised competencies, 2001
Demonstrates positive attitude towards reading Reflects on personal knowledge, and reading skills and strategies Sets personal goals for reading	*Reflection* Ability to think about own learning as a reader
Uses a variety of strategies to make and check meaning in context Previews, asks questions, sets purposes when reading	*Oral Reading Skills and Strategies* Ability to use a variety of strategies to read
Recognizes and connects ideas before, during, and after reading Responds critically to text	*Reading Comprehension* Ability to understand and draw conclusions from text

Source: Developed by author from government documents.

stand and implement the new policy. Considerable effort went into emphasizing the way in which the new assessment policy was closely connected to the existing curriculum and to good teaching practice. We invited school districts to designate teams of people, including administrators as well as teachers, to manage the implementation of the policy in their district. Because the policy announcement was so late these sessions were planned for the late summer and fall of 2000, limiting the time schools would have to get ready for the new policy.

To assist teachers in assessing the various competencies, the department designed and distributed a booklet of assessment tools. These were not tests, but a range of different tools teachers could use with children if they were unsure of the children's skill level on the various competencies. These tools were linked to the curriculum and could be useful to teachers in many ways, but they were intended as examples and options, not as requirements. Many of the tools in the resource booklet were intended for use with individual students, because we assumed that teachers would use them only when they were in doubt about a particular student's level on a particular competence.

The initial stages of implementation went reasonably well. Many Grade 3 teachers started out positively disposed because they were so happy to be rid of the standards test. There were certainly grumbles, and not without justification, about the short timelines for implementation. The Manitoba Teachers' Society urged that we delay implementation for a year to allow more time to develop the policy and work with teachers and schools. This was a reasonable suggestion, but given the importance of the election commitment it was simply not feasible. A new government cannot start out by postponing a key commitment for a year because the details are not worked out. We thought we had a reasonably good plan and would have to make improvements as needed.

We did build some flexibility into the policy. For example, some schools wanted to integrate the reporting to parents with their regular fall report cards. We allowed this as long as there was clear reporting on the required competencies. We also allowed flexibility in when the reporting to parents was done and in the format that was used, again as long as the required competencies were clearly included. In fact the implementation varied quite a bit across the province because different school districts had very different starting points in terms of their own assessment and reporting practices.

The policy of flexibility created some problems itself, within the department as well as for districts and schools. Some department staff were used to issuing orders to districts and having them obeyed (at least nominally), and had a hard time with the idea that we should focus on meeting the intent of the policy rather than on making sure it was carried out exactly as detailed. The same was true in schools, where some people were uncomfortable with the idea that they should use their discretion as to how to proceed. It is an irony of the relationship between the department and the schools that the latter often ask for very detailed rules on department policies only to criticize the rules as unworkable.

What we did not anticipate, but should have, was the effect of the previous assessment regime on the system. After five years of worries about testing, teachers and schools tended to treat the new Grade Three Assessment policy as if it were another test. Many teachers referred to it as a test, even though there was no test. The policy called for assessment of students' abilities using a range of vehicles, including daily classroom observation. We assumed that after six weeks or so of working with students, teachers would be able to judge most students' skills on most of the competencies based solely on their daily work. Our idea was that teachers would only do extended diagnostic work with those few individual students where they had doubts about a student's skills.

Many Grade 3 teachers, however, did not see it that way. Because the policy called for a report to parents, many teachers felt they had to have compelling paper-and-pencil evidence for each of the competencies. The set of assessment tools that the department provided as a resource for teachers became, for many teachers, a requirement they had to go through with every student. Some school districts, despite the department's direction that the assessment was to rely on teachers' professional judgment, insisted that all teachers conduct a full range of formal assessment practices with each student on each competency. For many teachers this meant a very large investment of time working with each individual student for several hours to do a formal assessment on all twenty-one competencies. In some classrooms teachers spent weeks on this task, virtually to the exclusion of their regular teaching. In Winnipeg School Division, the largest in the province, the new policy was complicated further because the division had its own policy on assessment in primary grades that involved very extensive data collection by teachers – considerably more than the department was asking for. Teachers, understandably, did not distinguish as to the source of the problem; to them it was all one large imposition.

As teachers and schools began to implement the new policy in the fall of 2000, we started to hear about how much time it was taking and how burdened many Grade 3 teachers felt by the approach. While teachers were strongly supportive of the cancellation of the Grade 3 standards test, by late fall there was quite a bit of anger with the policy and it was clear that we needed to make some changes. I visited several schools and discussed the policy directly with Grade 3 teachers. In December other staff and I attended a meeting of Manitoba Teachers' Society representatives on the policy, and were made very aware, in very direct language, of teachers' concerns.

At the same time, the department was surveying principals, teachers, and parents to gather their reactions to the new approach more formally. These surveys showed strong awareness of and support for the new policy among the 2,500 parents who responded. Three-quarters of the parents reported discussing the report with their child's teacher. It was also clear from parents' responses that there were too many competencies and that our three-point scale for reporting was not clear. The surveys of teachers reinforced the high level of concern about the work required.

In the face of these legitimate concerns we began to look at changes in the policy to make it more workable for teachers. Unless the policy was sustainable given the other demands of teaching, it could not be effective. The department's working group went back to work. Several groups of Grade 3 teachers and school principals were also involved in discussions about potential changes.

In preparation for the 2001 school year we made several important changes. First, we reduced the number of competencies to be reported on in mathematics from fourteen to eight, and in reading from seven to three. This would in itself dramatically reduce the requirement for teachers while still giving parents a good picture of their child's progress. We changed the three reporting categories, to make them clearer for both teachers and parents. Another step was to reinforce the message that teachers were not expected to go through a whole range of new assessment vehicles with every student, that the whole point was to integrate assessment with ongoing teaching so that the two reinforced each other. This point was stressed in all the revised materials the department produced, and in the 2001 round of professional development sessions, which were earlier and more extensive than in 2000. We also worked more closely with principals and superintendents to reinforce this message. As well, in the face of decisions made in 2000 by a few school districts, we strongly discouraged districts from requiring all teachers to conduct a full and intensive round of data-gathering with all students; we felt it important to emphasize to all parties the importance of building, supporting, and respecting teachers' professional abilities to assess student learning in a variety of ways. A revised policy document was distributed in May 2001, and in the fall we produced a short brochure for parents that explained the purpose and nature of the assessment.

These changes made a substantial difference in 2001. Many Grade 3 teachers still felt that the policy took too much work. Sometimes this was because teachers lacked the skills to integrate assessment into their daily work with students. Sometimes it was because they continued to feel the need to have extensive documented evidence for their conclusions in case parents raised questions. Sometimes schools and districts continued to exert pressure to make the assessment more intensive than really was required. Even so, in the fall of 2001 the process went quite smoothly. We heard very few complaints, and more comments on the ways in which the assessment actually reinforced and supported good teaching of the curriculum. Some schools and districts began to look at ways of extending the principles of the Grade Three Assessment to other grades and subject areas, an idea that makes good sense because it links assessment to good teaching and learning practices.

Schools and school districts were also asked to report to the department the proportion of students at each of the three levels on each competence. In the first year, as we anticipated, the reporting was inconsistent in timing and quality. Some school districts did a careful job and reported results well, while in others the implementation was much weaker and the district results less reliable. Some districts never reported results at all in the first round. On most of the competencies, something between 60 per cent and 70 per cent of students were reported as meeting expectations, another 20 to 25 per cent as doing so with some support, and about 15 per cent were described as 'requiring ongoing help.' The proportions varied, of course, across skills. The department published a report on these results on its web site and in print, but reported only gross provincial data. The report occasioned relatively little attention, partly, no doubt, because we did not report school-by-school results. School districts also differed in their use of the data, with some but certainly not all schools and districts using the assessment to inform their own planning and professional development.

None of this was surprising. It was clear from the beginning that a change in assessment would take several years to work its way into the system fully. In subsequent years we did see increasing interest in and use of the Grade Three Assessment in many schools and districts. All districts reported their results, and many made use of the results in their own internal planning and public communications. As teachers became more familiar and more comfortable with the assessment, the focus shifted from getting it done to integrating the assessment with instruction and planning. In 2002 the department expanded its follow-up to the assessment by holding a series of 'making meaning' sessions in which teachers and principals from different school districts came together to talk about what the results meant and how they could use them to support improvements in teaching and learning. Gradually the sense has spread that the policy really is about improving students' learning and supporting good practice.

In a paradoxical and certainly unintended way, the mistakes we made with the assessment in its first year actually served a useful purpose. The willingness of the department to hear the criticisms and make changes in response gave a positive message to teachers that they were important partners in shaping educational practice. It reinforced the feeling that there was a new approach in education from what had been in place in the 1990s.

Extending Good Accountability Practice

Beyond the Grade Three Assessment, the rest of the department's agenda for schools, discussed more fully in Chapter 8, builds on many of the same ideas around effective assessment. Provincial testing plays a relatively minor role, but schools and districts are strongly encouraged to use a range of data on student outcomes both to provide information to the public and to inform their own planning and goal setting. All schools were already required to develop school plans as part of the New Directions program of the Conservatives. Beginning in 2001, the department increased efforts to connect the school plans to local data on student achievement using a variety of indicators. The K–S4 Agenda (see Chapter 8) calls for all schools and school districts to provide an annual public report on student outcomes, but does not prescribe the specific outcomes or data sources to be used. Given the strong interest among parents and the public in knowing how well our students and schools are doing, this kind of approach to data-informed planning and reporting is vital. The goal is to encourage local discussion of goals and results rather than impose a single standard across the province. The approach is based on the belief that improvement is most likely to occur when parents, teachers, students, and others in the community discuss students' accomplishments and challenges and work together to decide on useful strategies based on the evidence. Schools can work to improve their own previous performance rather than being compared unfairly to other schools in very different circumstances.

In September of 2002 the department released its own report on student outcomes in Manitoba. This report reviewed provincial data on several outcomes, including national tests such as the School Achievement Indicators Program, results on provincial grade tests in several grades, the number of students 'retained in grade' (failed) in elementary schools, the proportion of students graduating from high school, and high school course marks. The goal is to give a rounded picture of the outcomes of schooling in the province. The report contained no comparisons of schools or districts but did include some analysis of results by gender. The intent is to continue this provincial report while expanding the indicators it includes and doing more analysis for regions of the province, and for particular subgroups, so as to give a fuller picture of the successes and challenges facing the system. The report received extensive media coverage but did not raise concerns from any of the major educational organizations. We had circulated a proposal for this document several months earlier, so people in the system were well aware of what was being planned and had had a chance to comment on the project.

I believe that people can and will become more informed users of information about school outcomes if the information is made available to them in reasonable ways. The media can and should continue to play an important role in reporting on school outcomes, though many reporters need to learn more about understanding or interpreting numbers. At the same time, schools and districts need to do much more public reporting themselves, which also means being willing to identify shortcomings and problems.

All of this will take continued work. The effective use of a variety of data concerning school outcomes to inform both the public and professional planning for improvement is a long-term effort. Although it seems an obvious activity, the fact is that educators are not particularly used to collecting or analysing student outcome data to guide their own practice. Many schools simply do not have good data on student success rates in different skills or programs, or on what happens to students after they leave the school, which is one reason there is public support for provincial testing. For example, the 2002 provincial report on student outcomes revealed that about 10 per cent of students require more than eight years to complete Grade 8 (which means that they have in effect 'failed' a grade, despite the public impression that almost no student fails any more). When this number was reported in the media, a number of educators expressed doubts about it, though they did not have accurate data from their own school or district. Once people have reliable data, they also need to learn how to use it to guide planning and resource allocation.

An approach that emphasizes giving lots of information to as many people as possible has its problems. There is always the danger of misinterpretation of data. Educators cannot reasonably object, though, to giving people information on the grounds that it might be misused. The educational stance has to be to make good-quality information available to people and then help them learn how to use it effectively. It is not an easy challenge, but it is consistent with our valuing of education and of democracy. In proposing and developing the Grade Three Assessment, the Manitoba government helped move educational practice in a positive direction, one that does not assume that more testing is a good thing, but one that recognizes the public desire and need for better information on student outcomes, and keeps the focus on approaches that can actually help improve teaching and learning.

CHAPTER 4

College Expansion: Unforeseen Problems in Meeting a Commitment

> The Commission believes that community colleges are crucial to the economic growth of Manitoba ... It is our view that a concerted and determined effort is required to increase the capacity of community colleges to develop a broader range of diploma programs ... *The Commission recommends, as a reasonable target, the doubling of the participation rate in community college diploma programs over the next five years.*
>
> Report of the University Education Review Commission,
> December 1993, 41–3; original emphasis

A pledge to increase enrolment in community colleges was a central NDP commitment during the 1999 election. The campaign announcement promised to 'double college enrolment' by increasing funding, to expand co-op education programs, and to implement a more flexible system of transferring credits between colleges and universities. The commitment was estimated to cost $6 million per year in additional funding for each of the next four years. This promise was made part way through the campaign, after the Progressive Conservatives had announced their billion-dollar package of $500 million in increased spending and $500 million in tax reductions.

The genesis of the promise lay in the Roblin Commission report on university education in 1993. Although asked to review university education in Manitoba, Roblin also recommended a large increase in the community college sector. In 1999 the province's participation rate in university education was about the Canadian average, but Manitoba ranked last among all provinces in the proportion of 18- to 24-year-olds attending college. Manitoba's college sector was underdeveloped by national standards. This was partly because the colleges had been part of the government bureaucracy from their inception in the 1960s until 1993. When I was assistant deputy minister with responsibility for the college sector in 1985 and 1986 it became clear to me how undesirable this arrangement was. For example, in 1986 Red River College ran out of money in its budget to buy books for its bookstore, even though it sold the books to students at a profit. In order to buy more books we had to go back to the Treasury Board to get an increase in the budget. Because this could be portrayed as an unexpected mid-year spending increase due to a lack of budget discipline by the government, Treasury Board was reluctant to approve the request, although they did eventually do so. To take another example, a college department head, because the position was so many levels down the hierarchy, sometimes did not have enough signing authority to order a textbook. The move by the Conservatives in 1993 to give the colleges greater, though still limited, independence was an important positive step. Under the new arrangement colleges became much more dynamic institutions, with stronger links to employers and the community.

Some serious problems remained, however. Funding to colleges and universities had been limited or cut throughout much of the 1990s, though in their last two years in office, in response to the Roblin recommendations, the Conservatives had funded a number of new college programs. The colleges' buildings were owned and operated by the Department of Government Services, whose own budget pressures had led to some college buildings being in less than optimal condition. Very few new college facilities had been built in the previous twenty years despite the rapid changes in many areas of college education, such as the technologies. Capacity in many programs was inadequate, leading to long waiting lists to enter some popular programs. In some programs admission requirements were unreasonable, while in others attrition rates were too high. College tuition fees were among the lowest in Canada, which further limited the revenue available to the institutions. All in all, despite the valiant efforts of many college staff members, and some infusion of money and energy in 1997 and 1998, the sector was not strong in 1999.

The four Manitoba colleges are very different. Red River College is by far the largest and most comprehensive, with, as of 1999, about 7,500 enrolments in its regular programs. Assiniboine College, in Brandon – 200 kilometres west of Winnipeg, and Manitoba's second-largest city – serves a much smaller population and has a smaller enrolment – about

2,300 – but still tries to have a reasonably full set of program offerings. Keewatin Community College, a much smaller institution (1,100 enrolments) with campuses in The Pas and Thompson in northern Manitoba, has a particularly difficult set of challenges. It serves a total population of about 70,000 spread out across more than 150,000 square kilometres, large parts of which are not easily accessible. Its population also has the lowest level of formal education, so many adults do not have the prerequisites for college entry. More than half of the population of northern Manitoba is Aboriginal, raising additional issues for Keewatin around both its programs and its identity. There is increasing pressure from Aboriginal people and communities to have their own institutions that reflect their identity. Keewatin was not always seen as being sensitive to the needs of Aboriginal people, though the leadership and many of its staff clearly understood how important this issue was for their success. L'École technique et professionnelle (ETP) in St Boniface – Winnipeg's main francophone district – with only 150 enrolments in the college sector, had a very different identity issue, trying to serve a small francophone population that had traditionally emphasized classical education rather than technologies and trades. Although Manitoba needs people in many fields who can work in French, it has often been difficult for ETP to come up with enough students in any one area to make a program reasonably cost-effective.

The NDP election commitment to expand colleges was an exciting opportunity, one where there was a clear promise of additional funding. Moreover, the promise was not politically controversial, since it built on a direction taken by the Conservative government. A main concern of course was meeting the very ambitious target to 'double enrolments' within the time and resources we had. From the beginning it was evident that we would have to keep a strong focus on that target while also keeping in mind the long-term goal of creating not only a larger college sector, but also one that was highly accessible, had high success rates, and was involved in dynamic programming in vital areas of the economy and with close links with employers. This would be, it was clear, a tall order even though the colleges were ready and willing.

We began by commissioning a couple of policy papers from people outside the province who had worked in Manitoba and knew our colleges sector, in order to get a sense of what the best possibilities and options were. We soon realized that a commitment of this size would need substantial attention from the department. The Council on Post-Secondary Education had a very small staff and was already heavily committed on a number of fronts, not least the promise to cut tuition fees by 10 per cent. Because the college expansion commitment was so central politically, we decided to create the College Expansion Initiative (CEI), a small secretariat specifically to lead this effort. Dr Curtis Nordman, at that point dean of continuing education at the University of Winnipeg but with substantial experience in community colleges, was hired to direct this effort. While CEI was to be a separate office within the department, it was also intended to work closely with COPSE to ensure consistency in approach. The council's approval would be required for all new programs and policies funded through CEI, and all the money would flow through COPSE's accounts.

This kind of hybrid institutional structure is difficult to operate because it does not follow the normal hierarchical approach of government. It is not surprising that there were tensions from time to time among the various actors. Sometimes the council felt that it did not have enough involvement in CEI decisions. CEI and COPSE staff did not always see eye to eye on issues, and, especially at the outset, the colleges were not always sure of the respective roles of CEI and the council. CEI staff were highly aware of the ambitious nature of the government's election commitment and were quite prepared to put pressure on the colleges to meet the goal. The colleges were generally not very happy about the degree of scrutiny that CEI placed on their program proposals. At the same time, the creation of CEI gave a level of drive and visibility to the initiative in keeping with its importance as a central government commitment. I doubt the expansion would have moved as rapidly as it did without having a unit dedicated to it specifically. Given all the pressures, the system worked reasonably well and got steadily smoother as time went on, a tribute to the commitment and effort of staff not only in CEI and COPSE but also in the colleges.

The CEI office was set up in February 2000. Work began immediately with the colleges and COPSE to identify areas for expansion. A mandate statement was produced for CEI that not only emphasized creating more places, but also stressed improving success rates in the college system and strengthening the links – already very good in many areas – between the colleges and the employers of their graduates. An initial emphasis was placed on reducing waiting lists by improving capacity in popular program areas such as civil technology and creative communications. At the same time, we wanted to look towards the future and begin development of a new generation of exciting programs in important emerging economic areas such as the new technologies.

The colleges were asked to develop and cost four-year program expansion plans.

Challenges to Implementation

The College Expansion Initiative ran into a number of 'bumps' almost immediately. These included the problem of suddenly redirecting system energies, the need to meet pressing short-term concerns, and the huge amount of attention that went towards developing a new campus in central Winnipeg for Red River College.

The challenge of doubling enrolments in career-technical programs in four years was immediately apparent. It meant more than 4,000 new places for students as well as new programs with the requisite staffing and facilities. For institutions that had, until the last couple of years, been spending all their time figuring out how to keep all their current commitments given limited resources, it was a dramatic shift. The colleges simply did not have the capacity to do what was needed. None of them had a significant program-planning capacity. Although they had all been involved to some degree in strategic planning work, there had been no point spending time on grand visions that were not going to be implemented, so the background work in terms of identifying a wide range of new program opportunities had not been done. Yet now all of this had to be done, and very quickly.

Because the colleges are so different, there were always great concerns about whether the CEI funds were being distributed fairly. These concerns were expressed not only by the colleges, but by the communities they represented. Because Winnipeg is so dominant in Manitoba, making up about two-thirds of the population, other towns and regions are always worried that they will be left out and not get their fair share. Brandon, as the second largest city, is very sensitive to its relative attention vis-à-vis Winnipeg. The government had two cabinet ministers from Brandon, including Education Minister Drew Caldwell. An important substantive task, as well as a political challenge for CEI, was to make sure that new programs and services did recognize the needs of the entire province and were sensitive to regional issues.

One important pressure on the College Expansion Initiative was the need to support other priorities of government that were linked to training. Two key examples were nursing and aerospace.

The NDP's most important single election commitment had been improvements in health care. One of the critical issues in meeting this commitment was to increase the number of nurses. In the 1990s in Manitoba, as in other provinces, many nursing positions had been eliminated as part of the drive to reduce costs and balance budgets without increasing taxation. By the end of the decade, as effect of these cuts on health care quality became an increasingly important political issue, there was a mad scramble to find more nurses. Many of the nurses laid off earlier had left the country or the profession, so training more nurses became imperative.

In Manitoba, the need to train more nurses became a priority for the College Expansion Initiative. The task was made more difficult because Manitoba, again like other provinces, had largely eliminated two-year, college-level training programs for nurses, moving to a model in which all nurses would begin with a four-year degree provided by a university. The two-year nursing diploma programs that had been operated by Red River College and by several hospitals had been folded into the four-year BN offered by the University of Manitoba. The new government, through the Council on Post-Secondary Education, immediately began discussions to restore a diploma program at the college level, but a program that would be fully articulated with the BN so that students who wished could readily continue on to earn the degree.

The restoration of diploma training in nursing was strongly opposed by the professional body, the Manitoba Association of Registered Nurses, but strongly supported by the Manitoba Nurses Union. There were some very tense moments as COPSE worked with the professional groups, the colleges, and other parties to develop and implement a college-level nursing program to be funded by CEI and to begin as soon as possible. The government also wanted to support training of nurses in the north, where the shortage was particularly acute, and to create a college nursing program at L'École technique et professionnelle to train French-speaking nurses to meet needs in Manitoba's bilingual health system. Re-establishing a college diploma program that was fully articulated with the university's degree required considerable effort and a great deal of goodwill from all the parties. This single program initiative took a huge amount of time and energy during 2000. The result was a twenty-five-month nursing diploma program at Red River College that began in the fall of 2000 and graduated its first nurses in the spring of 2003. Nurses are graduating from ETP in 2004.

Another example of a single initiative that ate up energy and resources was in aerospace. Manitoba has a significant aerospace industry, with four large companies – Air Canada, Boeing, Standard Aero, and Bristol Aero – and a myriad of smaller firms. The industry had developed a very strong sector council, the Manitoba Aerospace Human Resources Council (MAHRC), and was working hard to improve its training efforts. MAHRC had been able to bring together both the large companies and the many small players who could not afford to run extensive training programs but who also needed skilled workers.

By 1999 there was a serious shortage of aircraft mechanics of various types in Manitoba and nationally. The province ran an apprenticeship program for aircraft mechanics through the Stevenson Technical Training Centre (STTC), located at a former air force base in Portage la Prairie, about 100 kilometres west of Winnipeg, but it was too small to provide enough people, and some companies, notably Air Canada, were unwilling to participate in apprenticeship training, preferring to hire fully qualified tradespeople. MAHRC approached the province for assistance in strengthening training capacity so that the industry could continue to grow. The companies wanted not only an increase in the apprenticeship program, but also the creation of a two-year, college-based, full-time program that could lead directly to employment.

Aircraft mechanics positions are highly skilled and well paid, so there was strong interest in trying to meet this need in the province. However the proposal had substantial costs. Creating an entirely new program would mean new facilities as well as staff. The industry preferred to have the new program in Winnipeg rather than in Portage, as all the main companies were Winnipeg-based. The government, however, did not want to diminish its presence in an important rural community. The parties also agreed that they wanted to find ways of bringing more Aboriginal students into the aerospace field as training capacity grew.

The negotiations around this program were handled primarily through the department rather than through CEI, with the director of Stevenson, Bob Knight, playing the key role on behalf of the government. CEI was involved as a potential funder of the new program, and also because the program was to be a college program that would contribute to the 'doubling' goal.

The program came into existence after intensive discussions over many months, and a huge amount of work in getting all the pieces lined up – not just facilities and staff, but also approval from Transport Canada, which has to certify the training of all aircraft mechanics. The industry made some significant contributions in the form of equipment and skilled staff. An unused building near the Winnipeg airport was renovated to house the new college program while the Portage facility remained in operation to train apprentices. The process of getting the building ready proved taxing, as additional costs cropped up that had not been anticipated while the deadline for opening seemed to approach all too rapidly. It took enormous effort from many people to make the project work.

Another important element in the aerospace program was the creation of a new governance structure. I had seen this development from the outset as a chance to move the operational responsibility for Stevenson Training Centre from government to Red River College, which was the appropriate location for such a high-skills training program. Industry, however, liked their strong role in Stevenson and was nervous about turning over control of the program to the college. As a means of resolving the differences, an agreement was struck to operate the Stevenson program as part of Red River under a separate advisory board, with substantial industry representation. Red River, used to working extensively with industry advisory groups, had no difficulty with this approach, while the companies were reassured that they would continue to have a strong voice in the operation of the program. The requirement to transfer staff to a different union with different pay rates and working conditions added an additional difficulty to the process.

In the spring of 2002 a grand opening was held at the new facility involving the industry partners, Stevenson, Red River, College Expansion, and the government. The finale of this event involved opening the hangar doors to the facility to watch a DC-9 donated to the program by Air Canada taxi up with engines running. It was an exciting moment.

Both nursing and aerospace were success stories in that important new programs were put in place to meet pressing economic and social needs. At the same time, they put a great deal of pressure on the College Expansion Initiative, not only in terms of organization but also financially. The original planning for college expansion had been based on the average cost of places in existing college programs, which was about $4,000 per place per year. New programs, however, were often much higher-cost because they involved new areas of operation, new facilities and equipment, and programs that involved sophisticated technology, carried higher operating costs, and required highly skilled staff. The expansion of nursing at Red River and elsewhere required nearly $2.5 million per year for about 250 new places, while the aerospace initiative took more than a million dollars annually from CEI for about ninety more students. Both programs were worth doing because they were tied to important areas of economic and social policy and prepared people for good jobs, but it was also clear that the College Expansion Initiative could not meet its target if the new places cost more than $20,000 each.

Princess Street

The most difficult issue to face the entire college expansion project was the proposal to build a new campus for Red River in downtown Winnipeg. This project originated outside the expansion commitment. The City of Winnipeg owned some old buildings on Princess Street in the Exchange District and was looking for proposals to use or redevelop the buildings, which were in very poor physical condition but had significant heritage value. In 1999, not long before the election, Red River and the Department of Government Services looked at whether those buildings could be the basis for a new Red River campus. The fact that the city was willing to provide the land and buildings for a dollar for an appropriate use was a strong inducement.

In late September 1999, between the election and the swearing-in of the new government, the Department of Government Services, working with Red River, issued a Request for Proposals (RFP) to developers for a new Red River campus using the Princess Street buildings and site. As a way of getting around the very limited capital spending in government, the project was envisioned as a public-private partnership. A private developer would build it and lease it back to the college or to the government. Even though the cost of a new campus would eventually be paid entirely by government, the RFP had not been discussed with COPSE or sent to the Treasury Board, had not been approved by the outgoing government, and was not brought to the attention of the transition team for the new government, either. Government Services apparently saw it as nothing more than an exploration to see what the level of interest might be.

In fact, the idea took off beyond the intentions of Government Services or Red River College. Half a dozen consortia of architects and developers put in proposals. The idea of a college campus in the Exchange was exciting to many people, and rapidly became a key part of various plans to revitalize downtown Winnipeg. The mayor, Glen Murray, became a forceful advocate for a Red River presence in the area, and the media, especially the *Winnipeg Free Press*, began to champion the idea. Other businesses began to look at sites nearby as potential locations for services to the Red River students, such as restaurants or entertainment centres. Several small software and technology companies were located nearby and loved the idea of having the Red River students available to them. By the end of 1999, many people in the community were talking about the new campus as a done deal, even though the project had never been approved by the provincial government nor had any funding allocated to it.

For several months the department resisted seeing Princess Street as a fait accompli. It was clear in the department that Red River College could not possibly manage the huge increase in enrolment that was being planned in its existing facilities, so new space would be necessary. A downtown location of some kind certainly made sense; the main Red River campus was on the edge of the city and quite difficult to reach except by car. As well, a downtown college campus could be a significant part of downtown revitalization, which was a policy goal of Mayor Murray as well as of the provincial government.

The College Expansion staff suggested an alternative location for a new Red River campus, next to the University of Winnipeg. There were some good arguments for this location, most notably the possibility of building very strong links between the college and the University of Winnipeg. The two institutions already operated a number of joint and integrated programs in which students could combine college and university study. It would be possible to share services such as food, bookstore, and athletics, and so reduce the size and cost of the new college campus.

The University of Winnipeg site was actively discussed, including substantial media coverage, for several months. Over time the factors favouring the Princess Street location were overwhelming. These included strong support from the City of Winnipeg, the business community, and the *Winnipeg Free Press*. Princess Street also fit better with larger goals for urban renewal, and of course the college itself was strongly committed to that location. In November 2000, the government committed to the Princess Street location. The possibility of an alternative location did lead the City of Winnipeg to offer some additional inducements for the Princess Street location, including much enhanced property-tax credits, streetscaping, parking, and public transportation services. These made the project both more attractive and more affordable.

It was apparent from the beginning that the building of a new campus would be an expensive project. The initial estimates from the development teams were in the order of $30 million, which would make this the largest single post-secondary education capital project in the province's history. However the $30 million was only a preliminary estimate. One of the problems with the Princess Street project was the way it developed: plans and budgets for the building were being discussed publicly while discussions were still going on as to what programs would be housed there.

During this period the issue was discussed by both the cabinet and the Treasury Board on several occasions. Ministers, especially those on the Treasury Board, were understandably quite unhappy that huge momentum had developed for a large capital project that they had never approved. The government was already facing tight budgets and was concerned about how it would finance the capital and operating costs of the new campus. At the same time, a large capital project in the downtown was very attractive, especially a college campus that would bring young people into the area. After the question of location was resolved, the discussion inside government revolved around a number of issues, including how big the project should be, what additional spinoffs it might generate, and how it would be financed.

The original call for proposals for the new campus had suggested a building of about 150,000 square feet to house approximately 1,000 daytime students and about 150 staff. However the commitment to College Expansion in the election made it reasonable to think about a bigger building. After all, Red River was now expected to absorb more than 2,500 additional students, and, as already noted, the main campus and its current satellite centres would certainly not be adequate to do so. As the larger plans for College Expansion began to develop during 2000, it was also clear that Red River's growth would centre around programs in the technologies, so a new facility would also be needed to accommodate the kinds of high-tech programs that did not fit well in the thirty-five-year-old buildings on the main campus. The size of the proposed building was upgraded so that it could serve 2,000 learners, day and evening.

While the main purpose of the building was clearly to house Red River College students, any major public capital project is also expected to contribute to other economic and social policy goals. When the City of Winnipeg first put out the idea of using the Princess Street site it had two goals: to maintain some heritage buildings that were vacant and in bad condition, and to help revitalize the Exchange District. These goals would remain no matter what kind of building had been decided upon. The province also had some broader policy goals. Like the city, it was interested in maintaining heritage buildings and wanted to show leadership in that area. Accessibility for disabled persons would be another requirement, in keeping with the NDP commitment to increase the participation of people with disabilities in higher education and work. The NDP also strongly supported a public daycare system so it would be important to ensure that a major new project had a daycare centre in it or nearby. Yet another goal was to create a 'green' building, one that embodied the latest environmental systems and controls so as to reduce energy use and waste.

Each of these concerns had to find its place and balance against the primary educational use of the building and the concern to keep the costs manageable. Different ministers naturally advanced their own policy goals within the overall project. Some of the issues were quite complicated. For example, daycare turned out to be a problem partly because it would take space away from classrooms and other educational purposes, and partly because the building design did not allow any green space, which a licensed daycare must have available for children. Even a plan to put a green space on the roof was considered, but turned out to be prohibitively expensive. On the environmental issues, the government eventually agreed to provide additional capital funds for a package of the latest energy and waste efficiency measures. These measures were projected to pay for themselves in operating savings within ten years, but they did increase the capital cost of the building by well over a million dollars.

A major issue concerned the ownership and financing mechanism for the building. The initial plan developed by Government Services and Red River had been a public-private partnership. However there was considerable doubt as to whether this would be cheaper, and the NDP has a commitment in principle to public ownership of public resources. Another option was to have the new building owned, built, and operated by Red River. In Manitoba, universities built and owned their own buildings, but the college buildings were still owned and operated by the Department of Government Services. When the colleges became independent in 1993, they were offered the option of taking over ownership of their buildings, but decided against this because of their well-founded concern that they would not be given enough funds to maintain the buildings properly.

The discussion of ownership options went on for well over a year, even while the design was completed and construction began. Various proposals and cost figures were circulated on the options. Although the technical procedures for cost analysis are well defined, twenty-five- or thirty-year financing projections are inevitably uncertain because a great deal depends on the assumptions made about interest rates, tax levels, and ongoing utility costs, all of which are likely to change significantly over a couple of decades.

Another consideration was how the different ownership and financing options would affect the government's overall accounts. Government is unique among large financial entities in recording large capital expenditures in full in the year they are made. Moreover, in government accounting a capital asset has the same status as a program expenditure, even though the former creates something of lasting value. Almost all other entities amortize capital costs over the life of an investment and show the costs against assets on their balance sheets. The unusual approach in government, often driven by the demands of auditors, means that a substantial capital project can distort the government's overall financial position. Part of the attractiveness of public-private partnerships for some governments is that instead of showing the full capital costs of a project in one or two years, much smaller annual lease expenditures appear on the books, even if, in the long run, the cost of the lease is significantly greater than an initial capital outlay would be. In the end the government decided, with the agreement of the board of Red River College, that the best option was for the college to own the building. Financing would come from annual operating grants to the college from CEI via COPSE.

As in most large projects, Princess Street also involved many actors with different and not always complementary agendas. Provincial government departments included Advanced Education (for the primary tenant, Red River), Government Services (as the project manager and possible owner), Intergovernmental Affairs (which was responsible for relations with the City of Winnipeg and urban development), Tourism and Culture (for heritage buildings), Environment (for green building issues), Energy (for energy conservation), Finance (which would manage any debt or loans related to the project) and the Treasury Board (which controlled spending in government). Keeping everyone informed and on the same page in terms of plans was a large task. In the midst of all the discussions in government, Red River College sometimes felt as though it were being left out of decisions on a building where it would be the primary user. As well, the consortium eventually chosen for the project, the Princess Street Consortium, included a development company, an architectural firm, and a construction company, and the three of them did not always see eye to eye on important issues, either.

Once the decision to locate on Princess Street was made, there was growing urgency to move the project rapidly forward. Given the money being invested in new programs in the colleges, Red River would soon be unable to accommodate all its students in its existing facilities, and it would be expensive to find and fit up temporary facilities for many of the high-tech programs that would eventually be housed at the new campus. From a political perspective, the new campus would be a very tangible expression of the government's commitment to college expansion and downtown revitalization, so there was strong interest in having the facility up and running quickly.

Active work on the project began almost immediately the final location decision was made. An interim agreement was made with the consortium to begin the construction pending final resolution of the issue of ownership. By the end of 2000, construction, final program planning, and decisions on ownership and modes of financing were all taking place simultaneously.

To complicate matters still further, progress on construction immediately ran into a problem when the owner of a small piece of property that was to be expropriated for the new campus took the issue to court in an effort to get much more money for his property. His case was dismissed as frivolous by each of the courts that heard it, but between delays in court hearings and appeals to further courts the case lasted months and threatened to derail the construction schedule badly. To avoid a major delay in opening the building, as well as a significant cost increase, the developers proposed that the phasing of the project be changed. Another section of the campus was moved ahead and the main building was rescheduled to be the last part completed. Although the most effective and cheapest alternative, this change in plans also increased costs by some $500,000.

Despite all the issues swirling around it, the construction itself proceeded very smoothly. The first phase of the new campus was opened by Prince Philip as part of the Queen's visit to Winnipeg in October 2002, just after I had left the government. It housed several hundred students, primarily in an old warehouse that was now completely renovated to house programs in computer technology, media, and broadcasting. The main part of the campus opened in 2004.

One of the truths illustrated by Princess Street is that the short-term vicissitudes of major projects, grist for the political and media mill in the short term, are usually forgotten entirely in the long run, and what remains is the lasting accomplishment. After all the effort and the scrambling to work out all the arrangements, the result is an impressive and useful building. When all the issues around the site and construction of Princess Street are long forgotten, the building still will be a an important legacy to post-secondary education in Manitoba and to the City of Winnipeg.

Indicators of Success

The government's commitment to college expansion in the 1999 election was to 'double college enrolment.' In the course of developing CEI, the explicit fulfilment of this commitment was an important focus and led to some particular policy approaches. One issue was to determine precisely what 'doubling' meant. Colleges run a wide range of programs, from one day to two or more years. They are extensively involved in continuing education, apprenticeship, and a wide range of workplace education programs.

Given the background to the election promise and the analysis in the Roblin Commission report, CEI was set up to focus on programs that met Statistics Canada's definition of a career-technical program. That definition includes one- or two-year programs that normally require high school completion for entry. These definitions are rather arbitrary. Statistics Canada has recognized for years the complex nature of community college programs in Canada, and the problems of categorizing them in ways that are useful and consistent. Nonetheless, the career-technical definition was generally accepted across Canada. Moreover, doubling enrolment in these programs, which were strongly linked to strong or emerging areas of the economy, was a more meaningful goal than doubling all enrolments, including the thousands of students taking evening courses in a wide range of areas from home wiring to computer applications.

The problem with the existing Statistics Canada definition was that both elements of the definition could work against the range of educational goals of colleges. Many college programs are one year or even less. Colleges and high schools or adult education programs also have articulation agreements designed to allow students to move more easily from one program to another, which, though beneficial to students, may result in a program not 'counting' in the right category.

Admission requirements are also a problem. Many post-secondary institutions, especially universities, use entrance requirements as a way of reducing the number of applicants and simplifying admissions even when the requirements are not clearly linked to eventual student success. For example, a program may require Grade 12 English or mathematics even though a strong link cannot be demonstrated between this requirement and success in the program. Because colleges are concerned to make education and training as widely accessible as possible, they often try to avoid setting this kind of arbitrary admission requirement, but the result may be that a program would not count under Statistics Canada's definition. The admissions issue was particularly critical for Keewatin Community College in the north, since high school completion rates in the north are substantially lower than in southern Manitoba, especially for adults. Many of Keewatin's students began their college program without having completed high school, yet were expected to complete, sometimes with additional time and support, the same program as that of a high school graduate. Given the critical importance to Manitoba of increasing the skill levels of many adults without high school, including many Aboriginal people, we could not exclude people from programs on these grounds.

Considerable discussion took place in CEI, the Council on Post-secondary Education, and the colleges concerning how to approach these issues. The need to reach the target set for CEI was important, since failure to do so would be reported in the media and attacked by the opposition. A response to the criticism that stressed the importance of accessibility would be seen as making excuses even if it was in fact a legitimate explanation. At the same time, the purpose of CEI was not to reach a particular target but to provide appropriate training and educational opportunities for Manitobans. It would not make sense to provide those opportunities in narrow ways that worked against learner needs only in order to meet a target that had, after all, been set rather quickly in the 1999 election campaign.

As the CEI developed, its office worked closely with the colleges on ways of meeting both objectives. Priority was given to new or expanded programs that met the Statistics Canada definition. We also found that the colleges had a number of existing programs that could fit the definition but had not in previous years. For example, in some programs nearly all students had completed Grade 12, even though this was not an official entrance requirement. Changing the general admission requirement in these programs would improve the count of students in career-technical programs, thus balancing other programs that were important for students but did not 'count' towards the target. Using the colleges' discretion concerning admissions to ensure that the formal change did not disadvantage needy students, would allow the programs to continue to accept learners who did not meet the formal requirements. In 2001, as part of a wider change in high school graduation requirements, the government introduced a policy of dual credits, in which students could take college or university courses and apply them towards their high school graduation. This allowed the colleges to admit students who were a few courses short of high school completion, and to have those students complete high school at the same time as they were working on their college diploma.

These changes, however, were relatively small in relation to the expansion of new and existing programs supported by CEI. During its first three years CEI invested or committed $20 million towards expanding programs in areas of high demand and adding fifty-five new programs in many other emerging areas, providing the resources that the colleges had long needed to renew themselves programmatically. Several thousand new places for students were created. The examples of nursing and aerospace have already been discussed, but many other new program areas were also developed, including digital and information technologies, broadcasting, precision agriculture, and new programs in various aspects of business administration. CEI also contributed to better accessibility to college programs by supporting substantial distance education developments, satellite campuses in a number of communities, and the redesign of courses at Keewatin Community College to increase the success rates of students whose previous academic preparation was not strong. By the end of the 2002–03 year, the accomplishments were impressive. The initial problems of implementation had been largely overcome, and, as a result of hard work by all parties, enrolments and program choices had grown significantly.

The College Expansion Initiative is an example of an election promise that was popular and uncontroversial, yet proved very challenging to implement. In the public mind the issue may remain a simple one, such as how many new places were created in colleges. For those trying to make it happen, the issues are inevitably more complicated and more difficult. A substantial literature in education and in public policy describes the complications of policy implementation (e.g., Howlett & Ramesh, 1995; McLaughlin, 1987), but inevitably governments give more attention to the announcement of policies than to their implementation. The college expansion story shows the importance of allocating resources and attention specifically to managing the implementation of important policy commitments, and of recognizing the likelihood that unforeseen complications will arise and have to be managed. Better implementation is possible if governments take it seriously.

CHAPTER 5

School Funding: Managing the Intractable

Very early in his tenure, Minister of Education Drew Caldwell met with a school board. The school board's issues focused entirely on issues of money and the board's need to get more of it from the province. After about forty-five minutes of this, the minister looked across the table and said, 'We're nearly out of time, folks. Would you like to say anything about education while you're here?' It was probably an impolitic remark, but I was silently cheering.

In education in Canada, as in health care, no issue gets as much media and public attention as funding of schools. Even issues around test scores – such as the supposedly poor results on the Ontario high school literacy test in 2001 – play second fiddle to coverage of school funding.

There are four key questions around school funding in every jurisdiction. First, how much money is enough? Second, who pays? Third, what does the money buy? Fourth, how is the money distributed? There can never be a final answer to these questions since no matter what arrangements are put in place, somebody will not like them. The annual decisions on these four questions are therefore among the most important education policy events of the year and so of great significance to the government.[1]

How Much Money Is Enough?

The funding picture for schools in Canada changed significantly in the 1990s. During the 1960s and early 1970s, the system expanded rapidly.

---

[1] This chapter focuses on political questions and provides only a very limited account of the issues in financing education. Interested readers can find a fuller discussion in Chapter 5 of *Understanding Canadian Schools* (Young & Levin, 2002).

Not only were there more young people, but more students finished high school and went on to post-secondary education. New programs and services were developed, facilities were improved, and new schools, colleges, and universities were built and staffed all over the country. In the mid 1970s the picture began to change as enrolments fell and government revenues came under pressure for both economic and political reasons. By the late 1970s many provinces were making efforts to restrain spending in education, but even so, spending per pupil in schools rose throughout the 1980s. Even as enrolment dropped, numbers of teachers rose and class sizes fell while new services such as special education were developed.

Despite all the talk of deficit fighting in the 1980s, and a few attempts to make real reductions such as the Quebec wage rollback of 1982, it was only in the mid to late 1990s that per pupil spending on schools in Canada fell, for the first time in fifty years. Many provincial governments either froze or cut their spending on education in order to finance tax cuts and deficit reductions.

Determining an appropriate funding level is always a matter of judgment. Spending on K–12 education in Canada is relatively high in comparison to other countries (OECD, 2002b). On the other hand, one would expect higher costs in Canada given our climate, our geography, our many small schools and many students who have to be bussed to school, and our diversity with so many different language and cultural groups to accommodate. It is not reasonable to think that schooling in Canada should cost the same as in densely populated, homogeneous countries such as Japan or France. The $40 billion spent in Canada on schools in 2001 is a lot of money, but to put it in perspective it is less than the $47 billion Canadians spent on new cars and trucks in the same year (Canadian Global Almanac, 2003, p. 202). To put it another, way, Canada spends in total about $7,500 per student per year for our schools. This amounts to about eight dollars per student per hour, based on about 900 hours of school time per year – about what one would pay a babysitter.

One frequently hears the objection that we can't improve education by 'throwing money at schools.' The charge is made that more spending is not connected with better results. In reality nobody has ever suggested the money should be 'thrown'; this metaphor is itself a way of discrediting calls for more spending, as if they were frivolous. The debate about the relationship between spending and outcomes remains unresolved (see Burtless, 1996, for a fuller discussion). In a system such as education one could always put more money to good use – by reducing class sizes, enriching programs, buying more library books or computers, hiring specialists in areas such as music or physical education, and so on. A case can always be made that a given level of funding is inadequate. Canadian polling data (Livingstone, Hart, & Davie, 2003) shows continued support for government spending on education as a high priority. However almost every other area of public activity also can and does make a strong case for more money. Governments inevitably face hard political choices around balancing the many competing demands on their budgets, not only in education, health, and other program areas, but also with regard to the pressure for tax cuts and debt repayment.

Who Pays?

Canada has long supported a system in which the costs of public schooling are paid entirely from public funds raised through taxation, and there are no direct charges to students. In post-secondary education, although there has always been a contribution from students through tuition, about 60 per cent of the total funding comes directly from public sources (Canadian Education Statistics Council, 2000).

Until about a decade ago, the costs of schooling in most provinces were shared between provincial governments and school boards, which generated their share through local property taxes. However through the 1990s most provinces changed their funding system so that the province provided all or virtually all the money. Ontario made a huge and complicated shift in financing in 1997, moving the responsibility for about $6 billion in education funding from local to provincial hands while at the same time shifting a similar amount back to municipalities in the areas such as social assistance and transport. The province now controls all education funding, including the amount raised from property taxes in each district. By 1999 Manitoba and Saskatchewan were the only provinces that still had a significant local property tax component set by school boards as part of their funding model for schools – about 40 per cent in Manitoba and as much as 60 per cent in Saskatchewan. In the rest of Canada, education is funded from various provincial revenue sources, one of which is property tax. Although property taxes are often described as particularly unfair, there is an argument that taxing property has a legitimate part in any overall tax regime, especially when other forms of wealth are not taxed.

The freezes and cuts in provincial support to schools have also had the effect of increasing the cost of education to parents. As noted by People for Education (www.peopleforeducation.com), parents are increasingly being asked to pay not just for extras such as field trips but also for books for school libraries, computers, and sometimes basic school supplies. Parent contributions are still very small in comparison to the total cost of education, but they pose an increasing annoyance to many parents and a real problem for the substantial number of Canadian families living on very modest incomes.

What Does the Money Buy?

The money spent on K–12 education in Canada is used primarily to pay salaries. More than 80 per cent of the total operating expenditure goes to payroll. About three-quarters of that amount is for teachers, principals, guidance counsellors, resource teachers, and other professional educators. The remainder of the salary budget is for teacher assistants, secretaries, bus drivers, maintenance staff, and everyone else. Beyond salaries, the main costs are for supplies, building maintenance, pupil transportation, books, computers, and other such costs.

The most important determinants of budgets, then, are the numbers and pay levels of staff, especially teachers. Education remains a labour-intensive industry, and, despite all the talk about the impact of technology, there is no sign that staffing requirements will decrease in any foreseeable future. In fact, the rising demands on schools laid out in Chapter 2 lead to calls for more staff. There has not, however, been much attention paid to the ways that resources are deployed across the system, such as concerning the ratio of classroom teachers to specialists or the ratio of teachers to paraprofessionals. Education policy might also benefit from discussion of questions such as why secondary schools are more richly resourced than primary schools when the evidence suggests that the primary grades are more important to students' long-term success.

In fact, resources in education are deployed in highly standardized and often unimaginative ways. There is little thinking about how to match resources to purposes (Levin, 1994). Most school systems provide a teacher for every 20 or 25 students, one or two school administrators per school, and, as budgets permit, a variety of specialists such as resource teachers or music teachers. Overall staffing ratios vary across Canada. In 2000–01, Newfoundland had one professional educator (including principals and specialists) for every 14 students, while in Alberta the ratio was 1 to 18.3 (Interprovincial Education Statistics Project, 2002). With its 540,000 students Alberta would need 9,000 more teachers if it were to try to reach the same ratio as Newfoundland had! Pay rates for teachers also vary; the average teacher salary in 2000 ranged from about $47,000 in Quebec to $61,000 in Alberta.

Because more than 80 per cent of the education budget goes into paying people, efforts to control education costs often involve efforts to control salaries. In the 1990s provincial governments took a number of steps in this direction, including legislated rollbacks in salaries, legislated restrictions on the scope of collective bargaining, authorization for school districts to require teachers to take days off without pay, and so on. Similar steps have been taken in other countries. In the United States there have been many instances in which school districts have had to cease operations weeks before the end of the school year in order to meet budget deficits; a similar situation is developing in 2003 in the face of very large state deficits, leading to cuts in funding to schools.

At the same time that provincial funding was frozen or cut, governments quite often increased the proportion of the smaller pie targeted to particular purposes such as technology. In one sense this was a shell game, in that the additional funds for purpose A had to be found by reducing spending on purpose B, and the practice was seen by school boards and teachers as cynical. When budgets are tight most organizations react by eliminating anything new and sticking to what they are already doing. Yet new issues do need to be addressed and funds have to be reallocated. Sometimes the only way to shift local spending priorities to address emerging issues may be by targeting provincial funds.

In the short term it is certainly possible to limit teachers' salaries and thus control education costs. In the long term this strategy is likely to be counterproductive. Teaching in Canada now requires four or five years of university education. Why would our best young people want to spend those years qualifying to teach, which is often very demanding work, if they could earn more money and have better working conditions in other fields? Why would good people want to stay in teaching? Jurisdictions that have limited teachers' pay have often found themselves with serious shortages of qualified teachers as the current staff retires early and new applicants either do not want to enter the profession or only stay in teaching for a few years. This has been the situation in England, New Zealand, and many parts of the United States. It is no coincidence that several Canadian provinces are also facing teacher shortages after years of limiting teachers' pay and working conditions. The basic market principle of supply and demand applies to teachers as well as to any other occupation. People do not enter teaching for the pay; even the best salaries in education are not all that high in comparison with the corporate world or even other areas of the public sector. We cannot expect to attract and retain excellent teachers unless we pay them reasonably well and treat them with some degree of respect.

How Is the Money Distributed?

Whatever formula a government devises to fund schools, it is a certainty that half the schools or districts will get less than the average. As Machiavelli said long ago, those who are opposed to a policy are almost always more outspoken than those who benefit from it. No funding formula is perfect; there could always be many other reasonable bases for allocating the money. So whatever approach is used, there is sure to be vigorous criticism of its adequacy and its fairness.

When reporting on the Manitoba school funding formula the *Winnipeg Free Press* usually preceded its report with the adjectives 'complex and convoluted.' Strictly speaking, this description is correct; the provincial formula for funding schools had more than twenty components and many of these involved rather complicated calculations. Many school board members, and even some superintendents did not really understand the formula in any detail. Few members of the public would be aware of the formula let alone understanding its details.

The problem with the *Free Press* criticism is the implication that there can be a simple, straightforward, yet fair way to fund schools. No province has that. Provinces that provide 100 per cent of the funding for schools have formulas that are at least as complicated as the Manitoba system. Funding formulas are complicated because they try to take into account the many different factors that affect the cost of education. The key concepts here are 'horizontal equity,' which means treating everyone the same, and 'vertical equity,' which implies treating people differently in light of different needs. Although the former has an intuitive appeal, it does not take much thought to see that the latter is just as important. Schools and districts face very different cost pressures. For example, rural districts require more funds to transport students. Older schools require more maintenance and may have higher energy costs. Urban and remote districts may have to pay teachers more because of higher living costs. Schools with high concentrations of poor or needy students need more funds to support them. Students who do not have English or French as a first language need additional support to learn one of our official languages. A provincial system of funding to schools has to take all these factors into account. That is why the formulas are complicated. A simple formula would be unfair because it would not recognize important differences in costs.

It is quite clear that the move in Canada to 100 per cent provincial funding of schools has not solved the problems of school finance. BC, Alberta, Ontario, and Nova Scotia, all provinces that provide 100 per cent provincial funding, have had much more uproar over education funding in the last few years than has Manitoba. All four provinces have seen teacher protests and strikes, school closures, and staff cuts when provincial support proved to be less than was needed to maintain the system. In Ontario the provincial government took over the financial operations of three large school boards – Toronto, Hamilton, and Ottawa – in 2002 because the boards would not make the budget cuts necessitated by the level of provincial funding. The funding formulas in Alberta and British Columbia are substantially more complicated than that in Manitoba because all the possible factors need to be taken into account provincially. There is no magic answer to the collision between the needs of schools and the revenue limitations of governments in the face of other spending pressures, demands for tax cuts, and legislation that requires balanced budgets.

School Funding in Manitoba

Throughout the 1990s Manitoba ranked relatively high among provinces on most school spending indicators such as pupil-teacher ratio, expenditure per student, and per student expenditure as a proportion of provincial GDP. In 1999–2000 total spending for schools was about $1.4 billion.

While other provinces were centralizing their finance systems in the 1990s and eliminating property taxes levied by school districts, in Manitoba local school districts continued to use local property taxes and fund on average about 40 per cent of the operating costs of schools. About 20 per cent of the provincial funding for schools comes from a provincial property tax specifically in support of education – the Education Support Levy (ESL) – though as of 2002 the government began to phase out the ESL for residential properties. The ESL is in addition to the Special Levy, which is the property tax for education levied by local school districts. Due to a policy put in place about forty years ago, the Education Support Levy is funneled through an entity called the Public Schools Finance Board (PSFB), which is made up of seven people appointed by the cabinet. Although the PSFB has no real authority over these funds, which are controlled entirely through the overall provincial budget process, PSFB funds do not appear in the provincial consolidated revenue and expenditure statements, which therefore significantly understate education spending. The full picture of school spending in the province, from all sources and for all purposes, is available through annual reports on combined school district revenue and expenditure that are issued by the department and posted on its web site.

The Manitoba formula has to take into account the fact that the value of local property varies greatly from one school district to another. The same tax rate will raise much more money in some districts than in others. The provincial funding formula attempts to offset these inequalities by giving more money to those districts with poorer local tax bases. The province also tries to provide more funds to districts with additional issues, including high levels of poverty, which are known to have a strong influence on educational outcomes. However districts vary not only in how much money they can readily raise, but also in how much they want to spend. As a result some districts that could raise more money choose to spend less and keep local taxes lower. Other districts choose to have higher taxes and provide more services. Yet others have to levy higher tax rates just to provide an average level of service. These decisions are made by each school board.

To add further complication, Manitoba, like several other provinces, provides property tax rebates to renters and homeowners. At first glance it seems strange to allow taxes to rise and then provide rebates, but there are several reasons why the rebate system is attractive. Everyone gets about the same rebate, so people who own very valuable houses do not get a greater benefit, as they do with a tax rate reduction. The rebate can be adjusted to particular purposes. It can be made higher for seniors or people with low incomes. It also applies to renters, who may otherwise not feel the impact of lower taxes paid by their landlords. The rebate is directly attributable to the province and appears clearly on people's property tax bills and income tax returns, so there is, at least in theory, more political credit to the province for the credits. Finally, provincial governments suspect that if they provided more cash to school districts the money would be used for additional spending, not for tax reductions. Thus, while tax credits complicate the funding picture, they are likely to remain in place.

In Manitoba the province's share of school operating expenditures, including PSFB money, peaked in the early 1980s at just under 80 per cent, and fell steadily thereafter under both NDP and Conservative governments. For the first several years under the Filmon Conservatives provincial spending on public education rose. But beginning in 1993, when the Conservatives began a determined effort to reduce the provincial deficit by cutting spending, provincial funding for schools was frozen or reduced for five years in a row. The overall decrease amounted to some $50 million, or just over 6 per cent of total support, not including the effects of inflation. The Conservatives tried to offset the impact of the cuts somewhat by allowing school districts to require teachers and support staff to take days off without pay, and by passing legislation to restrict the scope of teachers' collective bargaining rights in an attempt to have smaller salary increases.

These adjustments were not enough to allow school boards to maintain existing staffing and programs. Boards faced a difficult choice. They could either cut their budgets or increase their local property taxes. Over the five-year period most did both. Some 600 teaching positions were eliminated across the province (about 5 per cent of the total teaching force of about 13,000), along with many other expenditure reductions. School boards across the province also made substantial increases in their local property taxes in an attempt to sustain their programs. From 1994 to 1999, local education property taxes in Manitoba rose overall by more than $90 million, nearly 30 per cent, and the province's share of funding dropped from 66 per cent in 1994 to 60 per cent in 1999. Even after all this, in 1999 Manitoba was still among the higher-spending provinces on a per pupil basis, and had among the lower pupil-teacher ratios (Canadian Education Statistics Council, 2000), but there is no question that the cuts of the 1990s were keenly felt by schools that had to reduce staff and services.

The politics around school funding involved two very different agendas. Many people, especially parents, were concerned about the impact of the cuts of the 1990s. However the rapid increase in education property taxes had also sparked considerable concern, especially given the mounting overall political pressure in Canada for tax cuts in all areas. These dual pressures applied to the provincial government and also to school boards. The NDP used both factors against the Conservatives in the 1990s, arguing that insufficient provincial funding was the root cause of the property tax increases. In opposition, however, one does not have to have solutions, only criticisms.

These difficulties had created a high-profile political debate over school funding. Each year when the province announced its operating support for the coming year, often at a high-profile press conference, school boards responded that the increase would be insufficient and would require them to increase property taxes or cut programs. The province would blame the school boards, the school boards would blame the province, the municipalities would complain about having to levy taxes over which they had no control, and the media would report the conflict. Teachers and the Manitoba Teachers' Society were especially unhappy since the cuts had the effect of increasing workloads while salary increases were reined in quite sharply. The MTS was strongly opposed to all the reductions. Since even many insiders had only a vague understanding of how the funding system really worked, it is no wonder that the public debate was typically about who was yelling how loudly at whom. Important issues of how much money was needed, what it was spent on, and how it should be raised, tended to get lost in the melee.

For the NDP going into the 1999 election, a position on education spending raised some difficult issues. On the one hand, the party was firmly committed to a strong public school system. On the other hand, the NDP is always worried about being portrayed as a 'tax and spend' party that cannot manage public finances.

In the election the NDP's promise on school funding came in two parts. On 30 August, in the announcement that focused on the Grade Three Guarantee, the press release also committed to 'Tackle the legacy of user fees, fundraising, and tattered textbooks through stable school funding. We will invest in our public schools at a rate no less than the growth in the economy.' A few days later, in a release titled 'An achievable property tax reduction for all Manitobans,' the party promised to increase the property tax credit in Manitoba by $75 per household per year for each of its first two years in office, with the intention that this would offset any increases in school board or municipal property taxes. As well, the release, issued 2 September 1999, said that 'In year three of our initiative, an NDP Government will begin to phase out the Education Support Levy [the provincial property tax for education] on residential property subject to ensuring health care priorities are sustained and education and training are properly supported.'

The government made good on both commitments. The property tax rebates were increased in 2000 and 2001 as promised. Provincial funding for schools rose each year by an amount equal to or greater than GDP growth, which ranged between 1.5 and 3 per cent per year. In dollars, excluding support for adult learning centres, the increases were just under $25 million in 2000, $22.5 million in 2001, $16 million in 2002, and a little under $24 million in 2003, or more than $87 million in new funding in total over the four-year term. This compared with $15 million in new funding in total over the last four years of the Conservative government. By 2003 total provincial operating support was about $860 million.

While the government did meet its commitment, this did not solve the problems of funding schools. The increases in provincial funding were insufficient to provide both status quo programs and status quo local tax rates. Because the province was providing only 60 per cent of the operating costs of Manitoba's public schools, an increase of 2.8 per cent in provincial spending provided school boards on average with only 1.7 per cent more total income, less than built-in increases in costs such as salaries. School boards continued to face the choice of cutting their budgets or increasing local property taxes, though much less dramatically so than in the earlier years when provincial support had actually declined.

Most boards continued to increase local taxes to support their programs. From 1999 to 2002, local property taxes for education rose a further $85 million, or 21 per cent, and the provincial share of overall operating spending continued to decline, though more slowly, to 57.5 per cent. School districts blamed the province's limited funding for both tax increases and budget reductions. The province argued that it was the responsibility of school boards to manage their budgets within the available resources and that the government was meeting its stated commitment on school funding.

The government also pointed out, correctly, that in addition to its operating funding, it provided 100 per cent of the cost of approved capital projects (about $45 million a year after 1999), 100 per cent of the employer cost of teacher pensions (which had risen to about $90 million in 2002, and will continue to increase substantially), and about $150 million in property tax credits to offset local education taxes. If all education costs were considered, the provincial share was closer to 75 per cent. Needless to say, this fact did nothing to reduce the pressure for more provincial funding.

In Manitoba the announcement of school funding occurs every year in mid or late January for the following school year. The intention is to give school boards enough time, after the provincial support is known, to set their budgets and tax requirements, and to inform the municipalities, which collect the property taxes on behalf of school boards so that they can set their tax rates. The entire process is completed by 15 March each year. The process involves many actors – the province, school districts, and municipalities – yet it is hard to see how the process could be simplified as long as all three bodies are recipients of property taxes.

Within the provincial government the process of making decisions on school funding is also quite complex. The amount of money is large – about $800 million in 2000 – so it is quite appropriate to have substantial discussion and debate in government. The Schools Finance branch of the Department of Education typically begins by preparing a number of different scenarios for funding, which are then reviewed by department senior managers and by the minister. A more limited set of options is then sent forward to the Treasury Board, and, eventually, to the cabinet. The discussion at each level has to take into account the same four questions raised at the beginning of this chapter:

1 *How much money is enough?* What amount meets the government's political commitments? What will the impact of a given level of funding be on the overall provincial budget? How will an increase in funding for schools compare with the amounts provided for colleges and universities or adult education, or with health or highways? What will be the likely effect of a given level of provincial funding on school board taxation levels? What message will the public take about government priorities from a particular level of funding?
2 *Who pays?* How should the provincial share be raised? Should the provincial Education Support Levy be increased or decreased? If so, what are the implications?
3 *What does the money buy?* How much of the funding should be targeted to particular purposes and how much left to the discretion of school boards? Should new money be left to school boards to spend, or should it be targeted to particular provincial priorities?
4 *How is the money distributed?* Prior to 2002 Manitoba had some fifty-four school districts that varied enormously in enrolment and geography and in the challenges they had to face. There are endless

ways to distribute any given amount of money through the funding formula. The impact of any given distribution will affect each school district differently depending on changes in enrolments, local tax capacity, and cost pressures.

Each of these elements has both a political and an educational aspect to it. The department considered carefully, in making its recommendations on funding, the likely effects of any given allocation on each district's ability to operate its schools and programs. Politicians, on the other hand, are interested in what any given funding decision says to voters about the government's priorities. They are also intensely interested in the effect of an allocation on their constituency. MLAs are understandably unhappy with any allocation that results in their area getting less money than some other areas. Yet because school districts vary so much, there is no way to avoid unequal allocations. If every district were to get exactly the same amount per pupil, that would also be unfair, as some districts face larger cost pressures than others and some districts can raise money much more easily through local property taxes. So school funding is always a process of trying to reconcile highly divergent interests. Meanwhile, the Treasury Board and the Department of Finance have to consider how any given level of funding for schools will affect the budget as a whole and the province's overall fiscal situation.

Because the issues are both very important and quite complicated, school funding goes through an intensive review process. In a typical year it will be discussed by the Treasury Board three or four times, sometimes for several hours, which is a huge amount of time for a group of cabinet ministers to devote to any issue. It will also be discussed, sometimes at length, in cabinet and in the government caucus, as backbench MLAs also have a very strong interest in the issue.

One significant problem with the school funding process is that the timing of the announcement means that decisions on school funding are largely made outside the main provincial budget process. Typically, final decisions on the budget are not made until at least February, and sometimes March or even April. Federal funding, critical to the budget in Manitoba, is not known until the federal budget is tabled, which used to be most often in February. The decision on additional money for schools thus has to be made before the government has decided on its overall budgetary approach. There is a natural tendency for the finance minister and for Treasury Board officials to be cautious under these circumstances, so as not to overcommit themselves, but the pressure to give more money to schools is also very real.

The government's first school funding announcement, early in 2000, came less than four months after it took office. There was simply no time, either in the department or at the cabinet level, to look at significant changes. The emphasis was primarily on more money for schooling. Overall provincial funding was increased by nearly $30 million, including new funding for adult learning centres, the largest increase in nine years and much more than the previous government had provided in its entire last four-year term. Most of the money was provided in a block amount for school boards to spend as they wished. Still, the announcement amounted to less than 61 per cent of total school board operating spending. As in previous years, the immediate response from school boards, not unreasonably, was that this amount would require increases in property taxes even to maintain a status quo budget, let alone recover any of the ground lost during the preceding years.

Political pressure to change the funding formula began to build. Several sources of pressure were particularly important. The Manitoba Teachers' Society had long advocated a very different funding system. The Association of Manitoba Municipalities (AMM), the organization representing the province's 200 or so municipal governments, was a strong advocate for reducing the property tax burden for education. Some school districts also made strong cases for reform. For example the Winnipeg School Division had the highest education property taxes outside the far north, in part because its large inner city required substantial additional resources. Other districts with relatively poor local property tax bases also believed that the existing formula penalized them excessively. Because the NDP tended to elect members in poorer parts of the province, many of the school districts with the biggest problems were represented by NDP legislators, including several cabinet ministers. Meanwhile the *Winnipeg Free Press* ran frequent stories, especially at budget time, on the problems of education finance and the need for a new formula, without managing to say anything about how the underlying dilemmas could be resolved.

While the problems were easy to identify, the solutions were not. Prior to 1999 the department had had an advisory committee on school finance that included representatives of the main groups such as teachers, trustees, and superintendents. However this body had not been able to solve the problems. Its last report to the Conservatives had recommended a funding increase of $65 million, or nearly 10 per cent, in provincial support – a recommendation that no government would be in a position to support. We abolished the advisory group; there seemed little benefit in having a forum that produced recommendations that were entirely outside the realm of possibility, and we were told that several of the participating groups were unhappy with the committee's membership and operation. At the same time, Minister Caldwell expressly asked for ideas and suggestions on the funding formula from all school districts and provincial organizations, though we received very few.

The Manitoba Teachers' Society had been very active on school finance issues. MTS had produced several lengthy reports on education funding over the years, showing the problems created in the 1990s by cuts in provincial support. Their analysis of some of the problems was cogent. Their solution was to move to 100 per cent provincial funding of the full cost of a defined program. Under this system the province would outline the programs and resources that schools should have, and would then pay the total cost of those programs, whatever they turned out to be, including such items as salary differentials across the province. Such a system would have required at least an extra $480 million in provincial spending to replace school district property taxes. It would also have led to increased spending in many districts that were currently spending below the provincial average, and thus had driven up overall spending levels on education. If the province paid the total cost of a defined program, schools would be highly likely to spend up to the maximum amount available. While most of the required funds were in theory available through property taxes already levied by local school districts, moving to 100 per cent provincial funding would have meant very large shifts in tax burdens across the province, with some districts paying much more and others paying much less. If education were to continue to be funded from property tax, but with the local tax replaced by the provincial tax, school districts that had either low levels of spending or were property rich likely would face substantially higher tax levels. If education funding was no longer funded from property tax, as is often advocated, the province would have to find another source of $600 million. In Manitoba that would mean a one-third rise in income tax, or an increase in the sales tax from 7 per cent to nearly 11 per cent, shifts that would be impossible to manage politically. Unless provincial general revenues grew rapidly – and they were not growing as rapidly as were the pressures for spending, especially in health – a major shift in education funding would be very, very difficult to do.

During the 2001 budget process the department put forward a number of options that would have involved significant change in the funding formula, including options that would have increased the share of funding going to school districts that had higher needs, as evidenced by higher poverty levels and less capacity to generate local revenue. However, there were costs to all these options in that giving more money to some districts necessarily meant giving less to others. The overall budget situation was tough and the government was struggling to meet all its commitments within the framework of balanced budget legislation and available revenues. There were concerns that a substantial change in the formula would produce too loud an outcry from those districts that would be the biggest losers. In the end the formula was left relatively intact for 2001–02. Provincial funding was again increased by the rate of economic growth – about 2.8 per cent. Once again school district budgets increased by more than the provincial funding increase, and local property taxes rose. Another set of editorials and media comments appeared, complaining about the government's failure to solve this problem. The *Free Press* was one of the voices calling for the province to pay 100 per cent of the cost of education and eliminate all local property taxes for education.

One change we did make in 2001 was the format of the announcement on school funding. The practice under the Conservatives, and in the first NDP funding announcement, had been to hold a press conference with a formal announcement and plenty of media coverage. This format had set up conflict between the government's line and the response of members of some of the organizations, such as school districts, who typically had not seen any of the details until the announcement was actually made. At the suggestion of some of the stakeholder groups, in 2001 we moved to a lower-profile approach that we hoped would defuse some of the conflict around funding that had the effect of making citizens feel all parties were unreasonable. We briefed the various groups but did not hold a formal press conference. Instead, a media release was issued and the minister made himself available for a media scrum in the hall outside his office at the legislative buildings. This was a small but helpful step in creating a more constructive public debate.

A number of government supporters, including people in some of the school districts with high poverty levels and high tax rates, were particularly unhappy with the lack of change in 2001. They had understood in 2000 that it was not realistic to expect changes when the government had been in office only for a few months, but had expected more this time. Since almost every interest group saw the issue from its own perspective, each felt there was a fairly straightforward way to make improvements. As long as they benefited they were less concerned about who might lose, and many advocates took the view that losses could be prevented simply by providing enough new money, which is true but was not a realistic option.

The clamour for a 'new funding formula' grew. My staff in the department and I did not see a new formula as the answer, because any new formula would have to face all the same difficulties around equity and transparency that confounded the current formula. We did think the formula could be improved. In particular I felt the formula needed to do more to generate equity in local tax rates. In a fair system, school districts that spend about the same amount per pupil should have about the same local tax rate. Manitoba has nothing like the disparities in spending that are found in the United States, where some districts spend five times more per pupil than other districts in the same state. Still, we did have some districts that were spending 25 per cent more than others without imposing a higher local property tax. Greater equity could be achieved by changing the existing formula rather than having a 'new' one, but the problem, clearly recognized in the 2001 decision, was that a substantial shift would create some real losers, with some districts having to raise local property taxes substantially while other districts were able to reduce theirs. The fact that the increases would be in areas that currently had low tax rates would, I knew, do nothing to offset the political outcry. Districts with low tax rates tended to attribute this to good management rather than to the good fortune of having high property wealth, lower needs, or declining enrolments.

Still, it was becoming increasingly clear during 2001 that some kind of substantive change in the funding approach would have to be made for 2002. There was no way to address the whole set of pressures, and particularly no way to make substantial reductions in the property tax effort for education without huge upheaval, but there was simply too much political pressure to continue with the status quo.

In 2000 the Association of Manitoba Municipalities had created its own task force on education finance with the mission of finding a way to reduce property taxes for education. The department had actively supported the work of the task force, including making staff available and providing data, in the belief that the more people knew about how the system worked, the less likely they were to think a miracle solution could be found. Indeed, when the AMM task force reported, in the spring of 2001, they were unable to recommend any specific measures other than the need to keep working on the issues. However the government did agree, after some internal discussion, to set up another working group with the AMM, MAST, MTS, and other parties, to look further at options for financing education.

At the same time there was increasing internal discussion, including in the Treasury Board and the Department of Finance, concerning the possibility of eliminating the provincial Education Support Levy on residential property. This was an approach favoured by the premier because it would simplify the education tax structure and would get the province out of taxing residential property for purposes of education. On the other hand, the ESL actually helped increase funding equity in the system because the funds it generated were redistributed to higher-need school districts; thus a cut in this tax would not improve equity in funding. The ESL was bringing in about $200 million per year, of which a little less than half was from residential property and the rest from business and commercial property. The plan was to try to find a way to remove the ESL from the former, but not the latter; it would be hard enough in the context of the budget pressures to find $100 million, even over several years.

These issues were discussed extensively inside the government during the fall and winter of 2001–02, leading up to the 2002 funding announcement. At least ten options were presented to ministers at one point or another. Each option involved several pages of tables showing the impact on each school district based on some assumptions about what would happen in each district to local property wealth and to spending. While the lead-up to funding decisions is always intensive for staff in the department's Schools Finance unit, this year proved to be especially demanding, with many evenings and weekends of work including the Christmas holiday period. In addition to the Department of Education, the Departments of Intergovernmental Affairs and Finance were also involved in looking at the impact of changes in various local property taxes. The changes had to be considered in terms of how they would affect municipal governments and the province's overall fiscal picture. Although the departments had somewhat different interests, staff in all three worked so well together that the interdepartmental discussions were generally smooth.

The challenge was once again to determine how much change could be effected, and at what cost, within the government's commitment to increasing funding at the rate of economic growth, which was expected to produce about 2 per cent, or about $16 million in new funding. With 2 per cent more provincial funding, school districts already would be short of what they would need to stay even, so that any redistribution would exacerbate the difficulties in at least some districts. It was difficult to find an adjustment to the formula that would actually help those districts in greatest difficulty without either unfairly rewarding or penalizing other districts.

In addition to internal discussions, a few people outside the government were contributing suggestions. Most of the external suggestions were not workable; it was difficult for any single external organization to have a full understanding of the ways that a change would work out over more than fifty school districts in quite varying circumstances. However we did get an idea from an external source that proved very useful. The suggestion was to earmark an amount of money for those districts that had below average property tax wealth and above average per pupil spending levels. That combination would indicate a high perceived need in the community along with limited ability to raise local funds to meet the needs. Only a few districts fit that description, including many of those who were in the greatest difficulty under the existing rules. Here was an affordable way to address one major issue.

The funding announcement for 2002–03 was made late in January of 2002. It included a $16 million increase, corresponding to economic growth of about 2 per cent. Built into the calculations, but not announced until the provincial budget in April was the government's commitment to the elimination of the residential ESL over five years, including a $10 million reduction in 2002.

The 2002 announcement introduced major changes in the way money was distributed. We substantially simplified the funding formula by tying more of the money directly to enrolments. As well, about $4.5 out of a total increase of $16 million was allocated to supplementary funding for high-need, low-wealth districts. The overall impact of the changes was not dramatic in most cases. Most school districts received modest increases. A few of those with substantial local property wealth or declining enrolment got small decreases. The announcement was, as always, a balance between competing objectives. Clear signals were sent of a change in approach, while at the same time trying to avoid too much change too quickly.

While the changes in the formula were generally well received, the underlying problem of affordability remained. Most school boards could not maintain all existing operations with the additional provincial money and were once again faced with the need to reduce spending or increase local taxes. Overall, local education taxes rose by nearly $38 million, or more than 8 per cent, and the provincial share of total operating spending fell slightly again. Following the announcement there was a further round of calls for more change. MTS met with the minister several times to go through their own proposals. The government renewed its commitment to follow up on the work of the AMM Task Force by establishing a new working group to look at the issues. In the fall of 2002, when I left the government, the issues on the table were pretty much the same as they had been in 1999 – or, for that matter, in 1989 or 1979.

Accomplishments and Continuing Dilemmas

What were the results of three years of hard work on school funding in Manitoba? They were as much as could be expected under the circumstances. On the positive side, after years of decreasing provincial support the picture changed. After years of real cuts, provincial funding rose, as promised, by at least the rate of growth in the provincial economy. Schools were able to plan their finances with some degree of confidence. As well, some of the changes in the formula helped the system – by directing more money to high-need districts, by simplifying some elements of the formula, and, less visibly, by changing some of the parameters on some of the elements of the formula. For example, the approach to additional funding for Aboriginal students was changed to focus on improving outcomes rather than on counting the number of Aboriginal students. The process for funding special needs students was simplified. These are significant accomplishments.

On the other hand, the basic dilemmas around school funding were not resolved. An education funding regime is always trying to balance equity, efficiency, and differing local needs and desires. It is not possible to maximize all these competing values at the same time. In Manitoba, while provincial funding rose at the rate of economic growth, school-district spending rose more rapidly so that local property taxes continued to increase.

There is no way to have a funding system that recognizes differing needs and circumstances yet is seen as fair by all parties, and equity will remain an important concern. While some of the biggest disparities in the funding of districts were reduced, substantial differences remain among Manitoba school districts in level of spending and in local tax rates, due in part to differences in wealth and in part to different local priorities for education. The Manitoba system accepts the idea that locally elected school boards should reasonably have some control over the programs, policies, and expenditure levels of local schools, something that is largely lost when provinces move to 100 per cent financing.

Most significantly, it is not possible to have more money for schools and lower taxes, let alone eliminate a tax worth several hundred million dollars. You cannot provide school boards with local autonomy in making decisions about priorities and also impose limits on how much they can spend. These tensions remain in school funding in Manitoba and across Canada. If we want good public schools with skilled teachers, reasonable class sizes, and decent facilities we will have to be prepared to pay for them. Governments are trying to accommodate both calls for better public services and for tax cuts. It will not be possible to do both indefinitely. I believe the evidence is clear that Canadians prefer, as we should, the former to the latter.

CHAPTER 6

School Division Amalgamations: Giving the Public What It Wants

> School division amalgamations will neither save money nor improve education.
>
> Submission by Ben Levin and J.A. Riffel to the
> Norrie Commission on school boundaries, 1993

At the end of my first week as deputy minister, I drove with a colleague to Brandon to a meeting of the Manitoba Association of School Superintendents. This would be a good chance for me to talk with superintendents about their concerns and some of our plans. That morning the *Winnipeg Free Press* carried a headline quoting Drew Caldwell as expressing a strong interest in reducing the number of school districts in the province. I was taken aback by this headline, as, for me, school district reductions would be an unnecessary distraction from what I thought were more important educational concerns. However, I assumed Caldwell's statement was probably off-the-cuff and not serious. I was quite wrong.

By the fall of 1999, Manitoba was one of only two provinces that had not taken action to reduce the number of school districts. New Brunswick had entirely eliminated its school boards, although it restored them, in a modified version, in 2002. Alberta went from 140 districts, a few of which did not actually operate any schools, to 60. Nova Scotia went from 27 boards to 10. Newfoundland, through a constitutional amendment, moved from a system of multiple religious boards to a single public system with only 10 boards. The process in Ontario had been particularly difficult, with the creation of mega-boards such as the Toronto District School Board with 300,000 students. Only Manitoba and Saskatchewan had not moved in this area.

Manitoba had 54 public school divisions and districts[1] in 1999. The largest district, Winnipeg School Division, served about 30,000 students. The City of Winnipeg also had eight other school districts, most of which had between 5,000 and 10,000 students. These districts conformed largely to the boundaries of the separate municipalities that had been in place prior to the creation of a single city of Winnipeg in 1971. While a single City government was created, school districts were not changed at that time. By 1999 many rural districts had enrolments below 1,500 students and several had fewer than 1,000 students. In northern Manitoba several remote communities had independent districts with a single school, though most provincial schools in the north were part of the Frontier School Division.

The last major reorganization of school districts in Manitoba had occurred in the 1950s and 1960s, when the province moved from more than 2,000 districts, most with only one school, to about 60. That process had been very difficult and produced considerable political conflict. Many small schools had been closed by the new larger districts. Closing a school in a small rural community is a serious blow and may threaten the community's survival, so rural communities remained nervous about further reductions.

Reducing the number of school districts had been considered by the Conservatives, who in 1993 appointed a commission chaired by Bill Norrie, a former mayor of Winnipeg and former chair of the board of the Winnipeg School Division, to make recommendations for changes in boundaries. At the time I was a professor in the Faculty of Education at the University of Manitoba. My colleague, Tony Riffel, and I presented a brief to the Norrie Commission in which we argued that school district amalgamations would neither save money nor improve education, and should therefore be given a low priority. The potential savings from administrative efficiencies, we argued, were small in relation to overall education spending and could easily be taken up by costs for such things as harmonizing salaries. We saw no evidence that creating larger school boards in Manitoba would have any significant impact on students' learning; in general, research in education has not shown any strong links between organizational variables such as district size or spending level and pupil outcomes. Our brief got little attention at the time but resurfaced in 2001 and 2002.

---

1 Manitoba uses the term *school divisions* for most of its units, but the difference between a district and a division is of no significance to this account. I mainly use *district* because it is a more common term across Canada.

The Norrie Commission reported in 1994. It recommended that Manitoba redraw school district boundaries completely, moving from fifty-six to twenty-one districts. Every boundary in the province would be changed.

The Conservative government considered the report for some time and finally decided not to act on it. Presumably this was because the changes were not regarded positively in rural Manitoba, where the bulk of the Conservative caucus was located. They did, however, even prior to establishing the commission, pass enabling legislation to permit a minister to change district boundaries or create new districts following the report of a commission. Instead of taking action, the PCs decided to try to encourage voluntary amalgamations, and two such mergers actually took place, one in Winnipeg and one in rural Manitoba, between 1994 and 1999.

Government Decides to Amalgamate

This was the situation when the new government came in. Despite Drew Caldwell's statements about amalgamation at the very start of his tenure, not much happened on that front for several months thereafter. However by the spring of 2000, both the minister and the premier were clearly in support of reducing the number of school districts. The issue was discussed a couple of times in the cabinet. Not surprisingly, views on what should be done varied quite a bit among ministers, but with the minister and premier both supportive, development of various policy options began.

From a bureaucratic point of view, amalgamation was a highly complex process. Not only would the change process itself be complicated, but there would be substantial ongoing implications for many administrative operations and for the system of school financing. It would be important to line up all the required elements so that the process unfolded smoothly and in a timely way. All this had to be done by staff who were already fully occupied with other tasks. The cuts in the department's staffing during the 1990s had largely eliminated any extra capacity that could be devoted to new, large undertakings of this kind. Although the staff members involved were capable and conscientious, the process really stretched the department's capacities.

There were some weighty factors in favour of amalgamation. Ever since the Norrie report, enrolments in rural districts had continued to shrink. Quite a few rural districts now had fewer than 1,000 students.

The Manitoba Teachers' Society had been a strong advocate of fewer school districts for years, arguing that the existing units were simply too small to provide good service. Voter turnout for school board elections was low, seldom reaching much above 50 per cent in regular elections and falling to below 10 per cent in many by-elections. A large number of school trustees made it into office through acclamation – about half of all positions were filled in this way during the mid and late 1990s.

Reducing the number of school boards was undoubtedly popular. It would be difficult to find many voters in Winnipeg who thought the city needed nine school districts. Presumably this was why so many other provinces had taken the step, giving it a sense of inevitability. School boards would be against amalgamation, but as has been pointed out already, school boards in Canada do not have much political clout these days and find few defenders against provincial governments. The Manitoba Teachers' Society had been a consistent advocate for amalgamation, arguing that having so many small districts resulted in inequalities in programming.

My personal view continued to be that while there might be reasons for amalgamation, the process would take a great amount of energy and would distract everyone from focusing on things that had more potential to benefit students. When reorganizations of any kind occur, people shift their attention to the impact of the reorganization and give other tasks shorter shrift. Amalgamation would throw into question jobs (presumably there would be fewer central office staff), work locations (in rural districts some boards offices would close and people would have to move), and school programs (in new districts new decisions might be made about where to offer specialized programs such as French Immersion). Many administrative issues would require harmonization, from agreements to computer systems to personnel policies to bus schedules to program standards. The attention given to all these issues would be attention not given to issues of teaching and learning. I also made the minister and central political staff aware that I was on the public record as saying that changing boundaries was not good education policy.

A central issue in the discussion within government concerning amalgamation was how forceful to be. The process in most provinces had been highly directive and rapid: six months in Alberta and about ten months in Ontario, from the announcement to having the new organizations in operation. However the Manitoba government was not anxious to be that directive. Voluntary amalgamation had been tried by the Conservatives, with only two amalgamations resulting in four years. In September 2000 the minister asked – or, more accurately, required – that all school districts review their options for amalgamation and report to him on their conclusions. He said he hoped that school districts would decide to enter into voluntary amalgamations as a result of their reviews, but if they did not he would make decisions about what amalgamations would occur. He stated that changes would be made in time for the elections for school boards that were scheduled for October 2002. Boards were offered grants to defray any costs, such as legal consultant fees, that might be incurred in investigating amalgamation possibilities. Reminders were sent to school districts again in January.

The reports filed by school districts in the spring of 2001 made interesting reading. A few districts took the exercise seriously, meeting with their neighbours and analysing the various elements that an amalgamation might require, such as staffing and tax rates. A couple of districts indicated they were willing to move ahead on amalgamation but that none of their neighbours were. Most districts did not give any serious consideration to the activity, filing reports that basically said everything was fine as it was, or, in some cases, would be fine if only the province provided more money. Some school districts submitted approximately the same report they had made to the Norrie Commission eight years earlier. Very few boards took advantage of the funds we had made available for investigation of amalgamations. It was clear that districts were not going to help the government move this agenda forward.

The Decision Process on Amalgamations

During the late spring and summer of 2001, attention in government focused on how many and which amalgamations to do, as well as on the legislative and policy infrastructure that might be needed. By the end of the summer of 2001 the government had a target of fifteen to twenty amalgamations, bringing the number of districts down by about a third. It was also clear that amalgamating existing districts would be much less disruptive than redrawing all the boundaries to create a whole set of new districts, as Norrie had recommended. If existing units were merged, the existing political and administrative structures could be in place to manage the work.

The government also decided that there should be amalgamations in Winnipeg as well as in rural Manitoba. While the existing Winnipeg districts were all of reasonable size already – the smallest had more than 5,000 students – it would be very difficult to justify amalgamating rural and northern districts while leaving Winnipeg with nine school districts. Comparing Winnipeg to other Canadian cities of similar size, Calgary, Edmonton, and Hamilton had two school districts each, while Ottawa had three.

Decisions on which particular districts to amalgamate were based on several criteria. Some were relatively obvious. In two or three cases the partners had already agreed that amalgamation was something they could undertake. In the north there were still three small towns that had single school districts; these could be folded into the Frontier School Division, which already encompassed most of the small communities in the north and had an effective decentralized governance structure in place that gave its far-flung communities considerable autonomy.

There were two other one-school districts in eastern Manitoba that were candidates for amalgamation, but in each case there was a complicating issue that forced us to defer these changes. In one case, Pinawa, the federal government provided substantial funding for the school under an agreement that would end if the district were amalgamated. In another case the school had been built to support a pulp and paper operation and there were a number of legal issues that had to be resolved before the school could be transferred to a public school district.

In rural Manitoba we looked at amalgamating the smallest districts in terms of enrolment, but we also considered amalgamations that were most logical in terms of existing transportation and commercial links. The resulting rural districts were going to cover large areas – though not nearly as large as those in Ontario or Quebec – so it made sense to focus on creating units that people could travel around relatively easily. In some cases there was one willing partner, creating a positive factor, as compared to districts with two boards, both opposed, needing to merge. The biggest problem in rural Manitoba turned out to be in a rural area where we had two small districts – Turtle River and Duck Mountain – that were prime candidates for elimination. There was no reasonable way to change both of these units and leave the new districts at a manageable size, so one very small rural district was left intact. Turtle River was left unchanged and later expressed disappointment, yet their brief in the spring of 2001 had made it very clear they did not think any change was warranted.

The urban decisions were reasonably easy to make. The decision to try to reduce the number of districts by about a third meant three urban amalgamations. It was preferable to leave the Winnipeg School Division unchanged since it was already the largest in the province. Carving pieces out of Winnipeg was also an undesirable option since even a small change would create considerable disruption. That left three real amalgamation possibilities, each of which involved bringing together two districts that currently shared a quadrant of the city. In one case, the decision to combine two districts was made easier because of a public squabble over which of them would build and operate a new high school in the area between them. It was precisely that kind of argument over turf that increased public support for amalgamations.

Another difficult issue in deciding on the final map had to do with splits of existing districts. Our preference was to merge whole existing units, but there were at least a couple of places where that approach would not work. One was in the northwest of the province, where Duck Mountain School Division had a small enrolment and a very weak tax base spread over a large area. The geographic distribution of communities in Duck Mountain suggested that the best solution would be to divide it among three neighbours. A second problem was in eastern Winnipeg, where the Transcona-Springfield School Division was already an uneasy amalgamation of rural and urban areas. The Transcona-Springfield board had almost voted to split itself the year before, defeating such a motion by a vote of five to four. Amalgamating the rural area of Springfield with neighbouring Agassiz would produce a rural district with a strong population and tax base and a reasonable area. The urban area of Transcona could then be merged with neighbouring River East School Division.

One factor that did not play a role in the amalgamation decisions, despite all kinds of rumours, was the political orientation of the community. There was much discussion at the political level as to which amalgamations should be made, but there was no discussion whatsoever of trying to amalgamate areas that voted for one party or the other. The eventual amalgamations, rural and urban, included as many areas that supported the NDP as those that supported the Conservatives.

The announced set of amalgamations reduced the number of urban districts from 9 to 6; the rural districts from 36 to 26 (with 2 of these on hold pending resolution of the issues mentioned earlier), and the north from 8 to 4. More than 20 districts, with about 60 per cent of all students in the province, were not changed at all. Winnipeg School Division, by far the largest, was left intact, as were a number of other larger districts across the province. I regarded the final map as a reasonable accommodation between the government's wish to make some substantial change and a desire to avoid disrupting the whole system.

Other important implementation issues concerned timing, legislation, protection of small schools, and money. On almost all these issues we had substantial and sometimes heated debate among staff in the department as to what to recommend. Some people favoured a highly directive approach, as had been used in most other provinces. Others, myself included, preferred a softer approach that gave the amalgamating districts more control over how they implemented the changes. We eventually adopted a process that specified the particular amalgamations and set some basic parameters around them, but gave the amalgamating units quite a bit of discretion as to how to proceed. For example we allowed a wide range of interim management structures, as long as the partners involved thought it would work. Although we received some criticism for lack of direction, this flexibility actually worked well in allowing adaptation to local circumstances across the province.

One important question was how much notice was needed for the new districts to be in place and ready for the election of new boards in October 2002, when local elections were scheduled to take place. A year was determined to be a reasonable period – requiring steady work on implementation, but not as hurried as in Ontario or Alberta. A debate took place inside the government as to whether the amalgamations required new legislation or could be carried out under the existing authority of the Public Schools Act that had been put in place by the Conservatives. Lawyers in the Department of Justice felt that although the current legislation provided a reasonable legal basis for action, it would be safer to introduce new legislation that would provide a completely clear legal status to the amalgamations. However legislation was potentially a problem in terms of timing. The Manitoba legislature usually sat for a few weeks in the fall and then for several months in the spring. Political staff worried that legislation could be held up in the House by the opposition in the spring of 2002, with a danger that vital deadlines would be missed and the process put at risk. For several months during 2001 the decision as to whether there would be legislation was under discussion without a final decision, although department staff worked with the lawyers in Justice who draft legislation for government to prepare a draft bill just in case.

A good example of the impact of administrative factors on policy concerns school district fiscal years. In Manitoba, school districts budget and are funded from 1 July to 30 June. If the new school districts did not come into place until October 2002, when the new boards were elected, the existing boards would have to be funded for several months in the 2002–03 fiscal year. The department would have to have a partial-year funding formula, the districts would have to file audited financial reports for those few months, and then there would have to be another round of funding, accounting, and auditing for the remainder of the year – all of which would create substantial additional work and expense. As an alternative, we proposed to bring the new school districts into existence on 1 July 2002, with interim governing boards made up of people from the amalgamating boards. New boards would then be elected in October at the regular municipal elections. This would mean a single funding, accounting, and financial reporting process for 2002–03 based on the new districts. The interim boards could begin the process of amalgamation but would only be in place for about four months, and so would act largely as caretakers. However there was no provision in existing legislation for interim boards, so that implementation model would require new legislation.

Many rural people were concerned that another round of amalgamations would again lead to the closure of schools in their communities. Alleviating this concern was an important policy need. Manitoba already had school closure guidelines in place that required nearly two years lead time before a school could be closed. We decided to prohibit the closing of schools in the amalgamating districts for a three-year period to reassure communities about their schools' future in light of amalgamation.

Another debate concerned the financial provisions that should be put in place to support amalgamation. The government had earlier offered a small incentive of $50 per student in a one-time grant to districts amalgamating voluntarily. What incentive, if any, would be given to the districts forced to amalgamate? Amalgamating districts would face some costs for items such as merging information systems. However other provinces had provided little or no additional money, in part because there was a general presumption that reducing the number of administrative units would actually generate savings. After the amalgamations were announced, Minister Caldwell extended the $50 per student to all the districts involved, but no other monetary incentives were provided.

From the beginning of the amalgamation discussion there had been debate about the financial implications, some arguing that there would be savings and others that there would be increased costs. The government decided that it would reinforce the message about resources by limiting the amount that a school district could spend on administration, a provision previously adopted in Alberta. Just as with the amalgamations as a whole, the intent was to demonstrate a commitment to move funds to educational purposes from what were seen to be administrative purposes. A cap was set of 4 per cent in urban districts, 4.5 per cent in rural districts and 5 per cent in northern districts. As yet another step in the attempt to avoid financial problems, amalgamating school districts with surpluses were asked to avoid spending the surpluses except after consultation with their new partners.

The department organized several supports to the amalgamating districts in recognition of the many questions that were likely to arise, from relatively mundane matters such as fiscal years to more charged issues such as collective bargaining and the successor rights of unions. In consultation with a group of school district administrators, and building on the experience in Ontario and Alberta, a resource manual was produced that addressed many of these questions. This guide outlined the various tasks that amalgamating districts would have to undertake, and gave advice on timelines and strategies as well as on some of the less tangible elements such as merging organizational cultures. As well, staff in the Schools Finance and School Administration units of the department were available to provide advice and support to the process in terms of procedures. As an additional support for amalgamating districts, the department entered into a contract with a consultant who had previously been a senior staff member with the Manitoba Association of School Trustees, to provide neutral and independent support to districts, at no cost to them, in areas such as planning for amalgamation and dispute resolution. This service provided a third-party mechanism to help the new organizations move forward effectively.

We anticipated that despite the supports there would still be serious disputes on some matters, such as the location of the board office in rural districts. We advised amalgamating districts that if they were unable to agree on specific items, the minister would impose binding arbitration, the costs of which would be shared by the disputants. This would, we felt, give the parties a strong incentive to settle any differences on their own.

The Announcement and Implementation

The final decisions on amalgamation were made in the fall of 2001 and an announcement date was set for Thursday, 8 November. Even in the week before the announcement, however, there were some proposals to change the list of amalgamating school districts. From a political perspective these were understandable and quite in keeping with the last-minute nature of much political decision making. From a bureaucratic perspective, however, they were impossible. The announcement was a complex event, and several days' lead time was absolutely necessary to make sure it happened correctly. I was already quite worried about the risk of inadvertently sending out two different lists of amalgamating districts or two different sets of instructions because of the many changes that had been made during the process.

The announcement plan was to advise all school districts by fax on the morning of 8 November, including those that were being changed and those that were not. This would happen a couple of hours before a press conference at which the minister would outline the new arrangements for the media. Each school district needed a somewhat different letter. Several in the north were being merged into Frontier School Division. Two districts – one urban and one rural – were being divided and their parts merged with more than one other district. In a couple of cases the mergers were voluntary, so our letter would only confirm what had already been agreed. The remaining 10 or so were straightforward mergers with two existing units. Each letter would have to take into account these varying circumstances. Moreover, we had to prepare the new maps so that they would be ready for the announcement, including posting them on the government's web site at the same time as the press conference. With other complex announcements, such as school funding, the department had had experience with them year after year, so we already had a 'to do' list. With amalgamation, as a one-time change, we ran a high risk of getting something wrong, with potentially embarrassing consequences.

By the time 8 November arrived, we were dealing with a further problem: the decision to terminate the Morris-Macdonald School Board and replace it with an official trustee (see Chapter 7) would be announced the same week. This meant that two education announcements of historic proportions would occur on consecutive days – something one would normally try hard to avoid, but in this case could not be helped. The new session of the legislature was due to open the following week. Because both issues were matters of considerable interest, it was important to get the announcements made before the session began.

The public announcement had several key elements. The list of amalgamating districts was the central element. The minister indicated that the amalgamations were intended to lead to 'more equalization of resources between divisions, lessening of inequalities, and a leveling of the playing field between the bigger and smaller divisions.' Larger divisions, said the press release, 'have a greater ability to enhance programming options, provide more top-quality services, access technological resources, and provide more career development options for teachers.' The government also announced the three-year moratorium on school closures in the amalgamating units and the limits on administrative spending. The announcement provided that a school board (with the exception of Frontier in the north and the Division scolaire franco-manitobaine, which served francophones across the province) could have a maximum of nine members, and that all school districts would have to have a ward system for electing their school boards. These latter changes affected only the small number of existing districts, those with more than nine trustees or at-large elections. In all, more than 130 school trustee positions – about 30 per cent of the total in the province – were eliminated through these measures.

The cap on administrative costs had an important unexpected effect. Throughout the amalgamation process we grappled with the issue of financial savings from amalgamation. This was a favorite media issue; we knew the minister would be asked whether the amalgamations were expected to save money, and, if so, how much. Throughout the debate on amalgamation Drew Caldwell had been avoiding any mention of savings, speaking instead of the ability to redirect resources from administrative to educational purposes. The actual November announcement made no mention of savings either, again focusing on better use of resources. Amalgamation was not being sold as a cost-saving measure.

One of the financial projections done by the department was an analysis of the savings that would result from reducing the number of school trustees and senior officials, including a calculation of the difference between what school districts were now spending on administrative costs and what they would be able to spend under the proposed new limits. Based on a number of assumptions, the total cost of both analyses came to around $10 million. At the 8 November announcement, in response to a barrage of questions on savings, Drew mentioned the $10 million figure. Although this number was a notional calculation that was never intended to represent an amount that could be 'saved' it immediately became widely publicized. Once the media reported it and the opposition began to use it in the House, it took on the independent status of a commitment from the government. No doubt at some future time the government will be asked to demonstrate that this money was indeed 'saved,' and no doubt it will be possible to produce an analysis making such a case. But in a system spending about $1.4 billion per year, with substantial changes in amounts and patterns from year to year, it does not make much sense to fixate on a $10 million item that is in any case largely a matter of interpretation.

The amalgamation announcement went relatively smoothly. If anything, there was some surprise that the reorganization was not larger in scale. I heard from a number of superintendents in later weeks who fully expected their districts to be on the list for amalgamation and were surprised when they were not. However fewer amalgamations definitely made the process less disruptive and more manageable.

In most cases the implementation also went reasonably well. Most of the districts involved, though they did not like the change, took seriously their obligation to make it work. Most of the school boards and senior administrators worked diligently to make the change happen. Many held public contests to name the new entity. A number held events of various kinds to mark both the disappearance of the existing entities and the creation of something new. The many operational details were generally handled efficiently and competently, though some of them – such as merging computer systems, or coordinating school bussing operations, or ensuring consistency in programming across the new units – will take several years to be completed.

Of course many small issues did arise. The staff in the department who were supporting the process worked very hard to respond to all the queries on the administrative and financial details. In some cases one of the existing superintendents resigned or retired, smoothing the transition to a new administration; but in one or two cases the amalgamating boards had to struggle over the appointment of their new CEO. Gradually, over a period of months, and quite often with help from the consultant provided by the department, the issues were dealt with. The compulsory arbitration provision was invoked in only two or three cases, and worked well in giving the parties an incentive to settle their differences themselves. But the process also benefited from the genuine efforts of most of those involved, who made things work.

In one case a change in the announced map was made. One of the small communities in the disappearing district of Duck Mountain asked to be placed in a district other than the one to which they had initially been assigned. Their request made sense, was supported by both of the other school districts involved, and was approved.

Only two issues arose that were more serious. One concerned the proposed dismantling of the Transcona-Springfield School Division, especially the merger of Springfield with Agassiz School Division. (As another instance of how the media shape stories through emotive language, stories in the *Free Press* on this issue usually referred not to the 'division' or 'split,' but to the 'ripping apart' of the former division.) This proposal immediately raised strong opposition in the Springfield area. A group of parents, with support from the local opposition MLA, began to organize a dissent. All sorts of rumours started to circulate about closure of schools, huge tax increases, the disappearance of programs such as French immersion or vocational education, the transfer of popular teachers to the most distant parts of Agassiz, and so on. Although the parents involved did have some concerns, much of this was, in my view, fear-mongering on the part of people who were opposed to the amalgamations, sometimes for partisan political reasons. In any change of this kind there is inevitably some uncertainty that gives rise to rumours based on fears, and these can be exploited for a variety of purposes. The leadership of the rural municipality of Springfield also got involved in the issue even though the amalgamation had little effect on the municipality. The problem was exacerbated because Agassiz had had a large deficit a couple of years earlier, caused by an incompetent secretary-treasurer and a too-credulous school board, and had had to make some significant program cuts to cope with it. In fact, though, Agassiz was a prosperous district that had a better tax base to support its operations than did Transcona-Springfield.

In December unhappy parents in Springfield held a public meeting. About 900 people showed up, and so did Minister Drew Caldwell. He spent a couple of hours there, listening to the concerns and absorbing the boos from the hostile crowd. The community meeting was a front-page media story.

Managing the entire amalgamation process with only one significant problem area seemed a pretty good record, but naturally the government was unhappy about the negative image the Springfield debate was giving to the issue. Over the next couple of weeks many meetings were held to discuss options for dealing with the Springfield situation.

The leaders of the opposition there, however, insisted that the only solution was for Transcona-Springfield to be amalgamated, as a whole, with River East. This option was not acceptable to the trustees in River East nor to the government because of the serious fissures that existed already between the rural and urban parts of Transcona-Springfield. The parents' concerns about programs, though we felt they were exaggerated, did need to be taken seriously. The minister provided a guarantee in writing to the Springfield community that their children would have access and transportation to specialized programs in Winnipeg if such programs were not available in their own district. Despite this, a determined group of opponents in Springfield launched a legal challenge against the amalgamation, a challenge that was later dismissed by the courts.

A second important concern arose regarding the reaction of some school districts on the financial front. Because some of the school boards were dominated by trustees who were politically hostile to the government, we had to anticipate that some boards might boost their budgets substantially in the spring of 2003 – likely the lead-up to a provincial election – and blame the increase on the cost of the amalgamations. The legitimacy of this concern was made clear when several of the amalgamating school boards began to make public statements soon after 8 November that amalgamation would be very expensive and would result in local property tax increases.

After much discussion in the department, and with the government's legal staff, the government decided to put a provision into the planned legislation that would give the Minister of Education the power to review and order changes in the budgets of amalgamating school districts in their first three years, and to require them to make changes, if, in the minister's opinion, their overall spending increases were too large.

As the process developed between November and the first part of 2002, the need for legislation became clearer. Creating the interim boards required legislation, but it was also increasingly evident that the process would be best served if it had a firm and clear legal basis that was beyond any dispute. In the spring of 2002 the cabinet passed regulations under existing legislation to provide for the election of the new boards in the fall. Meanwhile final drafting of the proposed Public Schools Modernization Act was taking place. The legislation went through many drafts and much discussion in the civil service, with the minister, and, on a number of key questions, with central political staff and in the cabinet. For example, there was discussion about whether the bill should authorize further amalgamations in future. Drew Caldwell felt that such a provision would create a great amount of uncertainty and that the government would be accused of having a hidden agenda on amalgamation; as a result the legislation as adopted made provision only for voluntary amalgamations in future – if a subsequent government wanted to mandate further changes in school district boundaries it would have to pass new legislation. The bill contained the provisions to limit the share of the budget that school districts could spend on administration, and to allow the minister to review the budgets of amalgamating districts. It also had a number of administrative provisions regarding fiscal years, interim boards, changes to boundaries in amalgamating districts, ward systems, and so on.

Once tabled in the House in May 2002, the bill was vigorously criticized by the Conservatives, at least some of whom saw it as a good opportunity to attack the government. The Conservatives did not come out against amalgamation, but suggested that the process used by the government had been badly flawed. The opposition in Springfield was frequently cited. The provisions on administrative spending and review of budgets drew the ire of the Manitoba Association of School Trustees, who saw in them a further erosion of the powers of school boards. During the debate in the legislature, the Conservative critic for education several times held up my 1993 comments on boundary changes and berated the government for not taking what he now saw as the sound advice of the deputy minister. Fortunately for me, Drew Caldwell was not particularly put out by this. He was able to point out, quite correctly, that ministers, not deputies, make policy decisions on behalf of government. He was also confident that most of the public did not know who the deputy minister was, nor did they care what his opinions were.

As June wore on, and we got closer and closer to the proposed target date of 1 July, pressure mounted for the bill to pass. There was worry about the handling of fiscal years and budgets if the legislation were not in place by 1 July. In the first week of July the bill was still before the legislature. However the politics around the issue were changing. The fact was that the amalgamations were generally popular, and that people, including those in the system, wanted the uncertainty ended and the process to move forward. The bill went to committee for public hearings in late June, hearings that were relatively quiet aside from some impassioned pleas from people in Springfield. In an effort to respond to those concerns, the government amended the bill to guarantee access to programs to parents in the new district. Other amendments were made to limit the minister's review of school district budgets in a largely unsuccessful attempt to mollify the concerns of MAST. The Public Schools Modernization Act was finally passed on 17 July, and the new structure was officially brought into existence.

Was the Initiative Worthwhile?

The experience with amalgamation is a good example of the unexpected ways in which political issues unfold and the variety of influences that can shape them. The idea of reducing the number of school districts was politically appealing. However the range of financial and administrative issues that had to be sorted out brought unexpected complexity to the process. The decision to amalgamate existing units rather than redraw the map entirely made the process much simpler in many ways, but it also meant that we could not resolve all the problems in the existing structure and still have districts that were reasonable in size and demography. The strong opposition in Springfield caused some anxious moments, though in reality we were fortunate to have only one heated situation out of 20 amalgamations. A policy that looks good and works well at a general level will almost always produce some local situations that are troublesome. There might easily have been other communities where people got riled up enough, whether justifiably or not, to cause serious complications.

My own view on amalgamations has not changed as a result of this experience. There were some good reasons to change school district boundaries, and I believe the amalgamations will, over time, be beneficial. The larger districts may be able to provide more mobility for staff, more cross-fertilization of ideas, and better professional development. However these are modest gains from a policy that took an enormous amount of time and energy from everyone, from the minister through to the staff of the department, and on to the hundreds of people in the affected school districts whose time was spent making the changes work. In some amalgamated districts it is clear that it will be several years before a new working equilibrium is reached. Larger districts may further distance school boards from their electorate; the impact, if any, on voter turnout or political participation will not be clear for years. In my view this time given to amalgamation could have been better spent on issues that were more likely to have a direct positive impact on students' learning, such as those outlined in Chapter 2. At the same time, I recognize and accept that decisions on priorities are made by elected people, and, as I have pointed out earlier, these people have to be sensitive to a range of issues and concerns in setting those priorities.

CHAPTER 7

Adult Learning Centres: From Crisis to Opportunity

With respect to MMSD, we concluded that:
- ... the Division overbilled the Province ... by using overstated ALC enrollment figures related to other ALC operations within the Division; and
- The Division provided an inappropriately low level of management, monitoring and quality assurance for The Program and other ALCs.

Provincial auditor of Manitoba, 2001. Investigation of an adult learning centre in Morris-Macdonald School Division No. 19

In October 1999, even before I took over as deputy, I was told that the department was overspent by some $10 million in its grants to schools, and that this was a result of increasing enrolments in what were called adult learning centres. This was my first introduction to an issue that would occupy a considerable amount of time and energy for the next three years. Its development shows the fine line between a political crisis and an educational opportunity.

The story behind adult learning centres in Manitoba goes back to 1996, when the Department of Education made what was thought to be a rather minor change in its rules for funding schools. The department decided to provide funding to programs for adults located in separate facilities outside of secondary schools. Students over the age of 21, though they did not have a legal right to attend high school, had always been enrolled in small numbers in various high schools. The Winnipeg School Division had operated an adult education centre, which was entirely dedicated to providing high school completion for adults, for many years, and had received provincial grants for it. Some other programs had existed as well prior to 1997, notably several alternative schools in Agassiz School Division, east of Winnipeg, which enrolled both students under the age of 21 and some who were older. The general feeling seemed to be that a change in the rules would recognize existing practice. Moreover, since Manitoba had a high proportion of adults who had not completed high school, it seemed desirable to make changes that would encourage these persons to upgrade their qualifications.

Adult Learning in Morris-Macdonald School Division

What nobody anticipated was the response of a few entrepreneurial educators to the rule change, most notably in the Morris-Macdonald School Division (MMSD), just to the southwest of Winnipeg. The superintendent of Morris-Macdonald saw an opportunity in the rule change to extend adult education programs very substantially, and, at the same time, to generate funds for the school division.

Under the Conservatives the overall policy environment for education included considerable emphasis on the virtues of partnerships, on the merits of working with the private sector, and on the importance of entrepreneurship. The Manitoba government, as in many other jurisdictions, believed that private-sector methods of operation should be used to strengthen schools, and that choice and competition were key to improvement. As usual, Canada was borrowing from the United States, although no jurisdiction in Canada has gone as far down the road to privatization and choice as have some U.S. states. In 1996 the Conservative government passed legislation to allow parental choice of schools in Manitoba, both within and across school districts, with the money following the students. The result was a growing level of competition for students, especially in secondary schools. Some school districts began advertising their schools in neighbouring districts, and even running bus routes into other school districts to attract students.

This was the environment within which the adult learning centre problem developed. Morris-Macdonald started down this road slowly, and probably without much sense at the beginning of how it would eventually develop. However, the division was running a variety of other so-called entrepreneurial programs, including a hockey school. It was running school buses into neighbouring districts to pick up children under 'schools of choice' – a policy allowing parents to choose the school their children attend – and one of its schools had offered parents the chance to have classrooms named for them on payment of $5,000.

In the case of the learning centres, MMSD began with one program: a partnership with an addictions treatment foundation. The division enrolled in its high schools the adults in the foundation's program who wanted to finish high school. These adults did not actually attend school in Morris-Macdonald; their program was physically located in the territory of another school district. But the students were enrolled in a Morris-Macdonald high school, thus provincial money flowed to the division for them as though they were regular high school students.

Most provincial operating grants are paid on a per pupil basis under a variety of categories in order to recognize different costs involved in running schools. Provincial grants are developed on the basis of average costs; that is, each regular student is assumed to need about the same amount to educate. However, as one learns in elementary economics, marginal costs are often less than average costs. Adding a few students usually is not very expensive because the basic infrastructure of schools, systems, specialists, and the like is already in place. If new students could be added to existing programs, the provincial grant money, even at only 60 per cent of average expenditure, could be greater than the additional cost. Moreover, the Morris-Macdonald leadership realized it was possible to run separate adult education programs less expensively than regular high schools, that the grants they received would be more than they spent, and could be used to offset other expenditures or to keep taxes low.

Over the next three years Morris-Macdonald dramatically expanded its adult education activities. By 1999 it was operating more than 20 programs for adults with more than 3,000 students enrolled, compared to fewer than 1,800 students in their K–12 schools. By 1999–2000 the department was providing the division with nearly $11 million in funding for these programs, compared to $350,000 in 1997–98. According to the provincial auditor's 2001 report, ALCs in 1999–2000 were generating about $1.9 million in surplus funding against the division's K–12 budget of less than $12 million.

Although Morris-Macdonald accounted for only about 1.5 per cent of total provincial school enrolment, it had more than 50 per cent of the adult learners. Most of the adult programs were delivered outside the physical boundaries of the school district. Although there was a requirement that school districts get provincial approval to operate programs outside their boundaries, no such approval was sought by or given to Morris-Macdonald.

Most of the Morris-Macdonald programs were partnerships between the division and other agencies, such that while the division enrolled the students nominally in its high schools, the programs were actually organized, staffed, and delivered by a variety of third parties including non-profit organizations, a labour union, First Nations, and for-profit training companies. At least one of these partnerships had been the subject of a press release by the Conservative government extolling the virtues of the program.

Morris-Macdonald operated with what they called 'site-based management,' in which school principals or the operators of ALCs were given authority over staffing and budgets without much oversight from the division administration or the board of trustees. In some cases the third-party organizations had almost complete responsibility for finances, the hiring of teachers, and for students' records, even though this was doubtful practice under Manitoba legislation and regulations. The division signed a collective agreement with its teachers under which school principals were paid an additional amount for every student enrolled in their school. The division also approved bonuses for the superintendent and secretary-treasurer based on increases in enrolment. Some $400,000 was paid in additional salary to school and division administrators in 1999–2000 and 2000–01 with respect to ALC enrolments. Senior administrators across the division thus had a strong personal financial incentive to show higher enrolments.

Because the adult students were all officially enrolled in the division's existing high schools, the Department of Education had no official knowledge of the adult learning centres. From the department's official point of view, these students were indistinguishable from any other student enrolled in any regular high school. Still, the adult learning centres were hardly secret. In 1998, staff in the department raised concerns about the developments with the ALCs, citing rising enrolments and the absence of any standards for operation and quality, but no action was taken.

Initial Efforts to Manage the Adult Learning Issue

When the new government took office in the fall of 1999, we found ourselves facing a $10 million overexpenditure to fund the increasing number of enrolments being reported by adult learning centres. At the same time, I very soon started hearing rumours that some of the ALCs were dubious operations, and that there were doubts about the validity of some of the student enrolment figures. Morris-Macdonald was not the only school district operating adult learning centres, but it had many more centres, in many more locations, with a much more decentralized and unaccountable management structure than anyone else. Morris-Macdonald was also the only district giving its staff a personal financial incentive to increase enrolments. The bonuses being paid to administrators were reported in the media in March 2000.

We began to take action on this problem immediately. First, it was important to learn more about the scope of the issue. It was clear that we needed to put a proper policy and fiscal framework in place around ALCs. We could not have a system that grew without any parameters, and with 40 or 50 centres we needed rules in place to operate them and to ensure quality programs. At the same time, providing high school completion to adults is an important educational goal, and we did not want to create problems for adult learning centres that were running good programs for legitimate students. Many of the centres were operating in high-need communities and enrolling substantial numbers of immigrants and Aboriginal learners. Others were being operated by community organizations with strong records of service. Over the following year I visited quite a few centres and heard many stories from students whose lives were being changed by the existence of these programs. Many parents had returned to school via the centres in an effort to provide more support to their children in school, giving the ALCs a doubly positive impact. So, from the outset, our strategy involved identifying and addressing any problems while also developing a solid, longer-term approach to the future of ALCs that supported good adult education practice.

We could not effectively move forward until we knew more about how the ALCs were actually operating; good public policy should not be made on the basis of some rumours or a couple of untypical examples (though often enough these kinds of factors do shape policy). An initial step was to commission an external report on adult learning centres by a consultant from another province. This work began in December of 1999 and took about two months, including visits by the consultant to quite a few centres. His report was strongly supportive, and recommended the centres' continuation and even expansion. While he did identify the need for a better policy framework, his report made no mention of any serious problems with student numbers, program quality, or financial arrangements.

One decision we made in the fall of 1999 was to ensure that adult learning centres were not being operated to generate a profit for the sponsoring school districts or their partners. We did this by substantially reducing the amount paid by the province for each ALC student, from about $4,000 per student to roughly $2,500. The lower amount, we believed, would still be enough to operate the centres, but would not allow sponsoring school districts to generate a 'profit.' The change in funding would also require, for the first time, that school districts report enrolment in adult learning centres separately from that of other high school students. However by the time this decision was made in November of 1999, school budgets were already fully committed for the 1999–2000 school year, so the changes in funding were to become effective for the 2000–01 school year. A second decision made early on was to eliminate support to adult learning centres run by for-profit organizations, of which there were three in 1999–2000.

In January of 2000 the department convened a meeting of all adult learning centres and their sponsoring school districts to discuss the current situation and possible alternatives. Over several hours there was a lively discussion about how we could support the good work being done in ALCs while also focusing on quality and keeping the numbers and funding under control. The centres expressed unhappiness about the funding reduction, but most felt they could live with it and saw it as a reasonable interim measure while we sorted out a long-term approach. Many people in the adult learning community were themselves worried about the same issues of quality, and so supported effort in this direction.

Minister Caldwell also met with the Morris-Macdonald school board, which agreed that the division would not expand its adult learning network in the coming year while provincial policy and funding were being clarified.

Adult learning centres also presented the department with an organizational challenge. In 1999 they were being funded through the regular schools funding system. The department had little policy capacity in the adult learning area and no supervisory mechanism other than enrolment reporting. Given the intention that ALCs should evolve as genuine adult-focused programs, it seemed more appropriate to house the responsibility for them in the adult learning part of the department. In the late spring of 2000 responsibility for ALCs was moved from the School Programs Division to the Training and Continuing Education Division.

During 2000, department staff worked closely with the adult learning centres to improve policy and administrative systems. A policy handbook and an accountability framework were published and a new program-based funding system was set up. A draft *Good Practice Guide* was released early in 2001. We planned to fund centres in 2001–02 through the review of applications that would set out each centre's intended clientele, programs, support services, and intended outcomes. A panel of community persons with interest or expertise in adult education would review the proposals and help the department decide which programs to fund.

Early in 2000 we also concluded that new legislation would be necessary. The Public Schools Act did not provide an appropriate legal framework to operate an adult education centre because the act focused on principally children – for example in terms of the legal responsibilities of teachers and students. Moreover, a new piece of legislation would stand as a clear statement of the government's commitment to a high-quality, coherent, and accountable approach to adult education.

By the end of 2000, we felt we had a reasonable framework that would allow us to bring order to the ALCs. We were confident that over a couple of years we could develop a system that was solidly grounded in principles of effective adult education, was well managed, closely tied to local communities, and firmly committed to appropriate outcomes.

The Agassiz Problem

In the fall of 2000 we became aware that enrolments in ALCs had increased substantially both in Morris-Macdonald School Division and in Agassiz School Division, a rural area to the east of Winnipeg. We were quite unhappy about these developments, as we felt we had an understanding with both districts that enrolments were not to be increased substantially in 2000–01. We instructed both districts to review their enrolments to ensure that the figures they had given us were accurate.

Morris-Macdonald hired a local consulting company to review its enrolments. After the review they confirmed to us that their substantial increase in enrolment was accurate. We later discovered, however, that the consultants had actually submitted a report to the division that concluded that at least some of the enrolments were highly doubtful, and had been instructed by division officials to change the final version of the report to eliminate these conclusions.

Agassiz, on the other hand, reported to us in December 2000 that the enrolment figures they had provided in September had been substantially overstated. This left us with a serious problem. Agassiz had already budgeted based on the higher numbers. Moreover, the division had a significant accumulated deficit from an earlier fiasco in which its board had received inaccurate information from its secretary-treasurer, with the result that their spending was far too high for their revenue. In order to restore a balanced budget, the board had made large cuts in spending and staffing. Losing another half-million dollars could provoke a major crisis in Agassiz.

Agassiz's adult learning centres were different from those in Morris-Macdonald in that they had been established much earlier and had a ten-year record for good-quality programs for adults and youth who were not succeeding in regular secondary schools. While they had grown in size since 1996, their growth was not nearly as rapid as that of Morris-Macdonald. Because the Agassiz programs predated the overall development of ALCs, I felt that we could reasonably continue to fund their ALC students at the old, higher rate that was in place prior to 2000. Because these centres had existed for many years, Agassiz would report its accurate, lower enrolment but get the funds these students would have 'earned' prior to the funding change.

This approach turned out to be very difficult to do. The funding arrangements to various districts had already been approved A change in the Agassiz formula would require significant additional work. It was already December and we needed to announce the next year's funding by mid-January. There might not be time to get everything done and to flow the money as proposed. We then considered another option to the same end, which was to fund the higher number of students in the Agassiz ALCs at the new, lower rate. The net effect in terms of funding to Agassiz would be the same, but no change in approvals would be needed. So that is the option I approved – a decision that turned out to be a big mistake.

The Scandal

Early in 2001 I was contacted by two people who were working at an adult learning centre in downtown Winnipeg operated by Morris-Macdonald. They made serious allegations about problems at their centre, including falsified enrolments, unqualified staff, inadequate teaching, lack of records, pressure to award unmerited course credits, and general chaos in the administration. The picture they presented was of a centre that was failing to provide any sort of reasonable education and was receiving funds for services it was not providing.

These allegations had to be taken very seriously, especially in light of the other concerns already mentioned. I asked the department's chief financial officer and our director of administration to interview these informants on an urgent basis, and to give me their advice as to how to proceed. They spoke with four persons from this same centre, all of whom made similar comments. My staff felt that the concerns warranted a formal follow-up. Accordingly, I discussed the matter with the provincial auditor and sent him a formal request to investigate.

The provincial auditor (now called the auditor general) is an independent official appointed by and responsible to the legislature of Manitoba, not to the government of the day. The auditor's job is to ensure that the financial and management affairs of the province are handled appropriately. He has wide-ranging powers in law to conduct investigations. In addition to the regular audits of government departments and agencies, the auditor's office is also called in when there are concerns about how an area of public policy is being managed. As the auditor's jurisdiction does extend to school districts, he was the appropriate official to involve in the adult learning centre problem.

The auditor's investigation went on throughout the spring and much of the summer of 2001. His staff seized many records from Morris-Macdonald School Division and from several of the ALCs operated by the division. He hired a forensic accountant to help determine whether money was misappropriated. While all this was going on, the Department of Education continued the work of developing an appropriate adult education policy. Under the department's new policy for funding ALCs, applications for operating grants for the 2001–02 school year were received and reviewed. Funding of $14 million for forty-three centres was announced in May. Work continued on the proposed legislation. But we all knew that the auditor's report would be vital.

The process used by the provincial auditor for a review provides an opportunity for the department to see and comment on a draft of the report, though the final report is the sole responsibility of the auditor. The report was released publicly at the beginning of October 2001. It found that there had been very serious problems in the administration of adult learning centres in Morris-Macdonald, not only in the one program that had led to the allegations but also more broadly. The division, the auditor concluded, simply did not manage its adult learning centres appropriately. Although records of enrolments were in some cases very poor or nonexistent, it was clear, the report said, that the division had submitted enrolment figures for some ALCs that their officials 'knew or should have known' to be false. The auditor concluded that a minimum of $2.5 million, and possibly much more, had been provided by the province to the division on the basis of those unsubstantiated enrolments submitted by the division. The auditor noted that Morris-Macdonald had used profits from its ALCs to keep its own property taxes lower than they would have been otherwise. The report also pointed out that some ALCs were of very poor quality, with appallingly low graduation and course-completion rates. For example, of more than 1,000 students enrolled in a group of ALCs in 2000–01, only 22 actually graduated. The auditor's conclusion: management practices at Morris-Macdonald ALCs were very weak.

Among the findings published in the report of the provincial auditor were the following:

- Non-certified individuals were observed to be instructing students on at least 13 different occasions after the start of this investigation.
- Students indicated that certain teaching assistants were the only persons teaching their classes. (Provincial Auditor, 2001, 28)
- During site visits by our Education Consultant, no curriculum frameworks of outcomes were observed to be available to teachers in the core subjects with the exception of the Senior 4 English Language Arts ... Curriculum.
- English Language Arts, as taught by a teaching assistant, was not at the level expected of a Senior 4 class. On at least six different observations, the only activity noted was students reading aloud to a teaching assistant with others following along, as well as conversation about a number of non-English Language Arts related subjects. (29)
- ... we have determined that the September 30, 2000 enrollment figure of 301.5 FTEs [full-time equivalency students] provided to MMSD by The Program was significantly inflated. Specifically, we estimate the attendance at September 30, 2000 was likely less than 50 FTEs and that no more than 100 students were ever in attendance. (33)

- MMSD submitted an enrollment declaration to the Department that its administrators knew, or should have known, was significantly overstated ... (34)
- MMSD did not ensure that the requirements of the Public Schools Act and regulations were met at The Program.
- MMSD administrators did not sufficiently act on knowledge they had, or should have had, that the quality of education being provided by The Program was deficient. (35)
- MMSD had no formal policies and limited procedures in place to monitor ALC activities. Some ALCs did not submit Monthly Enrollment Reports on a timely basis. (55)
- Based on the additional ALC revenues, it is reasonable to conclude that MMSD's involvement with ALCs contributed to a lower mill rate than if such revenues had not been generated. Department ALC funding intended for adult education was not all spent on adult education. (66)
- A poor decision-making process was used by the Board in undertaking ALC partnerships. Trustees noted that they felt that decisions with respect to ALCs were brought to them by the former Superintendent already premade and the Board simply ratified them ... In that respect, this was a 'rubber-stamping' Board. (72)
- Discussions with former and current Department staff suggest that even after the potential significant impact of the concept of ALCs and their funding was recognized, changes as recommended by Department staff in 1998/99 were not implemented in a timely manner. (95)

The auditor's report also included a brief paragraph criticizing the department for the decision we had made about funding Agassiz. When we saw the draft report we had raised concerns about the wording of the paragraph in question. The auditor's office agreed that the paragraph would be more accurate if changed, but in its final public version the change was not made – an oversight, I was later told by the auditor's staff.

Responding to the Auditor's Report

We knew that the auditor's report would create a storm of publicity and controversy, and it did. Media interest, both print and electronic, was intense. The coverage was, however, amazingly superficial. No journalists bothered to visit other adult learning centres or to follow up leads in any detail. No genuinely independent effort was made to pursue the story.

The auditor made some 60 recommendations, most directed to Morris-Macdonald School Division, but a number also to the province. As soon as the report was released the minister announced that the government accepted and would implement all the recommendations directed to us. He also announced that Morris-Macdonald would be removed from all involvement in adult learning centres as soon as possible. Two centres run by MMSD and identified by the auditor as especially problematic would be closed, and the others would be transferred to other school authorities. The Morris-Macdonald school board was required to submit a plan within thirty days, indicating how it would implement all the recommendations of the auditor that applied to it. Morris-Macdonald would also be required to repay the province, as the auditor had recommended, between $2.5 million and $4.2 million in money it had received for nonexistent students. Finally, the government requested that the RCMP investigate the matter to determine if criminal charges should be laid against any of the participants.

While the government was ready to move ahead with the recommendations, the big question was what to do with the Morris-Macdonald School Division. The auditor had made many recommendations to them as well. Two members of the board, including the chair, resigned as soon as the report was issued, leaving only four trustees. One of the four had formerly been an administrator in a high school that enrolled ALC students, and so had declared a conflict of interest on ALC issues and was not participating or voting on them. The board barely had a quorum. Our interaction with the division and the information we were getting from other sources also made it clear that the remaining members of the board were not committed to any real change in approach. A highly credible source told us that the board did not accept the auditor's findings and was prepared to spend several hundred thousand dollars to commission its own study of the matter in an attempt to exonerate itself. Although the division had a new superintendent as of the summer of 2000, all other key proponents of the ALCs, including a number of people who had received substantial additional salary because of them, remained in their roles; several of these were well connected politically, both in the local community and with the board.

By the time the thirty days for the Morris-Macdonald response were up it was clear to me that its board was not going to make the necessary changes. Accordingly, on 9 November (the day after the announcement of the school district amalgamations), the cabinet approved the department's proposal for an order under the Public Schools Act to remove the elected board of the division and replace it with an official trustee, appointed by the province, who would discharge the responsibilities of the board until a new one was elected in the regular municipal and school board elections scheduled for October 2002. The official trustee appointed was Alex Krawec, a former school board member (in another district), a former municipal reeve, and at one time a director in the Department of Education. Alex was widely respected in educational and municipal circles in the province and had a reputation as a person of great integrity. Also, he had no political connection with the NDP, important because Morris-Macdonald was an area that voted Conservative.

The decision to remove an elected school board was unprecedented in Manitoba, though at the time it had been done in British Columbia and Alberta, and since then has also been done in Nova Scotia, and, in a somewhat different way, in Ontario. Manitoba has a very strong tradition of school board autonomy. There was, predictably, a great deal of controversy, although the Manitoba Association of School Trustees, which was quite well apprised of the real situation in Morris-Macdonald, made no criticism of the provincial action.

As these actions took place, the legislature began its fall sitting. The opposition immediately turned their guns on Drew Caldwell with regard to the Morris-Macdonald decision. They suggested that the government had eliminated the Morris-Macdonald board for political reasons while not penalizing the Agassiz board. (As already noted, I believe this comparison is entirely invalid and that the situations in the two districts were not at all comparable.) The media reporting of the story was particularly bad, in my view. An enterprising reporter could easily have found many stories of the problems in the Morris-Macdonald enterprises had he or she simply interviewed students in some of the programs that were so unsatisfactory, and then drawn a fuller picture of the kinds of problems that had occurred in the district for the last few years. Alternatively, there could have been some reporting of the many centres that were providing good programs to students who would otherwise have had no opportunity to return to school. Efforts by department and government communications staff to draw attention to some of the positives had no result at all. Instead, media reporting focused almost entirely on accusations made by the opposition in the legislature, accusations that became more and more dramatic, if increasingly inaccurate, as the days went by and the opposition sensed that there might be some bite in the issue. Although there is a general agreement in the legislature that names of civil servants are not to be mentioned, accusations were leveled against me and at least one other deputy minister. The opposition suggested that the provincial auditor was biased. The minister was accused of fraud. At the zenith – or nadir, if you will – of the debate, the *Winnipeg Free Press* ran headlines that included 'Caldwell Admits "Error"' (20 November 2002) and 'This Is Fraud: Tories' (21 November). In all of this, any balanced assessment of the values and limits of the centres was completely lost.

November 2001 was the most difficult month I experienced in government, but I had an easy time compared to Drew Caldwell. The session lasted only four weeks, but he was basically the sole focus of question period every day of the session. He was, to be sure, supported by his colleagues, especially, as the session went on, by Premier Gary Doer and Finance Minister Greg Selinger. (Several other ministers greatly appreciated Drew's sacrifice, as it meant that few or no questions were directed to them). However, it was a very trying time for him, and for his staff. There were endless meetings in the House to discuss strategy, and, more generally, to determine how to respond to the various accusations and to look at what further steps might be needed with regard to the ALC issue.

Inevitably, when there is such intense political pressure, some people want to remove the source of the problem. There were certainly suggestions that the entire adult learning effort should be terminated. I could see how people might wonder why we were spending a substantial amount of money in an area that was proving to be a serious political headache. However, key people in the government, despite their unhappiness at how the issue was playing out publicly, maintained their support for the principle of an effective adult learning policy.

While all the turmoil was going on at the provincial level, Alex Krawec was having his own difficulties as official trustee. I doubt that Alex realized what a difficult situation he was getting himself into when he took on the job of official trustee. He was under intense pressure not only because of political opposition but also because the Morris-Macdonald School Division was facing budget problems because of the absence of revenue from ALCs that in previous years had kept tax rates low. The requirement to repay funds to the province exacerbated the difficulty. And to top it off, the voluntary amalgamation that had been agreed between the Morris-Macdonald and Red River School Divisions was now threatened because people in Red River were worried about the impact of Morris-Macdonald's problems on the new, amalgamated district.

MMSD also faced a staffing crisis. The superintendent hired by the former board in 2000, a former director in the Department of Education, had, in my view, worked hard to improve the situation, but left the job due to ill health early in 2002, forcing the appointment of a new acting superintendent. Alex Krawec had to move forward in managing the division while actors heavily involved in the ALC mess remained in key administrative roles. Some of the main figures were well connected in the Morris-Macdonald community. There was enough evidence of wrongdoing in Morris-Macdonald to invite an RCMP investigation, but the RCMP could not say when their investigation would be complete (and it was still not complete two years later when this chapter was being completed). The provincial auditor was not able to assign responsibility for the problems to any individuals. The state of the records in the division was a shambles and the question of who had known or done what and when was unclear. It was evident that personnel changes would be needed, but, given the situation, dismissal was not a realistic option and the division still had to be managed on a day-to-day basis.

Meanwhile, unhappy parents in the division held several public meetings, and the municipal governments got involved as well, fearing substantial increases in property taxes. As usual in situations of uncertainty, rumours were everywhere. The cancellation of the division's involvement in adult learning coupled with the potential requirement for repayment to the province threw into doubt the status of a large number of teachers from the ALCs, raising alarms that younger teachers in some of the division's elementary schools would lose their jobs as they were 'bumped' by people with more seniority in the adult learning centres. There were some very tense negotiations between the department, the division, the Manitoba Teachers' Society, the ALCS, and some of the other school districts during December 2001 and January 2002, but in the end very few staff outside the ALCs were affected. Still, a group of citizens in Morris-Macdonald hired a lawyer and sued the government, a case that was still pending in the summer of 2004 as this book was completed.

Despite all this, within a few months many of the most urgent questions had been resolved. The ALCs that had not been closed had been transferred to other sponsors. Most of the key actors in the former administration, including several principals as well as senior division officials, had left, mainly through early retirement or other mutual agreements. Alex Krawec worked effectively with many people in the community. He created an advisory group of parents and worked hard to provide information to them on the state of the budget and its implications. He held a series of public meetings early in 2002 to discuss the situation and his plans for the 2002–03 budget. He met frequently with municipal officials as well. The municipal councils in the area also commissioned a consultant to give them a separate analysis of the ALC situation. Although the report was not made public, to my knowledge, I understand that the consultants came to the conclusion that the province was being generous in limiting the repayment to $2.5 million, and that the problems had been every bit as serious as the auditor's report had indicated. The amalgamation of Morris-Macdonald with Red River did take place with a provincial guarantee that the adult learning centre fiasco would not have significant financial implications for taxpayers in the former Red River Division area. In July 2002 a new interim board took over management of what was to be the new Red River Valley School Division. In October 2002 a new school board was elected for the new division. The new board was determined to move on from the problems of the previous year and make their new organization work, and the issue disappeared from the public horizon.

Legislation and the Future of Adult Education

The provincial auditor had recommended in his report that the province develop legislation to govern the adult learning centres. In fact the department had begun work on that project early in 2000, when we concluded that it would be desirable to produce legislation that would provide a strong legal basis for the continued and appropriate provision of adult education. The events of 2001 had the dual effect of making the legislation much more important, while also preoccupying all staff in the area so that there was almost no time to devote to getting the bill ready. The scandal also created pressure to increase the regulatory components of the legislation. Once the auditor's report came out, we went back to very active work on a draft bill. There were various internal staff discussions concerning the bill, focused largely on how to balance the evident requirement for accountability with a system that embodied principles of adult education, gave some centres some flexibility in how they operated, and did not drown them in paperwork.

The legislation on adult learning centres was tabled and passed by the Manitoba legislature in the summer of 2002. The bill itself was not particularly controversial. Although the opposition made some attempt to revive some of the criticisms they had made the year before, from a political perspective the issue was largely spent. Only ten groups appeared before the legislative committee, and most of these were adult learners talking about how the existence of the centres had changed their lives in positive ways. The bill passed without much debate.

The Adult Learning Centres Act creates adult learning as a unique education enterprise in Manitoba, putting the province at the forefront of national efforts to provide education opportunities to adults with low levels of education. It is an attempt to preserve the positive features of the system that had come into being, but to eliminate the kinds of excesses that had developed in Morris-Macdonald. ALCs are to be rooted in local communities, in that each one is developed and operated locally. Yet they are also strongly linked to secondary schools and post-secondary institutions through their governance structures, and in many cases through joint programs with high schools, colleges, or universities. The act provides for new forms of program delivery and new credentials for students where appropriate. It fosters the use of instructors and program administrators with training in adult education, and enshrines principles of prior learning recognition and joint programming. Funding is no longer based on enrolment, but on an education plan provided by a centre linked to clear objectives and follow-up reporting as to whether outcomes have been achieved. A number of centres have had their funding reduced to a level that fits their goals and accomplishments, while others have grown significantly. The department has created a branch to support the centres, is providing appropriate professional development to teachers, and is developing strong links between the centres in areas such as planning, curriculum, and student supports. In 2002–03, forty-six centres received a total of nearly $13 million and served more than 6,000 learners. The centres do highly positive work, providing many adults with a solid opportunity to improve their lives through education. Many of the centres reach out successfully to populations that have low success rates in the formal school system (Silver, Klyne, & Simard, 2003). ALCs can and do have strong partnerships with high schools, as several continue to be operated by school districts, and with post-secondary institutions, thus building new bridges across sectors.

The work of building an effective adult learning system in Manitoba is by no means over. The Manitoba approach is currently different from anything else in Canada, and it will take several more years to put the system on a firm foundation and to judge its longer-term success. As with any new initiative, not all the fondest hopes of proponents will be realized in the end, and there likely will be some unforeseen drawbacks. But the ALC experience in Manitoba shows that it is possible to turn a political problem into an educational opportunity. If, in the midst of political turmoil, the focus can be kept on benefits to learners, then out of something bad something good can come.

CHAPTER 8

Focus on What Matters: Managing the Department and Looking After Education

One of the accoutrements in the deputy minister's office when I arrived in 1999 was a stuffed clown that was part of the provincial government's art collection. When I left in September 2002 a successor was not immediately named. My staff put the stuffed clown in my chair and sent me a digital photo. It was apparent they had found someone to do the job who was easier to work with, just as efficient, and better looking! When this news spread around the legislative building, other ministers asked whether they, too, could have a stuffed clown for a deputy, but then decided that the Treasury Board would likely scoop up any savings. Moral: As a manager in government it's best not to take oneself too seriously.

Managing issues such as those in the previous chapters, as well as all the others not discussed at any length in this book, is in itself a large, sometimes overwhelming task. Yet that is not enough to be successful in a senior management role in government. There is no guarantee that the most important substantive issues will reach the political agenda, or that they will get the right kind of attention once there. For example, in education we know that poverty is strongly related to poor outcomes, but poor people and poor communities tend to lack a strong political voice so their needs may get overlooked. Many of the most important educational issues, as outlined in Chapter 2, do not have the pizzazz to reach the public political agenda. The same is true in just about every other area of government. So one important job of senior managers is to look at their field of responsibility as a whole, try to assess what is needed, and bring those issues forward for government to consider and act on.

The conventional wisdom about government is that elected people set the direction and civil servants implement that direction. That is both true and simplistic. It is true in that important decisions either stem from or have to be reviewed and approved by those who have been elected. That is a fundamental element in our system of government. In fact, many decisions that are not all that important, either politically or substantively, also go through a political approval process such as the budget. Because it is always hard to know what might later turn out to be politically important, governments are inclined to want to try to control everything. However, as noted in Chapter 1, there are always many more issues to manage than there is time to manage them. And politicians have to give attention to issues that are politically salient even if these are less important in the long run. This means that a large part of what goes on in government happens 'below the political radar.' A large number of decisions, though generally on less important matters, get little or no attention from ministers and are left to the civil service. There is no way it could be otherwise.

This is why the beliefs and priorities of senior civil servants do matter. It is also why political parties want to bring in to the senior ranks people who share their general orientation and principles. At the same time, civil servants are always cognizant that a decision they make, if it generates controversy, will draw political attention, which leads most civil servants to exercise a considerable degree of caution.

I came into government ready to implement the education commitments the government had made during the election campaign. That is a vital part of a deputy minister's job. At the same time, the election commitments only dealt with a small subset of the important issues in education. I had some strong views about the ways education policy needed to develop, as outlined in Chapter 2. Having been asked to take on the deputy minister's role by the Premier, and having connections to a number of ministers and other key people in the NDP, I felt that the overall strategy I had in mind was quite consistent with the general views of the government. This meant that I could proceed to move the Department of Education in these ways even if we did not have explicit approval for every step. Of course all the main plans would need the approval of the minister, and often of the cabinet, but rather than wait for the government to set direction in each area I saw it as my job to move forward as expeditiously as possible.

I felt there were two main requirements to move the agenda forward in Education. One was to develop a strong strategic approach in the department, the other was to create an organizational culture that would support and sustain the work that was needed. The change in organizational culture needed to include not only the way the department worked internally but also the nature of its relationships with many external groups.

My approach to managing is to set clear strategic goals through a collaborative process and then to organize resources and work to focus on those goals. That may sound rather banal, but a large amount of what goes on in government as well as in many other organizations where I have worked, including school districts, universities, and private-sector companies, is not driven by strategic goals. Most work is shaped by some combination of past practices, the demands of the day, or the personal preferences of individuals. Very few organizations, in my experience, actually focus most of their energies and resources around a set of defined goals with a long-term focus.

In government the political process adds another set of demands. Energy is largely spent on two things: carrying on the tasks that are already in place, and responding to ever-changing political requirements. Resources in governments everywhere in Canada have come under considerable strain as a result of efforts to cut spending, cut taxes, and reduce debt, so most civil service bureaucracies are quite stretched even in doing those two things. Governments do have to look after an array of program and administrative functions. Cheques have to be issued, records maintained, laws created and enforced, and services – from parks to highways to health care – operated. The demands of the political process are large, importunate, and unpredictable. Developing and implementing a longer-term strategic vision is a hard thing to fit into the spaces. However it can and must be done if important goals are to be achieved.

Changing the culture of the civil service is key because goals cannot be achieved unless they are widely understood and shared by the people who have to carry them out. The minds and hearts of people are the main resources government has to achieve its purposes. Motivation and commitment by staff are absolutely vital for success, yet you cannot create them by fiat. These things have to be built through communication and trust. Government tends to operate very hierarchically, with the implicit (and sometimes explicit) belief that staff are just so many cogs in a machine, who should be told as little as possible and whose opinions are of no consequence. That is quite simply an unworkable approach that cannot yield positive results. One of the biggest challenges governments face is to create the kind of organizational culture that will provide excellent public service on an ongoing basis.

Changing the internal operations of the Department of Education is not enough, because education is delivered not by government but through schools, colleges, universities, adult education centres, and training programs. Just as the government's intentions are largely realized (or not) as a result of the work of civil servants, educational goals are achieved (or not) by the thousands of people in the education system. So the department's working relationships with those institutions and the people in them had to be, to the greatest extent possible, characterized by mutual respect, trust, openness, and a willingness to listen.

The need for the department to give very different signals to the education system about our priorities and method of operating was especially strong in the K–12 sector. After years of delivering a set of policies that were resented in the system, and forcing their implementation with very little opportunity for feedback, the relationship between the department and schools was not very positive. The department was used to issuing orders without much discussion, and the system was used to objecting to everything the department did, in a kind of dysfunctional symbiosis.

Changing this environment was difficult on both sides, as illustrated by the issues around the Grade Three Assessment (Chapter 3). Even where people wanted to work in a different way, and many throughout the sector did, they did not necessarily have the skills, and the operating systems did not support a more flexible approach. The department, to take one instance, had very well developed procedures for getting final approval on official documents and policies but these rarely included any substantive input from the school system. It wasn't only that the infrastructure for such discussions was lacking, but also that department staff were not used to building the support for such consultations into their operating plans and staffing allocations. Even the typical language in which documents were written was authoritarian, full of words such as 'mandated,' 'must,' and 'shall.'

We moved on several tracks simultaneously to try to make some changes. Drew Caldwell is a particularly gregarious and outgoing person, one who loves talking with people and is truly open to the views of others. He used those strengths effectively by holding a series of formal and informal consultations with people in the school system, beginning in his first days in office. During his time as minister, Drew not only met very frequently with teachers, trustees, parents, and others interested in education, but he visited more than 150 schools in all corners of the province. Given the many demands on ministers, and the temptation to stay in the legislative building, spend time with other political people, and deal with the endless paperwork and meetings, this is a remarkable accomplishment. As a result, when issues arose he had a good sense of what things were like on the ground.

As deputy I also tried to visit a school, college, university, adult learning centre, or training program at least once a week. I did not match Drew's record but I did get to many sites around Manitoba. These visits helped me stay grounded in the realities of teaching and learning. They were also a reminder of how many wonderful things are going on every day in our institutions of learning, whatever the headlines and political pressures of the moment might be.

In addition to Drew's meetings with the various organizations, the department held a series of consultations bringing together all the main stakeholder groups in education to discuss priorities and ways of working together. Several such meetings were held over the governments' first two years. Each involved about 50 people – teachers, school trustees, superintendents, students, parents, and other people from the community. These meetings were important in building some sense of trust that there would be a more open approach to policy-making, but it is pretty difficult in a group of that size to do more than have some interesting discussions around issues.

Within the department we also looked for ways to send some new messages about flexibility and openness. One of the main complaints about the department from the system had been its unwillingness to deviate from rules and procedures, so one way to signal a new approach was to provide more flexibility. Among the first steps were efforts to reduce paperwork and reporting on schools in the area of special education. In a number of other policy areas we made it clear that we would accept different ways of proceeding in different jurisdictions provided the intent of a policy was met. We made more effort to circulate policy proposals earlier and to give more time for comment before they were finalized. We changed the language in our letters and documents to be more collegial and to recognize the expertise and vital role of schools, districts, teachers, parents, students, and others.

I also made a substantial number of personnel changes in the department. In the very first days of the new government, as mentioned in Chapter 2, two assistant deputy minister jobs were combined into one and one of the incumbents, filling the role on an acting basis, was reassigned to another senior role. As it became clear that there would be substantial changes in the substance and approach that the department used in relation to schools, several other senior managers left. One was appointed as a school superintendent, another took retirement, and a third asked to be reassigned to a non-managerial role. We promoted some people from within the department and also hired some new people from the school system who had strong field connections. It is important in any organization to keep a balance in hiring between good internal people and people from outside with different backgrounds and perspectives.

In identifying these changes I am not casting any aspersions on the people who left or were moved. With very few exceptions these people were dedicated civil servants who had tried to serve the government and to defend what they saw as important educational principles. However after years of being closely identified with the Conservative agenda, it was very hard for them to be perceived as speaking effectively for a different approach. Some of them were probably disappointed with the new regime and felt that it was a good time for them to do something else. This kind of turnover is often the result of a change in leadership, not only in government but in schools and in the private sector as well. It is important to recognize and accept this, as long as those who are displaced are treated well and are not blamed for shortcomings that were not of their own creation.

I believe our efforts to change the way the department was perceived were successful to some extent. At the professional level, between department staff and superintendents, principals and teachers, we did gradually see improved relationships and a greater sense of trust developing. In several cases the department made significant amendments to initial policy proposals as a result of feedback from the system. Even the problems around the Grade Three Assessment actually helped create a sense that the department would listen and respond to concerns from the field.

The realities of government and politics are, however, that not everything can be done through full consultation, and that lobby groups will not always get what they want. While we made extensive efforts to talk and work with the major organizations in the school sector, the school trustees were never more than lukewarm towards the government and were often quite hostile, while the Manitoba Teachers' Society often felt its influence was not adequate either.

The reality is that a government sometimes cannot and sometimes will not, for all kinds of reasons, change positions to accommodate other views. Indeed, the more high profile an issue is, the more likely it is that positions will become entrenched. This is especially the case when issues move into the legislature, where they usually turn into a matter of scoring points, or when the issue is portrayed by the media, as is often the case, as a matter of who wins and who loses. It is ironic that increased media scrutiny can sometimes lead to less, rather than more, willingness to change position. For example, once the government committed in the 1999 election to taking the Youth News Network out of Manitoba schools (see Chapter 1) there was very little willingness to change this position. Once a final commitment to amalgamations was made, which only happened after more than a year of opportunity for influence from school districts, again there was little willingness to make major changes in the plans. The reduction in post-secondary tuition fees in 2000 and the decision in the two subsequent years to prohibit increases in fees were made against the advice of the universities, who quite reasonably foresaw revenue problems for themselves as a result. The process of building stronger relationships with the education system thus inevitably involves steps backwards as well as forwards.

It is also the case that government serves as a convenient foil for people in the system. It is often easier to blame someone else than to take responsibility ourselves, and for people in schools, school districts, or post-secondary education it can be convenient to put the blame for something unpopular on the province, in the same way that the provinces and the federal government blame each other for various matters. Having someone else to blame is important to allow the organization to move on. I recall after leaving one position in government advising my successor to blame me on a rather sticky situation; I did not mind, and having his predecessor to blame would enable him to put that particular issue away without damage to his own credibility.

Changing the Internal Culture

It is extraordinarily difficult to change the culture of a large organization such as the Department of Education, especially when it is part of an even larger organization – the government – that may not be changing in the same ways. Nonetheless, I began my work as deputy convinced that we had to alter the way we worked internally if we were to be able to create and implement broad and far-reaching educational strategies.

The most important single change to be made, in my view, was to give staff at all levels the sense that they and their work were important and valued. This is something governments often do badly. In the press of events and political pressures staff are expected to work endlessly, to reverse direction at the drop of a hat, to put aside what they care about to do something they find trivial, and to do all this while having their pay frozen or reduced and their numbers cut, as happened everywhere in Canada in the 1990s. We ask a lot from our civil servants! During the height of the adult learning centre crisis in November 2001 I attended a meeting with some senior political staff about 7 p.m. one evening. 'Look at that,' one of my colleagues said, pointing out the window at the parking lots. 'All the civil servants have gone home.' 'Yes,' said another, 'they have real lives.' Treating people as if they were cogs in a machine is not only unfair, it hurts productivity. People cannot be productive over time if their basic requirements for a decent workplace are not met. Government is often a difficult environment, but it should not be made more difficult than needs must.

I have found as a manager that people are quite willing to work very hard if they feel the work matters and their efforts are appreciated. Indeed, what is striking is how little reward it takes to encourage people to put in enormous amounts of effort. The requirements are a sense of purpose and some recognition.

Many of the vehicles open to private companies to reward staff are simply not available in government. You cannot give people bonuses. You cannot send them on holidays as a thank you for a job well done. It is even difficult, as a senior manager in government, to throw a little thank you party and buy your staff pizza and pop, let alone flowers or liquor. When I was assistant deputy minister in the 1980s, responsible for community colleges, my finance director came into my office one day with a bill. The president of one of the colleges had bought a rose for each college secretary, about two dozen in all. My colleague told me that the Department of Finance would not process it because buying flowers for staff was prohibited. I disagreed, thought the purchase entirely reasonable, and signed the bill, figuring that if Finance rejected it they would send it back to me. Finance did reject the bill, but instead of sending it to me, they sent it to the minister – at that time, Maureen Hemphill – for her approval. Maureen phoned me about it. I defended the expenditure as a very small recognition of the hard work of the staff, and she readily agreed to sign it, though she pointed out to me that she didn't believe she had ever received a rose as recognition! I laughingly reported this to the college president, who was happy to send Minister Hemphill a rose, as well, at his own expense.

Given the absence of real perks, are there still ways of recognizing staff? I believe there are. People do not join the civil service primarily for the rewards, but because they believe in the work. They are motivated, as I have said, by a sense of purpose and accomplishment. These can be provided even within the restrictive rules of government.

Among the most vital tools that senior managers have to this end is their communication with staff. As soon as I arrived in Education I began sending regular e-mails to the staff of the department – all 900 of them. One of the great features of e-mail is that it makes this kind of broad communication easy. A decade earlier it would have required something on paper, with printing, duplicating, and distributing – much more time-consuming and more expensive. I would send these e-mails every couple of months. Typically four to seven pages, they reported to staff some of the main accomplishments and challenges of the department, including a list of accomplishments of individual staff as I became aware of them. I put our work in the context of our plans and strategies, stressed the many positive developments that were occurring, and thanked people for their hard work.

The response to these messages was striking. Especially at the beginning I had many responses, primarily from front-line staff, secretaries, and people in some of our more far-flung offices around the province. 'This is the first time in my twenty years as a civil servant that a deputy minister has ever communicated with me about the department's goals,' was a typical comment. People were really happy to be treated as if they mattered. To me this is entirely obvious. In government the intellect, energy, and commitment of staff are by far our most important resources. People cannot support a plan or direction if they do not know what it is, so keeping them up to date on developments is absolutely essential. Yet it is surprisingly uncommon.

In addition to the regular e-mails, we made a point of distributing key policy documents to all staff. An early version of our strategic-direction document was sent to everyone in the department, and every unit was asked to discuss the document at a staff meeting and to provide any views or comments. The same was true, within each sector, for the sectoral plans such as the K–S4 agenda and the Manitoba Training Strategy. In the spring of 2000 I sent to all staff a statement of my hopes for our organizational culture and my expectations for managers, so that they would also be in a position to judge how well their supervisors were doing. After I had been in the job about six months, I e-mailed all staff asking for any feedback they might want to give me on my performance, giving them a way to provide this feedback anonymously. I also asked all staff in the relevant units for input whenever I did a performance appraisal for one of the people who reported to me. Whenever I visited our department's offices – and I tried to do so regularly, just to get around and talk to staff – I heard positive comments about the importance of this open communication, and the sense of confidence and participation it gave them. A relatively small amount of my time yielded huge returns in positive energy and effort.

Yet another step in this direction was an effort to have more decisions made at lower levels of the organization as much as possible. Many decisions that would be made at the operating level in other organizations have to get political approval in government because there is always the possibility that they could become sensitive. Although critics berate government for being bureaucratic, they berate it even more for failing to pay attention to details that later turn out to be more important than anticipated.

Still, it is possible even within these conditions to express confidence in your operational managers, to give them as much room as you can to run their operations, and to try not to second-guess. I asked people to report to me only what they considered to be important. With the agreement of both ministers we reduced substantially the number of briefing notes. I eliminated the practice of having managers on standby in the legislature for hours during the review of estimates, just in case a question came up in their area. In the 2002 estimates review, a few staff in the Finance branch and I were able to do the entire review without calling in any of the branch directors. These may seem small benefits, but experienced civil servants understand the constraints of government, and even small efforts to give them more scope to do their jobs are greatly appreciated.

Another important part of building the right kind of culture involves creating strong teams. Government departments, like most large organizations, tend to operate in separate units with little interaction among them. Staff are specialists who do their own jobs and don't always know much about what their colleagues are doing. My experience is that people much prefer to work in teams where they can support each other and have a sense of the larger enterprise. The problem with most teams in government, as in other organizations, is that they do not share a common sense of the task or the mandate to make decisions, and so often end up floundering amidst issues regarding turf and competing conceptions about purpose.

For these reasons, one cannot simply create teams here and there. The tasks have to be chosen appropriately and the groups have to have strong leadership. A number of teams we created in the department did not work well for the reasons just described, but in many other cases teams operated very successfully and built strong ties across the various units of the department. The senior management group of about ten people met every two weeks and looked at the entire range of strategic issues in the department. I tried to encourage an approach in this group in which everyone could contribute on all issues, even those not in their jurisdiction. Every few months we would bring together the department's 40 or 50 senior managers to look at some issues of common importance. Some of these meetings worked well but others were less successful; much depended on having an issue concrete enough for people to see the consequences of the certain actions, yet also general enough to be important across the organization. Having a well-designed process that gives people plenty of time to talk, and being willing to hear and recognize a range of opinions, are also vital. A strong sense of 'team' requires that people are able to disagree with the established line without fear of repercussions. On a couple of occasions we asked external people to facilitate, with mixed results; consultants who do not know government tend to have quite unrealistic ideas about how work can be organized. The team effort to create and implement the Grade Three Assessment, or the team that worked on adult learning policy, or the team created by Assistant Deputy Minister Pat Rowantree (appointed deputy minister after my departure) that developed the Manitoba Training Strategy are instances that worked quite well.

In addition to teams with real tasks, we tried to develop some other internal working groups to build communication. For example a policy analysts network was started to bring together people across all parts of the organization whose work involved policy development and evaluation. This group seemed to develop well, and it defined some useful work that it took on in its own right.

Another effort to change the organization was the development of a department approach to staff learning. As people began to feel a greater openness to staff needs, some colleagues began to talk about the need to support staff development. Spending money on professional development is one of those things that governments have a hard time doing because it is so easy for the opposition to criticize. An amount that in the scope of government budgeting is miniscule – some small fraction of 1 per cent of payroll – still looks large when put in absolute numbers.

Moreover, as noted earlier, even small amounts of money can churn up large amounts of political indignation. While I did not think we could put more money into staff development, there were other things that we could and did do, such as indicate to all staff that they had both an entitlement and an obligation to improve their skills in areas relevant to the work of the department.

I had a great deal of feedback from staff all over the department suggesting that these measures were meaningful and important, and that they did improve morale. Still, the obstacles to organizational change are daunting, and it would be wrong to suggest that the actions we took in the department were transformational or decisive. They were steps in a right direction, but measures of this kind need to be sustained, supported, and expanded over time. Most crucially, it is very difficult for one part of government to be too far out of step with the rest of the organization, and I did not feel that the civil service as a whole was embracing the same kind of cultural change despite the efforts of some outstanding people.

Creating a Strategy

A positive organization culture only matters if people also have a clear sense of and commitment to what the organization is trying to accomplish. Setting clear direction in government is difficult because of all the contrasting pressures described in earlier chapters. The Department of Education did have some elements of strategic planning in place when I arrived. In the post-secondary education and training area considerable time had been spent on a vision and on a mission statement. In the K–12 sector there was what was called a business plan, although not all managers and very few staff had actually seen it. In neither case could I see a strong link between the plan and the bulk of the work the department was performing. The planning documents seemed to me largely statements of intentions, not clearly enough linked to action plans. People in the department did not always see how their particular piece of the work – running a library or a school for the deaf or giving out student bursaries – was part of the larger picture or could best contribute to the overall department goals.

The process of agreeing on a set of goals and priorities in my view, needed, to be inclusive but also relatively brief. Large organizations are given to spending large amounts of time debating the wording of statements of goals. But too much time spent on vision or goal statements is unproductive. It is much more valuable and efficacious to have a general agreement on directions and to move forward with concrete actions. The environment is too unpredictable to spend a lot of time creating documents. If one has a sense of where one wants to go, the trick is to try to move forward using whatever levers or opportunities may present themselves – what Behn (1988) calls 'management by groping along.'

Even before I officially took over as deputy I had begun drafting ideas on a strategic agenda for the department. In my first week on the job we held a meeting of the forty or so senior department managers to talk about strategy and direction. Using the input from that meeting, from the various external consultations and discussions that were taking place, and from my own views about education policy I put together a document that outlined five main goals that would apply to all areas of our organization, and then proposed about forty specific strategies under the five goals that would guide our work.

The draft document was circulated widely within the department for comment from all staff. It was discussed at staff meetings of the units throughout the department. A further meeting of managers was held to discuss it. Quite a few modifications were made, although much more in the shadings and specifics than in the general directions, which were widely supported. It was officially tabled as our Strategic Direction for 2000–03, in the summer of 2000. It has since been revised and re-released as a guide for 2002–05, and is featured prominently on the department's web site. More importantly, the goals and actions in this document have guided all other strategic and operational planning activities in various parts of the department. Most staff have found the directions broad enough to be appealing and inclusive, yet specific enough to give them some guidance as to how to proceed in their own work.

The Strategic Direction document was a good start but we needed more specific strategy documents in each of the sectors of the department to guide both actions and resource allocation. Setting out such strategies posed a number of challenges. Any agenda had to be ambitious yet also reasonable. People in the system needed to be able to look at it as something that was worth doing and on which progress could be made given all the other pressures and constraints. Too often, reform agendas in education lay out proposals that are far too ambitious. When timelines are not met and goals are not achieved the result is increasing cynicism. The New Directions reforms in Manitoba in the 1990s had produced that reaction as the previous government reversed some commitments and failed to meet the timelines on others. The positive accomplishments of New Directions thus were buried under the problems. After 1999, though the situation was improved in many respects, educational institutions were still under considerable pressure financially and programmatically, and the department also had limited resources to support new initiatives. It was clear very early in the new government's mandate that money would continue to be tight, so that any strategy we developed had to be possible primarily through using or reallocating existing resources, both in the department and in the system. The few exceptions were areas such as college expansion, where there was a clear commitment by the government to additional funding. All of this meant that our agendas had to be limited in scope, relatively modest in their undertakings, yet still innovative enough to build staff and system commitment. It's a fine balancing act.

In general the development of planning documents was easier in the post-secondary and training areas than in the schools sector, for reasons described earlier: fewer interest groups and less controversy over the options. The process and strategy for college expansion has already been described in Chapter 4. In the training and continuing education (TCE) area, covering such areas as adult learning, literacy, apprenticeship, non-institutional training, and employment services, a number of teams worked for several months under Assistant Deputy Minister Pat Rowantree to create the Manitoba Training Strategy, which was made public in January 2001. This strategy stressed three main goals: building a skilled workforce aligned with labour market needs, enhancing access to learning, and building an integrated and high-quality education and training system. For each goal there were several more specific strategies, and then a series of even more specific actions in areas such as articulating programs across sectors, strengthening prior learning assessment and recognition, and improving employment services for social assistance recipients.

In the spring of 2001, TCE and the College Expansion Initiative collaborated to host meetings of community leaders in Winnipeg, Brandon, and Thompson to get feedback on our plans for training and for community colleges. The response was very positive, giving us a clear direction for implementation.

A strategy for post-secondary education (PSE) came a little later, pushed forward by the creation of a Department of Advanced Education and the appointment of Diane McGifford as minister in January

2001. Diane was a strong proponent of a clearly articulated strategy for her area. The post-secondary strategy was released in May 2001, and over the next several months the minister met with many post-secondary institutions and other interested parties such as faculty and student organizations to discuss it. The strategy was built on the same five goals but with a different set of action statements that were clearly related to post-secondary education. The plan gave a strong emphasis to increasing accessibility and increasing success for groups who were currently marginal in the PSE system. It also had the same focus on system renewal, integration across sectors, and stronger community input that characterized all our strategies.

Aboriginal education is a particular challenge in Manitoba given a large and rapidly growing Aboriginal population. Although educational outcomes for Aboriginal people have been improving steadily, and in some cases dramatically, they still lag well behind the population as a whole. There is increasing recognition in the province that our future depends in large part on the ability of Aboriginal people to contribute to and share appropriately in the benefits of our economy and society. Each of the strategy documents in the department gave considerable attention to Aboriginal issues, and at the same time we developed an overall Aboriginal education and training framework to guide our work. Senior management in the department were all agreed that Aboriginal education issues had to be on everyone's agenda, and that while our Native Education branch could provide leadership and support, success depended on effort and commitment across the entire organization.

The most difficult area in which to develop a clear action plan was for schools. Creating an ambitious yet feasible agenda for schools was more difficult, given all the years of acrimony between the department and the system. It was especially important to focus on priorities that might genuinely affect what happened to students. In our early consultations with the various stakeholders, we found a strong willingness on the part of the school system to have some clear directions from the new government, especially if these were seen as reasonable to carry out. In the summer of 2000 a letter from the minister to all schools, districts, and provincial organizations outlined six proposed priorities. During the fall of 2000 these priorities were then more fully developed, and early in 2001 we conducted a series of consultations across the province concerning what was becoming known as the K–S4 Agenda. Each consultation involved teams of people from school districts, including students, parents, and community members as well as teachers, administrators, and school board members. More than 450 people participated in these events, which were followed in May 2001 by a one-day provincial conference with 250 more people representing all sectors of Manitoba.

This way of proceeding was slow, in part because of all the consultative efforts, and also because so many other things, such as amalgamations and school funding, had to be handled at the same time. However the advantages of the process were also considerable. The contrast to other governments, who tended to announce sweeping plans for change without any consultation, was itself a positive feature of the process, giving people in the system some confidence that we would not be proceeding in an arbitrary way. The consultation also helped reinforce the message that K–S4 would not be just a department initiative but something that would be shared by all the major partners and would build on the many positive things that were already happening in Manitoba schools. Throughout the consultations the six priorities received substantial support as being a reasonable agenda. We also made it clear that the specific actions we would propose would be feasible for schools to undertake and respectful of the work that others were already doing. We would not claim that we had found all the answers and were now going to make the school system adopt them.

In the summer of 2001 the formal K–S4 Agenda was released, with six main priority areas and twenty-seven specific action commitments. It produced very little reaction from either the system or the media. The school system already knew what was coming, and so did not need to react in a strong or angry way. Because the agenda did not make grand claims or produce much conflict, it garnered little interest from the media. There is an irony here in that policies that have a longer-term and gentler focus, which are much more likely to be successful, will not generate the kind of public and political attention that governments need to convince voters that they are acting forcefully on important public issues. The Manitoba K–S4 Agenda is very different from most provincial government education programs in Canada because it sets modest goals, does not promote or promise a transformation of the system, and seeks to build on positive developments that are already occurring rather than replace them with new models.

Creating strategies is not always easy, but it is easier than implementing them effectively. To ensure that policies are more than simply announcements, a bureaucratic apparatus and commitment has to be created, as was done in the examples in earlier chapters. Once a bureaucracy is pointed in a direction – like the oft-cited oil tanker – it is very difficult to turn it around. It is the task of senior management to put the structures in place to ensure ongoing effort on the most important issues.

Across all the strategies the senior management team worked hard to build staff commitment through ongoing communication. We also tried to develop strong ties across the boundaries of the organization. Using the kind of team building that was described earlier, more issues began to be looked at across the sectors. Apprenticeship was linked more strongly to high schools, to colleges, and to prior learning assessment. The colleges began to work more closely with high schools, and increased the number of joint programs with universities. We began to look at the range of vehicles – such as bursaries, loans, employment programs and tax credits – that we used to support students. We developed some bridging mechanisms between the secondary and post-secondary systems. Although these connections did not always happen easily, on the whole, staff in the department liked the idea of working together in new ways so as to increase the impact of our policies and programs.

For me, work on the strategies was a prime concern. I knew that without strong support from the top of the organization, staff at other levels would not be able to keep the momentum going. In government there are, as already described, constant other demands on time and resources. Long-term strategies, especially where they are not high profile politically, tend to drop to the bottom of the pile despite all the good intentions. Thus it required relentless effort to allocate my time to our stated priorities and to avoid spending all my time on issues that were pressing politically or bureaucratically but did not have the same long-term educational significance. This meant not only keeping the strategies at the top of my own list of things that required attention, but also doing everything I could to keep other managers focused.

From 1999–2002, although both Ministers Drew Caldwell and Diane McGifford supported the strategies in their respective areas, many other issues also had to be addressed. (A chronology of the main issues and events is listed in Appendix A.) Some of these issues were important and have been described in earlier chapters, but many other concerns also arose. Every couple of weeks I put together an agenda of significant issues for discussion with each minister to whom I reported. Most of the time the lists would have twenty or thirty items that required attention. In addition were all the minor items that also reached the ministers or myself at some point or another. To take a rather trivial but not unusual instance, quite a bit of time was devoted one spring to a concern raised by a person in an important political role, that the posters, T-shirts, and hats produced for one of our programs were in the Conservatives' colour: blue. The first suggestion – actually more than a suggestion – was that all these items be recalled and replaced. But eventually the matter died down and no changes were made. The struggle to keep attention on the things that really matter is never-ending.

Putting in Place a Larger Agenda

The goals outlined at the beginning of this chapter were ambitious ones. One does not easily or quickly create an organizational strategy that truly guides action and changes the culture of an organization so that it is able to achieve its goals more effectively. Three years is a relatively short period of time to do so.

Some important progress was definitely made. We did develop a set of coherent, well-grounded, interesting, challenging yet achievable strategies. These goals were widely supported within the department, and structures were put in place to bring them into reality. The goals and priorities also had general support in the broader education community. They moved education in the province in positive directions without much public controversy.

Setting goals, though, is the easy part. Much harder and more important is to make genuine progress towards them. Here, too, I believe some significant progress was made. Many of the actions outlined in the various strategy documents were well on the way to implementation by the fall of 2002. New programs were put in place, better services to students were supported, some interesting innovations were developed, and substantial energy was devoted to things that mattered to learners and learning. All of this was done with modest resources and in a way that recognized existing positive efforts and accomplishments in the system. Once a bureaucracy has been set on a course it is not easily moved to another one. The same inertia that made it hard for me to change some things in 1999 will also act to keep the organization focused on its current goals and strategies even if some important circumstances change in future.

At the same time, it is easy to see how much more is left to do. With regard to both organizational culture and sense of direction, we were still only beginning. The Department of Education is a large organization. Many of its habits have been deeply ingrained, and the department cannot easily move too far from the prevailing attitude in the government as a whole. Developing a sense of strategy was made more difficult because of all the competing pressures, because people were often inundated with the daily demands of their jobs, and sometimes because staff did not have the background or expertise to see beyond those daily demands.

I have been asked why, given the scale of what we were trying to do, I only stayed three years. In part, the answer is a personal one: the life of a university professor is, for me, more satisfying than that of a senior manager in government. Although I have much less formal authority as a professor, I have much more control over what I do and how I do it, and far fewer frustrations. That is why I indicated before I was appointed that my intention was to stay for two years – though I ended by staying for three. When my time as deputy was over, I felt I did not have the same positive energy I had initially brought to the job. We also had built a strong team in the department and I felt confident that the main directions we had put in place would continue to remain intact. An organizational change that rests on the supervision of one person will never be sustainable. Organizations often require leadership transitions because different stages of change require different kinds of skills – people who are good at conceptualizing a strategy are not necessarily the right people to implement it. Thus I left feeling confident that the department had the people and skills to continue to move forward with a positive agenda.

The limits on our progress were the usual ones: not enough time, attention, and resources. Although I was quite ruthless about focusing on the big issues – to the point that I simply would not go to meetings that I did not consider sufficiently important, no matter what they were or who called them – the realities of government meant that inevitably quite a bit of my time was spent on things other than the priorities in this chapter, or even in this book. If I were to do it over again, I would be even tougher about allocating my time and keeping minor issues off my agenda. The issues of the day will get looked after one way or another, but if the CEO does not pay attention to strategy, nobody else is likely to do so.

While I wish many things had happened more quickly, the reality is that changes in education depend fundamentally on changed understandings of what is possible and desirable on the part of teachers, administrators, students, parents, employers, and others. These changes cannot be dictated. They have to be built slowly and steadily though ongoing effort. Resources are not the only important factor, but some resources are necessary, if only to keep the issues on people's minds. We struggled throughout those three years to find the people and money to move our strategies forward, often against the pressures of other demands on the government that seemed to be more pressing.

The Manitoba government has treated education as a priority area. Education has received substantial attention from ministers, and has been given more generous treatment in the budget than most other departments. However Manitoba is not a wealthy province, and because provincial governments are always struggling with balancing all the pressures they face, parts of the strategic directions developed by the Department of Education were never really on the central radar screen and so tended to be pushed aside.

There is an interesting paradox in the relationship between political attention and policy agendas. Political attention and support are often needed to create the conditions and provide the resources for substantive change. College expansion, for example, would not have happened if there had not been a political commitment to it because we could not have found the needed money and capacity internally. On the other hand, a high political profile brings much more attention both from the government itself – central agencies and political scrutiny – and from the opposition and the media. Of course this kind of attention sometimes makes change harder, for all the reasons that should be apparent from the stories in earlier chapters. Sometimes it is easier to move issues forward if they are not high profile enough to become a substantive object of political interest. This paradox, like many other contradictions of government, will not go away, but simply must be managed as best one can.

It is a challenge to build a meaningful and sustainable agenda for change and the kind of organization needed to support it. There are large obstacles. But it is possible. In Manitoba from 1999 to 2002 some important progress was made, and it continues today. In the final chapter I consider more generally the possibilities for change and improvement for government and education.

CHAPTER 9

Improving Government and Improving Education

It was a privilege to serve as deputy minister of education for three years. It may sound trite, but I truly did feel as though I were serving the people of Manitoba. My visits to schools and other educational centres, my conversations with educators or parents or students, all reminded me of how important public education is. Not everything the department did during my tenure was good or successful, but I am proud of quite a few things we accomplished, and just as proud that we chose not to do in Manitoba some of the negative things we felt were being done elsewhere in Canada.

To me, putting in place a longer-term strategy and moving the department in some different directions were central tasks. From the government's perspective, however, many other more specific issues in education were of greater salience at any given time. These specific accomplishments were also important. I am particularly proud that we made post-secondary education more affordable, reintroduced a bursary program, strengthened the community college sector enormously, moved away from an unhealthy reliance on provincial testing in schools, strengthened funding at all levels, addressed pressing capital needs at all levels, created a sound adult learning system, moved forward substantially on prior learning recognition, and improved support for workplace training. I wish we had made more progress more quickly on many of these issues, but not everything can be done no matter how good one's intentions may be.

Sometimes avoiding a bad idea is even more important than finding a good one. Unlike many other provinces, Manitoba from 1999 to 2002 did not provoke crises with its teachers, did not cut funding to its institutions, did not impose unreasonable or punitive requirements under the guise of accountability, and tried – not always with complete success – to treat all parties with respect. We recognized the importance of building capacity in the system rather than just issuing orders to it, and we worked hard, if not always with as much success as we would have liked, to build more positive relationships with educators at all levels. The latter is particularly important, since in education progress depends on everyone involved making their best efforts.

In the latter part of Chapter 2, I outlined my views on an effective education strategy for one Canadian province. This strategy goes well beyond the areas that have typically been of most concern, such as finance and governance schemes. Indeed, it takes a broad view of education and the factors that shape educational outcomes. Improving student outcomes means that we have to pay attention to factors outside the school, that we have to work closely with parents, families and communities, that we have to pay more attention to early childhood development and to adult education. Within schools, reforms need to focus more on the elements that actually influence student outcomes, such as teachers' skills and students' motivation. In post-secondary education we need to find ways of strengthening innovation as well as improving success rates and participation rates.

In most areas during my tenure as deputy we made only a beginning on that larger agenda. Many educators and other interested parties in Manitoba are unaware of or are not focused on the agenda. There is still not enough innovation in the system and not enough focus on a broad vision of progress. On many fronts, from special education to prior learning assessment, from reaching out to more northerners and adults to supporting effective learning in the workplace, we are still only at the very beginning of what is possible. After three years the K–S4 Agenda was only in its very initial stages. While we took some important steps in Aboriginal education, the gaps in outcomes between Aboriginal and other Manitobans remain far too great.

In this final chapter I want to draw on these experiences to speculate about the possibilities for improving both government and education.

As I have tried to show in this book, the imperfections of government – and there are many of them – result from the dynamics of political and bureaucratic processes much more than from the limitations of individuals. Not much is left of the craze in the early 1990s for 'Total Quality Management,' but its founder, W.E. Deming, emphasized the importance of 'blaming the system, not the people.' Government operates the way it does because powerful drivers push it in those directions. Politicians are generally rational people whose behaviour is governed by the vicissitudes they face in seeking election and making decisions on difficult issues with inadequate time and information. The limitations of our system of government are not amenable to solution simply by electing different people or by making calls for 'political will' or 'new approaches.' Of course who we elect does matter in terms of the specific policies they pursue, but a single set of politicians, no matter how well-intentioned, cannot reverse or ignore the powerful dynamics inherent in politics. Political history is littered with examples of parties that intended to change everything about politics, only to be changed themselves by the political process.

There have been some worrying trends in politics in Canada and in other countries in the last twenty or thirty years. Membership in political parties has declined. More people are more cynical about the political process, which leads them to stop participating, and even to stop voting. Levels of trust in politicians and political institutions have declined.

On the other hand, there have also been some positive developments. In part, increased cynicism results from a more intelligent electorate and from the realization that grand promises are rarely fulfilled. People are cautious about believing political promises because they know the promises are hard to deliver. In the 1999 election in Manitoba the Progressive Conservative promise of $500 million in new spending and $500 million in tax cuts was simply not believed by many voters. In response to public cynicism, political parties are being more careful about what they promise and more concerned to make sure that they carry out their commitments. That is not a bad development.

The decline in membership in political parties may be related to people's desire to judge each candidate and election on the issues rather than making a lifetime declaration to a single party no matter what, as was more commonly the case a generation ago. If so, the change, while harder for political parties, may be a good thing for the body politic as a whole.

In the bureaucracy, too, there are dynamics that are hard to change yet there are also powerful pressures for change. The civil service has long-standing routines and practices that are quite resistant to change, such as the urge to grow, the focus on rules, disputes about territory, and deference to hierarchy. As the minister said to his permanent secretary in the TV series *Yes, Minister*, there are three rules of bureaucracy: it takes longer to do things quickly, it's more expensive to do things cheaply, and it's more democratic to do things secretly (Lynn & Jay, 1984, p. 357). Many attempts have been made to change the civil service in Canada, with not much to show for most of them. Yet the same forces for change that are altering the political landscape are also affecting the way the civil service works, such as the demand for more consultation, the need to respect diversity, and the requirement to admit and correct mistakes. While perfection is not attainable, improvement is.

I have about the same view of education in Canada. While there is a lot of criticism of our education system, and while there are certainly important areas for improvement, some very positive things have happened in recent years as well. In part, the criticism of schools is itself a result of a better-educated population. In part, as discussed in Chapter 2, our expectations have increased. At one time not long ago we were content that only a minority of students would finish high school and only a few would go on to post-secondary education. Not long ago we accepted that students with disabilities had little prospect for a good education, or that girls would not take science, or that 60 per cent of Aboriginal young people would not finish high school. Those situations are no longer acceptable, so even though the performance of the system has improved, it has not improved as rapidly as our expectations. We have made significant improvements in our education system, and, with the right approach, we can continue to do so.

My approach to improving government and education requires three seemingly inconsistent orientations all at the same time: being visionary, being realistic, and being optimistic. Vision is necessary to see what might be possible. Realism is essential to recognize what can actually be achieved. Optimism is required to keep trying to move forward even when the circumstances are not propitious.

I believe that the stories in this book, while they illustrate the ways in which the dynamics of government can create difficulties and frustrations, also show that good and important things can be done when people want them to happen and are willing to work for them. There will be no improvement unless people have ideas about the best that might be possible. Government is the means of achieving many important social goals; we have to retain our belief that these things can be done. Education is intended to bring out the best in people, and we have to maintain our optimism about this purpose even when reality falls short of our hopes.

At the same time, we have to have a sense of realism. When he was 5 years old, one of my nephews told my father, his grandfather, that when the Messiah came lions would no longer eat lambs. 'Is that right, Daniel,' my father said. 'What do you think the lions will eat?' The answer came in a flash. 'Deer, rabbits, whatever they can catch.' Lambs would be off the lions' menu, according to biblical injunction, but after all, Daniel reasoned, lions would still be lions and were unlikely to start eating lettuce.

The same kind of realism is needed in politics and government. Many of the calls for political change or educational change seem to ask people to be what they are not. There is little point in hoping for changes that run against our natures. Equally, there is almost always more scope for change in certain situations than many people realize. If one has a good idea of what would be desirable, then one looks for the opportunities to move in those directions when and as they arise.

Many proposals exist for improving our schools. Some of these proposals are simplistic; it is also unlikely that any single change can do all the things we want done. Yet we do know a substantial amount about what we might do that would be helpful. Many proposals have also been advanced for improving our politics. My focus here is not on changes in institutional arrangements or voting practices or political financing, important as these may be. Instead, I now want to draw attention to six strategies that could help us improve the way government operates, even within existing institutional vehicles. These are also possibilities that are relevant to everyone involved with the process of government, including politicians and political staff, civil servants, the media, and those trying to influence government.

1. My first recommendation is for modesty. Wherever possible we should avoid grand promises in favour of real but feasible improvements. This seems an odd follow-up to a call for vision, but the vision that is required is a steady and sustained course towards improvement rather than a single grand design. Big promises are attractive politically because they feed people's wish to believe that our problems can be solved. But a great deal of experience tells us that complex problems are not easy to solve. It's also much easier to fail with a big promise, and voters are increasingly sceptical of them. There is room, however, to make meaningful improvements in almost every area of public policy. If political actors can focus on the modest but worthwhile scheme, we are likely to see better results. One way to help this process is for lobbyists of all sorts also

to be a little more modest in their criticisms of current policies and their proposals for change.
2. Modest promises support a second important potential element of improvement – a greater awareness of complexity. Simple solutions are attractive, which is why people write books with titles such as 'reinventing government' or 'saving our schools.' There are certainly arguments for simplicity of message. I have been told more than once by political people that what can't be communicated publicly in twenty-five words or less, cannot be communicated publicly at all, and therefore cannot generate public support. It is important to understand that there are many issues in the public domain at any given time and that most people outside of politics and government have many other things on their minds. But as the old saw goes, to every complex problem there is a simple solution, and it's wrong. Similarly, there is an old Yiddish proverb about advice that translates as 'Either it won't help or they already knew it.' In our hearts most of us recognize that important issues are rarely amenable to simple solutions. This is an area where the media could play an important role by increasing the degree to which their coverage takes into account the multiple dimensions of public issues. In journalism as in politics, simplicity works well in delivering a message. Yet as people are more educated and less likely to be taken in by easy blandishments there may be stronger incentives for media coverage along with political debates to pay attention to complexity.
3. Related to both of these elements is the need to design policies to take account of the mistakes that are likely to be made. One thing we do know about large-scale action of any kind is that it will produce unanticipated consequences. As the earlier chapters show, actions almost always produce results that go beyond what was expected, especially when, as is often the case in government, the decision to act is made quickly and with inadequate information. In education we have a long history of fastening on to some fad only to find some years later that it fell far short of doing what was promised. Error correction capacity is critical, as Wildavsky (1979) pointed out years ago. It is, of course, easier to correct errors or respond to unanticipated events if one's promises are modest and one begins by recognizing the complexity in events. This strategy, too, would be assisted if external parties were a little less inclined to

look for mistakes and assign blame rather than seeing implementation as an inevitable process of learning and possible improvement. Oppositions can and will look for mistakes, but they may find it is also in their interest to go beyond blaming to learning how to do things better.

In trying to advance modesty, the recognition of complexity, and error correction, increased attention to research and evidence has the potential to be very useful. A more educated public is increasingly interested in evidence. It is hard to pick up a newspaper or listen to a news broadcast without hearing at least some reference to a new research study or report. Not only are governments more interested in evidence, but other participants in the policy process, such as lobby groups, are getting increasingly adept at creating and using research, including opinion polling, to advance and support their positions. Education is one of the fields where research is increasingly brought to bear as part of policy and political discussion. There of course is a danger that people will become so confused by the welter of conflicting claims that the result will be cynicism exmplified by the old adage that 'you can prove anything with statistics.' But the very rapid growth in the use of the Internet by individuals to get the latest research on health or the economy is strong evidence that the demand for quality information is high and growing. Research is always a two-edged sword for governments, as discussed in Chapter 1, but growing public interest will inevitably foster more government interest through such vehicles as indicators, evaluation reports, and audits. Evidence will not resolve most policy debates, which are also matters of values, but it can help make them better informed and more constructive. Disputes over evidence can, when well handled, lead to deeper public understanding (Lindblom, 1990). Indeed, the use of research to inform – rather than to direct – policy and practice is itself an educational activity.

4. Another important task, and one that is also already taking place in many ways, is to increase opportunities for dialogue around important public policy issues. In a society as diverse as Canada, where views on many issues vary widely, it is important to create as many venues as possible for discussion of important issues of public concern. The chances for agreement and common action generally increase when people have a chance to debate their differences in a constructive way. Third-party information provision can help make

policy debates more productive. Governments are already working in this direction through the kinds of increased consultation mechanisms discussed briefly in Chapter 1, but there is room for much more to happen. Educational institutions, as an example, could use annual reports or budget reviews as venues not just for self-promotion but for serious discussion of issues and alternatives. Evaluation reports and other performance analyses provide another mechanism that can support informed discussion. Information on public opinion should also be an important feature of the discussion of issues, since public opinion does so much to shape what governments do.

5. A fifth requirement is to support more innovation. When we do not know how to do something well it makes sense to try a variety of things and see how they work. Governments are generally risk-averse for reasons already described, yet the requirement for innovation is high. Governments need to find ways to support new approaches to programs and services. To attract and keep good people we need to have organizations that allow them to generate and use ideas. This means, in part, bringing new people into the discussion and hearing from different constituencies. As a senior manager in a private company told me years ago, 'If you want to change what people think, change who they eat lunch with.' If innovation is treated as an opportunity to learn, without excessive expectations and with the likelihood of errors that will have to be corrected, it can contribute in important ways to revitalizing operations.

6. Finally, it is vital to think about political action in terms of creating lasting change as well as short-term interest. Much depends on the capacity of our public institutions to learn to do things differently. Over the last ten or fifteen years, with the ascendancy of views that are highly critical of the public sector, the work needed to make public institutions more effective has largely not been done. Often this debate is presented as a matter of money, with change said to require more of it. Money is, of course, an issue, but other changes are as important, including efforts to make our institutions more innovative, to strengthen their connections with the public, to build bridges across institutions and sectors, and to encourage ongoing learning and initiative by public servants. We in the education field have learned the hard way that changes are not effective if people in the schools do not understand them or do not know how to

implement them successfully. The investment in capacity is not politically exciting, but it still has to be done if governments are going to deliver effectively on their promises.

A focus on capacity building and sustainability requires more attention to the longer term as well as to the immediate. It is hard for governments to resist the temptation to get the applause right now. However the picture is not all negative here, either. The increasing use of indicators and targets by government, though it can be abused to produce short-term results, does help get people thinking about outcomes and the longer term. Third parties and interest groups can help here, too, by providing independent data and keeping public attention on substantive issues. In education, third parties such as the Manitoba School Improvement Program (www.msip.ca) have been effective catalysts for changes that would have been hard to make through more traditional vehicles.

There will certainly continue to be many occasions when it will be difficult to advance any of these strategies. Politics will not stop being an enterprise that produces winners and losers, and governments will often see serious political downsides in making more evidence available, or in promoting broader discussion, or in admitting any errors or imperfections in their plans. That is why a sustained spirit of optimism is important. Everything will not be done at once, and setbacks and disappointments are inevitable. Working in government requires substantial ability to cope with frustration. Everyone, from premiers to civil servants to external parties, feel that the system gets in the way of doing what is important and needed. Yet all sectors and groups can play a role in moving these strategies forward. As noted, many positive changes are already occurring, though probably too few and too slowly.

As an optimist I am always drawn to possibilities for improvement. My suggestions are not made only to governments, since governments are very much creatures of their milieu. Change is also needed from the media, interest groups, school boards, professional organizations, and individual citizens. I have tried to avoid suggestions that would require people to be something very different or to develop unusual virtues in short order. Calls for sainthood are unlikely to be effective. Small changes that people can make would still make our politics, our governments, and our institutions better. All parties to a process, whether it be politics or education, can help improve our systems if inclined to do so, and can support improvement without giving up their own interests or raison d'être. We can at least, like the lion, begin by taking lamb off the menu.

Often change is a matter of being alert to the possibilities of the moment. As Kingdon's (1994) work on agenda-setting points out, there are moments when circumstances combine to make new things possible if people are ready to take advantage of them. People need to keep their eyes open and their optimism alive so that when there is a window of opportunity they can take advantage of it to make changes that matter.

As a three-time civil servant I also want to say something to other civil servants. The requirements for vision, realism, and optimism apply to civil servants at all levels, not just to senior managers but to line staff who do much of the real work of delivering programs and services. In addition to these, I also suggest that civil servants need to do three other things. First, as much as possible, they need to get out of the office and meet different people. Nothing opens up one's thinking more than talking to someone who sees the world differently. When one serves hundreds or thousands of clients a year it's hard to continue to see them all as individuals. A few minutes of attentive conversation with someone about his or her life can do much to remind any of us of the real reasons we and our services are there.

Second, civil servants need to read the literature. It is important for civil servants at all levels to learn as much as they can about their field of service, to know what the best current ideas are, and to understand what we have learned from sometimes painful experience. Being aware of current research and thinking in one's field of service is essential to being innovative and seeing the opportunities for improvement.

Third, civil servants need to understand the political process. The kinds of dynamics described in this book have a critical impact on how government works, and we cannot improve them or take advantage of the opportunities they offer unless we understand them. Amazingly enough, many civil servants do not really understand very much about the political process. They may also, like many educators, see politics as an undesirable interference with the real work that they do. This can be true at times of course, but with all its limitations politics is the way we govern ourselves and make decisions about our life together. Civil servants do not have to like politics, and they certainly do not have to be partisan, but to be effective they have to understand in some depth how the process works.

The same suggestions apply to the work of educators. It is vital for people in schools to spend more time with people from other settings. It is vital for educators to be well-informed about recent changes in our ideas and knowledge about education. And, although many teachers actively dislike the political process as they understand it, because politics affects education so much it is vital for educators to understand how politics works and to play an active role in the process.

I have enormous admiration for the work that many civil servants and educators do, sometimes under quite difficult conditions. Retaining our sense of possibility and our spirit of optimism, coupled with realism about what is possible at any given moment, is critical to being successful, and I believe our success in these areas is vital to our future as a society.

APPENDIX

Chronology of Main Issues and Events in Education, 1999–2002

1999

21 September
Election of New Democratic Party government

22 September – 3 October
Transition period; former government remains in office but defers major decisions; premier decides on cabinet and initial actions planned.

4 October – 18 November
New government takes office 4 Oct.
My first official day as deputy minister 15 Nov.
Initial staff work begins on the Grade Three Assessment commitment and the shift away from a standards test to a teacher-led assessment.
Commissioning of two reports concerning potential approaches to meeting the commitment on college expansion
First discussions on funding of schools for 2000–01 begin.

19 November
Newspaper story suggests Drew Caldwell interested in reducing the number of school districts.
Awareness of large overexpenditures related to adult learning centres; first discussions on steps to be taken to address this issue; commissioning of a consultant to study the ALCs and report
First meetings of senior managers across the Department of Education to look at longer-term strategy and planning process

Planning for and invitations to first meetings of K-12 stakeholders
Preparation of budget for 2000–01
Work under way to cancel Youth News Network contracts in Manitoba schools
Reduction in senior management positions and changes in several senior personnel
Legislative session 18 Nov.–14 Dec.
New chair named for Council on Post-Secondary Education
Initial planning with COPSE and universities for tuition fee reduction for fall of 2000

2000

January–April 2000
Internal decisions on scope and nature of Grade Three Assessment policy
Creation of College Expansion Initiative office; appointment of Curtis Nordman as executive director
Initial discussions with colleges on short- and long-term plans for college expansion
Initial work on Manitoba Training Strategy
Increasing public and media attention to the proposed Princess Street campus
School funding announcement for 2000–01 made; school districts increase property taxes
Property tax rebate increased by $75 per household
Changes in adult learning centre funding announced; longer term policy proposals developed and made public
Morris-Macdonald board agrees not to expand ALC enrolments in 2001
Appointment of two new assistant deputy ministers
Continued negotiation and media attention to Youth News Network issue
Development of legislative options restoring some collective bargaining rights for teachers
Significant staffing reductions but without any layoffs made in the Department of Education as part of 2000 budget
Agreement with Canada Millennium Scholarship Foundation makes it possible to re-establish the Manitoba Bursary Program, abolished in 1994.
First large meeting with K-12 stakeholder groups
Building connections to other priorities such as early childhood and inner-city development
Announcement of $70 million in capital funding for universities

May–August 2000
Grade Three Assessment policy made public and implementation begins.
Colleges develop long-term plans for expansion.
Active development of options to increase nursing enrolments
Public and internal debate over best location for new Red River campus
Ongoing discussion of school district amalgamation options
Legislative session from 25 April to 17 August
Legislation (Bill 42) to restore collective bargaining rights for teachers
Legislation to change some provisions around home schooling
Work begins on Manitoba Training Strategy and on a strategy for post-secondary education.
Drew Caldwell makes public proposed six priorities for K-S4 Agenda for schools.
Internal discussion of possible changes in high school program
Initial work on department staff development policy
Resolution of problem with teacher pension account

September–December 2000
Implementation of Grade Three Assessment followed by increasing expressions of concern by teachers regarding workload; discussions begin on possible changes to the policy
Princess Street confirmed as location for new campus for Red River College.
Commitment to new aerospace training program and discussions on governance structure
First new and expanded programs begin in colleges
Development of school funding options for 2001–02
Association of Manitoba Municipalities creates task force on school funding
Minister requires school districts to investigate and report on possible amalgamations; commits to changes for fall 2002 elections.
Awareness of increase in ALC enrolments in Morris-Macdonald and Agassiz; both boards asked to conduct a review of these enrolments
Proposals for new funding model for ALCs tabled
Decision to fund ALCs in Agassiz School Division based on higher enrolments
Internal continuing development of strategies for K-S4, training, post-secondary education
Legislative session 5–15 Dec.
Proposals tabled for changes in high school program.

210   Appendix

2001

January–April 2001
Evaluation of Grade Three Assessment policy released; changes to policy for 2001 introduced.
CEI moving ahead rapidly on new programs, long-term funding
Construction of Princess Street campus delayed by dispute over expropriation
School funding for 2001–02 announced followed by further increases in school district property taxes
Change to new Aboriginal Academic Achievement grant made
AMM Task Force reports
School district reports on amalgamations largely endorse the status quo
Allegations of problems at ALC in Morris-Macdonald lead to investigation by provincial auditor
Manitoba Training Strategy released
Cross-province consultations on K–S4 Agenda proposals
New high school program rules announced with challenge for credit, option to take post-secondary courses for dual credit, community service credit
Diane McGifford appointed minister of advanced education
Active development of approach to University College of the North
Policy and legislation on private vocational schools developed

May–August 2001
New round of professional development on Grade Three Assessment
Student Financial Assistance Act passed, giving legal status to bursary program
Internal discussions and decisions on school district amalgamations
Legislative session, 10 April – 5 July
Bill putting Student Aid program into legislation introduced and passed
Development of international education office
Preparation for review of COPSE as required in legislation
Class Size Commission created and holds hearings
Hiring of stakeholder relations manager
Active development of provincial youth strategy
Creation of Commission on Governance of the francophone school system

September–December 2001
Second year of implementation of the Grade Three Assessment proceeds smoothly

Amalgamation decisions released 8 Nov.
Provincial auditor's report on adult learning centres released 4 Oct; government commits to acting on all recommendations; removes Morris-Macdonald School Division from adult learning work and asks RCMP to investigate possible criminal charges
Morris-Macdonald school board replaced by official trustee 9 Nov.
Legislative session 13 Nov. – 6 Dec.
Daily question period and media focus on adult learning centres and replacement of Morris-Macdonald School Board
Active negotiations on proposed new hydro developments in northern Manitoba
Report on University College of the North released
Department sponsors provincial consultation on Training Strategy and College Expansion Initiative plans
Report of the Class Size Commission received
Report of the Commission on Governance of the francophone school system released

2002

January–April 2002
New school funding model and grants for 2002–03 announced
Property tax increases by many school boards
Springfield lawsuit against amalgamation is dismissed
Funding decisions made for adult learning centres for 2002–03
Provincial budget includes reduction in provincial Education Support Levy property tax
K–S4 Agenda officially announced
Review of ESL in schools policies undertaken
Commitment to legislation on special education

May–August 2002
New Red River College aerospace training centre opens
Legislation introduced and passed on school district amalgamations
New amalgamated school districts come into place 19 July
First provincial report on students outcomes for K–S4 released, August
Active implementation of K–S4 Agenda ongoing
Legislative session 22 April – 9 August
Legislation introduced and passed regulating private vocational schools
Legislation introduced and passed on adult learning centres

Legislation introduced and passed to modify several minor provisions of the Public Schools Act
Legislation introduced and passed to change the governance structure of the Division scolaire franco-manitobaine
University of Winnipeg financial problems increasingly in the news
Consultations organized on implementation plans for University College of the North
Review of COPSE undertaken

References

Alcorn, W., & Levin, B. (2000). Post-secondary education for indigenous peoples. *Adult Learning*, 11(1): 20–25.
Arrow, K. (1970). *Social choice and individual values* (2d ed). New Haven, CT: Yale University Press.
Association of Manitoba Municipalities. 2001. Rethinking Education Funding: Challenges and Opportunities. Report of the Association Task Force of Education Funding, April. http://www.mast.mb.ca/Communications/Publications/AMM_Rpt.htm.
Axworthy, T. (1988). Of secretaries to princes. *Canadian Journal of Public Administration, 31* (2), 247–264.
Behn, Robert (1988). Management by groping along. *Journal of Policy Analysis and Management*, 7(4), 643–663.
Black, P., & William, D. (1998). Inside the black box. *Phi Delta Kappan*, 80(2). 139–148.
Blakeney, A., & Borins, S. (1998). *Political management in Canada: Conversations on statecraft* (2d ed.). Toronto: University of Toronto Press.
Bovens, M., & t'Hart, P. (1994) *Understanding policy fiascoes*. New Brunswick, NJ: Transaction Books.
Bracey, G. (1995). *Final exam: A study of the perpetual scrutiny of American education*. Bloomington, IN: Agency for Instructional Technology.
Burtless, G. (Ed). (1996). *Does money matter? The effect of school resources on student achievement and adult success*. Washington, DC: Brookings Institute.
Campaign 2000. (2003). *Poverty amidst prosperity*. www.campaign2000.ca.
Canadian Education Statistics Council. (2000). *Pan-Canadian educational indicators*. Ottawa: Canadian Education Statistics Council. cmec.ca.
Canadian Global Alamanac. (2003). Toronto: John Wiley.
Cappella, J., & Jamieson, K. (1997). *Spiral of cynicism: The press and the public good*. New York: Oxford University Press.

COMPAS. (2001). The educational experience: State of the nation. Poll for the *National Post* and Global TV (26 August). www.compas.ca.
Conference Board of Canada. (2001). *Training and development outlook.* Ottawa: Conference Board of Canada.
CRIC (Centre for Research and Information on Canada). (2002). *Portraits of Canada* (December). cric.ca.
Dror, Y. (1986). *Policy-making under adversity.* New Brunswick, NJ: Transaction Books.
Earl, L. (2003). *Assessment for learning.* Thousand Oaks, CA: Corwin.
Earl, L., Watson, N., Levin, B., Leithwood, K., Fullan, M., and Torrance, N. (2003). *Watching and learning 3: Final report of the OISE/UT evaluation of the implementation of the National Literacy and Numeracy Strategies.* Prepared for the Department for Education and Skills, England. Toronto: OISE / University of Toronto. www.standards.dfes.gov.uk/literacy/publications.
Edelman, M. (1964). *The symbolic uses of politics.* Urbana: University of Illinois Press.
– (1988). *Constructing the political spectacle.* Chicago: University of Chicago Press.
– (2001). *The politics of misinformation.* Cambridge: Cambridge University Press.
Education at a glance. (2002). *Education Quarterly Review*, 8(3), 48–49.
Gidney, R. (1999). *From hope to Harris: The reshaping of Ontario's schools.* Toronto: University of Toronto Press.
Guppy, N., & Davies, S. (1999). Canadians' declining confidence in public education. *Canadian Journal of Education*, 24(3), 265–280.
Hardin, G. (1968). The tragedy of the commons. *Science, 162* (3859), 1243–1248.
Howlett M., & Ramesh, M. (1995). *Studying public policy: Policy cycles and policy subsystems.* Toronto: Oxford University Press.
Human Resources Development Canada. (2001). The school to work transition of post-secondary graduates in Canada. *Applied Research Bulletin.* Special edition (summer). Hrdc-drhc.gc.ca/hrdc/corp/stratpol/arbsite.
Human Resources Development Canada and Statistics Canada (1998). *High school may not be enough.* Ottawa: Minister of Government Services. www.hrdc-drhc.gc.ca/hrdc/corp/stratpol/arbsite/research.
Hunter, H. (2000). In the face of poverty: What a community school can do. In J. Silver (ed.), *Solutions that work: Fighting poverty in Winnipeg* (pp. 111–125). Winnipeg: Canadian Centre for Policy Alternatives and Fernwood Press.
Interprovincial Education Statistics Project. (2002). Summary of school statistics from the provinces and territories, 2000–2001. www.bced.gov.bc.ca/schools/interprovincial.
Ipsos-Reid. (2002). Support for Kyoto accord softens since June but remains

strong. Poll for the *Globe and Mail* and CTV (7 October). www.ipsos-reid.com.
Kiesler, S., & Sproull, L. (1982). Managerial response to changing environments: Perspectives on problem sensing from social cognition. *Administrative Science Quarterly, 27*(3), 548–570.
Kingdon, J. (1994). *Agendas, alternatives and public policies* (2nd ed.). New York: HarperCollins.
Lapia, A., & McCubbins, M. (1998). *The democratic dilemma: Can citizens learn what they need to know?* Cambridge: Cambridge University Press.
Leithwood, K., Fullan, M., & Watson, N. (2003). *The schools we need*. Toronto: OISE/UT.
Levin, B. (1985). Squaring a circle: Strategic planning in government. *Canadian Public Administration, 28*(4), 600–605.
– (1986). Uneasy bedfellows: Politics and programs in the operation of government. *Optimum, 17*(1), 34–44.
– (1994). Improving educational productivity through a focus on learners. *Studies in Educational Administration, 60*(1), 15–21.
– (2001). *Reforming education: From origins to outcomes.* London: Routledgefalmer.
– (2002). Knowledge and action in education policy and politics. In A. Sweetman and P. de Broucker (eds.), *Towards evidence-based policy in Canadian Education* (pp. 1–15). Montreal: McGill-Queen's University Press.
– (2004). Government and the media in education. *Journal of Education Policy, 19*(3), 271–283.
Lindblom, C. (1990). *Inquiry and Change*. New Haven: Yale University Press.
Livingstone, D. (1999). *The education-jobs gap*. Toronto: Garamond.
Livingstone, D., & Hart, D. (1998). Where the buck stops: Class differences in support for education. *Journal of Education Policy, 13*(3), 351–377.
Livingstone, D., Hart, D., & Davie, L. (2003). *Public attitudes towards education in Ontario 2002: The 14th OISE/UT poll*. Toronto: OISE/UT.
Lynn, J., & Jay, A. (1984). *The complete 'Yes, Minister.'* London: BBC Books.
Mackenzie, D. (2000). May the best man lose. *Discover, 21*(11), www.discover.com/nov_00/featbestman.html.
MacKinnon, J. (2003). *Minding the public purse*. Montreal & Kingston: McGill-Queen's University Press.
Manitoba School Divisions/Districts Boundaries Review Commission (Norrie Commission report). 1994. Department of Education. Available at http://www.edu.gov.mb.ca/ks4/docs/reports/boundaries/index.html.
March, J. (1991). Exploration and exploitation in education. *Organizational Science, 2*(1), 71–87.

McCain, M., & Mustard, J. (1999). *Early years study*. Toronto: Publications Ontario.
McLaughlin, M. (1987). Learning from experience: Lessons from policy implementation. *Educational Evaluation and Policy Analysis*, 9(2), 171–178.
McQuaig, L. (1995). *Shooting the hippo: Death by deficit and other Canadian myths*. Toronto: Viking.
– (1998). *The cult of impotence: Selling the myth of powerlessness in the global economy*. Toronto: Viking.
Mehrens, W. (1998). Consequences of assessment: What is the evidence? *Education Policy Analysis Archives*, 6(13). Epaa.asu.edu.
Milner, H. (2001). *Civic literacy in comparative context*. Policy Matters Series 2/2. Montreal: Institute for Research in Public Policy.
Nadeau, R., & Giasson, T. (2003). Canada's democratic malaise: Are the media to blame? *Choices: Strengthening Canadian Democracy*, 9(1). Montreal: Institute for Research in Public Policy.
Naylor, C. (2003). Reconciling teacher unions' disparate identities. *Our Schools/Our Selves*, 12(2), 113–139.
NEA (National Education Association). (1957). Ten criticisms of public education. *Research Bulletin of the NEA*, 35(4), 133–175.
Neuman, R., Just, M., & Crigler, A. (1992). *Common knowledge: News and the construction of political meaning*. Chicago: University of Chicago Press.
Nevitte, N. (1996). *The decline of deference: Canadian value change in cross-national perspective*. Peterborough, ON: Broadview.
New Directions: The Action Plan. Department of Education, 1995. Available at http://www.edu.gov.mb.ca/ks4/docs/policy/action/index.html.
OECD. (2001a). *Education Policy Analysis*. Paris: OECD.
– (2001b). *Knowledge and skills for life: First results from PISA 2000*. Paris: OECD.
– (2001c). *Starting strong: Early childhood education and care*. Paris: OECD.
– (2002a). *Financing lifelong learning*. Paris: OECD.
– (2002b). *Education at a glance*. Paris: OECD.
– (2003). *Beyond rhetoric: Adult learning policies and practices*. Paris: OECD.
OECD and Human Resources Development Canada. (1997). *Literacy skills for the knowledge society*. Paris: OECD and HRDC.
Panel on Education Legislative Reform. (1993). *Report*. Winnipeg: Manitoba Department of Education and Training.People for Education. 2003. The elementary school tracking report:
Six years of the funding formula: Failing Ontario's students. www.peopleforeducation.com.

Plank, D., and Boyd, W. (1994). Antipolitics, institutionalization and institutional choice. *American Educational Research Journal, 31* (2), 263–281.

Proust, Marcel. (1928/1956) *Swann's Way*. New York: Modern Library.

Provincial Auditor of Manitoba. 2001. Investigation of an Adult Learning Centre in Morris-Macdonald School Division No. 19. http://www.oag.mb.ca/reports/reports_fr.htm.

Renewing Education: New Directions. A Blueprint for Action. Department of Education, 1994. Available at http://www.edu.gov.mb.ca/ks4/docs/policy/blueprin/index.html.

Rothstein, R. (2002). *Out of balance: Our understanding of how schools affect society and how society affects schools*. Chicago: Spencer Foundation.

Savoie, D. (1999). *Governing from the centre*. Toronto: University of Toronto Press.

Shapiro, Bernard. (1991). *Remarks at the Conference on Policy Studies*. University of Calgary, 10 May.

Shepard, L., & Bliem, C. (1995). Parents' thinking about standardized tests and performance assessments. *Educational Researcher, 24*(8), 25–32

Silver, J., Klyne, D., & Simard, F. (2003). Aboriginal learners in selected adult learning centres in Manitoba. Winnipeg: Canadian Centre for Policy Alternatives. www.policyalternatives.ca.

Smith, D. (2003). *As many liars: The story of the 1995 Manitoba vote-splitting scandal*. Winnipeg: Arbeiter Ring Publications.

Smith, S. (1991). *Report of the Commission of Inquiry into University Education*. Ottawa: Association of Universities and Colleges of Canada.

Ungerleider, C. (2003). *Failing our kids: How we are ruining our public schools*. Toronto: McClelland and Stewart.

University Education Review Commission. *Doing Things Differently*. Report of the University Education Review Commission (the Roblin Commission). Winnipeg: XXXXX, December 1993.

Vincent, C. (1996). *Parents and teachers: Power and participation*. London: Falmer Press.

Wildavsky, A. (1979). *Speaking truth to power*. Boston: Little, Brown.

– (1986). *Budgeting: A comparative theory of budgetary processes*. (Rev. ed.). New York: Transaction Books.

Willms, D. (2003). Raising the learning bar. Paper presented to the Canadian Society for the Study of Education, Halifax, Nova Scotia. May.

Wilson, J. (1989). *Bureaucracy*. New York: Basic Books.

Young, J., & Levin, B. (2002). *Understanding Canadian schools* (3rd ed.). Toronto: Nelson Thomson.

In addition to the publications listed above, the following were consulted:

Various reports on the Grade Three Assessment, including the evaluations done after the first two years of implementation and the final report of results. http://www.edu.gov.mb.ca/ks4/assess/index.html.
The Manitoba School funding framework. http://www.edu.gov.mb.ca/ks4/finance/index.html.
The FRAME reports on school spending. http://www.edu.gov.mb.ca/ks4/finance/facts/index.html.
The Department of Education's policy on adult learning centres. http://www.edu.gov.mb.ca/aet/all/index.html.
Current strategy documents, including Strategic Direction 2002–2005, the K–S4 Agenda, for Student Success, the College Expansion Initiative framework, the Manitoba Training Strategy, and Priorities for Advanced Education. www.edu.gov.mb.ca/strategy.html.
Manitoba Teachers Society proposals on school funding. http://www.mbteach.org/copy_of_mtsfps02i/acrobatfiles/edfinance/equity1.htm.

Index

Aboriginal education, 12, 49, 50, 51, 64, 71, 73, 82, 83, 103, 107, 116, 138, 161, 162, 190, 197, 199, 210, 216

Adult education, 5, 6, 16, 34, 51, 52, 53, 55, 63, 64, 71, 74–5, 81, 115, 159, 160, 162, 164, 168, 173, 174, 197

Adult learning centres, 39, 80, 129, 132, 158–75, 207, 208, 209, 210, 211, 217, 218

Adult Learning Centres Act: legislation, 164, 173–4

Aerospace education, 105–8, 117, 209, 211

Agassiz School Division, 146, 153, 159, 164–5, 168, 170, 209

Apprenticeship, 53, 72, 82, 107, 115, 189, 192

Assiniboine College, 102

Association of Manitoba Municipalities (AMM), 56, 132, 135, 136, 138, 209, 210, 218

Axworthy, Tom, 32, 213

Benson, Julian, 46
Blakeney, Alan, 25, 213
Brandon University, 50

Caldwell, Drew, 16, 27, 34, 35, 56, 105, 119, 133, 140, 142, 148, 151, 153, 155, 163, 170, 171, 179, 192, 207, 209

Canada Millennium Scholarship Foundation, 70, 82, 208

Carstairs, Sharon, 3

Changes to school year, 81

City of Winnipeg, 109, 110, 111, 113, 141

Collective bargaining (teachers), 41, 55, 56, 67, 81, 123, 127, 149, 208, 209

College enrolment, 50, 80, 101, 115

College Expansion Initiative (CEI), 27, 101, 104–8, 110, 111, 113, 115–17, 189, 195, 208, 210, 211, 217, 218

Collège universitaire de Saint-Boniface, 50

Commission on Class Size and Composition, 27, 81, 210, 211

Community Economic Development Committee (CEDC), 15, 46

Community service credit, 80, 210

Computer literacy, 80

Council of Ministers of Education Canada (CMEC), 63, 84

Council on Post-Secondary Education (COPSE), 49, 52, 70, 82, 103, 104, 106, 109, 113, 116, 208, 210, 212

Dewar, Bob, 25
Disabilities and education, 53, 64, 73, 112, 199
Division scolaire franco-manitobaine, 81, 151, 212
Doer, Gary, 3, 5, 12, 25, 35, 46, 88, 171
Duck Mountain School Division, 145, 146, 153

Early Childhood Accord (2000), 21
Early childhood development/education, 20, 21, 51, 60, 64, 71, 74, 75, 197, 208
Education policy, 5, 54, 56, 68, 71–3, 76, 79, 119, 143, 177, 215
Education property tax, 80
Education Support Levy, 125, 128, 130, 136, 137, 211
Educational success, 73, 75, 197
Eldridge, Jim, 46

Farthing, Gerald, 88
Federal-provincial accord on child development, 64
Filmon, Gary, 3
Flanagan, Donne, 25
Forum of Labour Market Ministers, 82
French Immersion, 90, 143, 153
French language education, 53, 81, 83
Frontier School Division, 141, 145, 150, 151

Grade Three Assessment, 80, 84–100, 181, 186, 209, 211

Grade Three Guarantee, 80, 87–8, 128

Healthy Child: Committee, 16; policy, 83
Hemphill, Maureen, 183
Home schooling, 81, 209
Hope for Young People, 79

Immigrant education. *See* New Canadians/visible minorities education

Keewatin Community College, 103, 116, 117
Knight, Bob, 107
Kostyra, Eugene, 46
Krawec, Alex, 170–3
K-S4 Agenda, 27, 98, 184, 190–1, 197, 209, 210, 211, 212, 217

Labour Market Development Agreement, 53, 72, 82
L'École technique et professionnelle, 103, 106
Leitch, Don, 45, 46
Lemieux, Ron, 52
LeTourneau, Leo, 50
Lifelong learning, 63, 72, 75, 216. *See also* Workforce education
Literacy, 64, 74, 83, 119, 189, 214, 216
Lyon, Sterling, 45

Manitoba Aerospace Human Resources Council (MAHRC), 107
Manitoba Association of School Superintendents (MASS), 140
Manitoba Association of School Trustees (MAST), 41, 56, 136, 149, 155, 156, 170

Manitoba Public Insurance Corporation, 82
Manitoba School Improvement Program, 204
Manitoba Teachers' Society (MTS), 49, 55, 56, 94, 95, 128, 132, 133, 136, 138, 143, 172, 181
Manitoba Telephone System, 11–12
Manitoba Training Strategy, 27, 184, 186, 189, 208, 209, 210, 218
Manness, Clayton, 67
McGifford, Diane, 16, 52, 189, 192, 210
Media, 4, 8, 9, 19, 21–4, 31, 38, 40–1, 61, 68, 74, 85, 99, 109–10, 115–16, 119, 124, 128, 132, 134, 140, 151–3, 168, 170–1, 182, 191, 195, 200–1, 204, 208, 211, 215–16
Minority language. *See* French language education
Morris-Macdonald School Board, 150
Morris-Macdonald School Division, 158–70, 172, 174, 208–11
Mulroney, Brian, 18
Murray, Glen, 109, 110

National Literacy and Numeracy Strategies (England), 76, 214
NDP 1999 election commitments, 12–13, 16, 30, 42, 47, 52, 79, 80, 87, 88, 89, 91, 94, 101, 103–5, 111, 115, 116, 117, 128, 177, 182, 198
New Canadians/visible minorities education, 10, 32, 64, 73, 162
New Directions, 67, 87, 98, 188, 189, 217
Nordman, Curtis, 104, 108
Norrie Commission, 140, 141, 142, 144, 217

Nursing education, 105–6, 108, 117, 209

Pan-Canadian Education Indicators (1999), 84
Panel on Education Legislation Reform, 67, 217
People for Education, 122, 218
Pinawa School Division, 145
Post-secondary education, 5, 20, 34, 50–61, 63, 64, 65, 68–75, 78, 86, 111, 115, 120, 121, 196, 197, 199, 209
Potter, Don, 46
Prior learning assessment, 71, 75, 189, 192, 197
Program for International Student Assessment, 63, 84
Provincial auditor (auditor general), 158, 160, 162, 166, 167, 168, 169, 171–3, 210, 211, 218
Public Schools Act, 40, 49, 67, 147, 164, 168, 170, 212
Public Schools Finance Board, 126
Public Schools Modernization Act, 154–6

Red River College, 102, 105, 106, 108, 172, 173, 209, 211; downtown campus (Princess Street), 109–15, 210
Red River School Division, 172, 173
Red River Valley School Division, 173
Riffel, Tony, 141
River East School Division, 146, 154
Roblin Commission report, 70, 101, 102, 115, 217
Role of media. *See* Media
Rowantree, Pat, 186, 189
Roy, Guy, 88

School Achievement Indicators Program, 63, 84, 98
School bus safety, 81
School division (district) amalgamations, 20, 80, 140, 142–57, 172, 173, 182, 209, 211
School funding formula, 124, 126, 131–7, 148, 218
School planning and reporting, 77
Schools capital program, 81
Smith, Stuart, 69
Special education, 53, 76, 120, 138, 180, 197, 211; review, 81
Special Levy, 125
Status of teachers, 48, 66, 73, 77, 85, 87, 89, 91, 93, 95, 96, 122, 123, 194, 197, 205
Stevenson Technical Training Centre, 107, 108. *See also* Aerospace education
Strategy for post-secondary education, 189–90
Student aid, 50, 51–3, 68, 71, 82, 192, 208, 210
Student assessment, 56, 66, 67, 76, 84–8, 99, 196. *See also* Grade Three Assessment; Grade Three Guarantee
Student motivation, 73, 77

Teacher pensions, 81, 129, 209

Technical education, 69, 81, 104, 105, 115, 117
Third International Mathematics and Science Study, 84
Transcona-Springfield School Division, 146, 153-6, 211
Trudeau, Pierre, 32
Tuition fees, 20, 68, 71, 79, 82, 102, 104, 182
Turtle River School Division, 145

University College of the North, 82, 210, 211, 212
University Education Review Commission, 70, 101, 217
University of Manitoba, 5, 50, 106
University of Winnipeg, 50, 82, 104, 110, 212

Vogt, Paul, 25

Winnipeg School Division, 95, 132, 141, 146, 158
Winnipeg Technical College, 81
Workforce education, 55, 60, 64, 71, 72, 79, 82, 115. *See also* Lifelong learning

Youth News Network, 28, 80, 81, 182, 208, 209